The Definitive Guide to Squarespace

Learn to Deliver Custom, Professional Web Experiences for Yourself and Your Clients

Sarah Martin

Apress®

The Definitive Guide to Squarespace

Sarah Martin
Humble, Texas, USA

ISBN-13 (pbk): 978-1-4842-2936-1
https://doi.org/10.1007/978-1-4842-2937-8

ISBN-13 (electronic): 978-1-4842-2937-8

Library of Congress Control Number: 2017960180

Cover image designed by Freepik

Managing Director: Welmoed Spahr
Editorial Director: Todd Green
Acquisitions Editor: Louise Corrigan
Development Editor: James Markham
Technical Reviewer: Nathan Paynter
Coordinating Editor: Nancy Chen
Copy Editor: Karen Jameson
Compositor: SPi Global
Indexer: SPi Global
Artist: SPi Global

Distributed to the book trade worldwide by Springer Science+Business Media New York, 233 Spring Street, 6th Floor, New York, NY 10013. Phone 1-800-SPRINGER, fax (201) 348-4505, e-mail orders-ny@springer-sbm.com, or visit www.springeronline.com. Apress Media, LLC is a California LLC and the sole member (owner) is Springer Science + Business Media Finance Inc (SSBM Finance Inc). SSBM Finance Inc is a **Delaware** corporation.

For information on translations, please e-mail rights@apress.com, or visit http://www.apress.com/rights-permissions.

Apress titles may be purchased in bulk for academic, corporate, or promotional use. eBook versions and licenses are also available for most titles. For more information, reference our Print and eBook Bulk Sales web page at http://www.apress.com/bulk-sales.

Any source code or other supplementary material referenced by the author in this book is available to readers on GitHub via the book's product page, located at www.apress.com/9781484229361. For more detailed information, please visit http://www.apress.com/source-code.

Printed on acid-free paper

*This book is dedicated to Professor Greg Kesden,
who pushed me out of my comfort zone and
started me on my web development journey.*

Contents at a Glance

Contents

About the Author

Sarah Martin is a creative entrepreneur with over a decade of digital marketing experience. After working at an in-house creative agency for a Washington, DC, area nonprofit, she launched her own company, River Stone Digital. Sarah integrates marketing strategy, tech requirements, and compelling design into highly effective websites.

Squarespace quickly became one of Sarah's favorite web platforms for its flexibility, user-friendly interface, and cost effectiveness. Sarah holds the title of All-Star Circle Leader in the Squarespace Circle Forum, an online community for Squarespace's professionals.

In her free time, she enjoys reading and running. Sarah recently completed her first half-marathon and is training for another.

About the Technical Reviewer

Nathan Paynter has been building and designing websites for 8 years with 3 years building and designing in Squarespace. Since beginning to work with the Squarespace platform, he has built over 100 websites and consulted on 20 others. Nathan is currently employed with Now Media Services, providing affordable websites for nonprofit organizations, small businesses, and individuals across the United States and Canada. His goal is to help grow the web presence of these clients, who would otherwise have very limited reach on the Internet.

Acknowledgments

First of all, I want to thank my husband and kids for their amazing support and encouragement. It was a whole family effort to ensure I had time to get to write – team Martin for the win! I also want to thank my parents who taught me the value of hard work and to step out and try new things.

The support of the Squarespace Circle Forum Community has been invaluable to me. Your questions in the forum provided the inspiration and your words of encouragement kept me motivated. Finally, I want to thank my editors at Apress. This has been an amazing experience, and I have enjoyed working with all of you.

o Squarespace

d flexible tool for building beautiful and compelling websites.
nesses and individuals to easily maintain their online presence.
Squarespace platform, with more being added every day. The
the flexibility and range of control. A user with no coding
ite using the built-in tools. Users with coding knowledge can
oduce highly customized websites.
eb hosting and a content management system into a single
vorks seamlessly together. Other web platforms require a
ularly update the site for security. Squarespace monitors every
ility. This frees the user up to focus on the content of the website.
platform runs on the same Squarespace content management
the website is the same no matter what subscription plan you
pages or users while others offer more advanced e-commerce
their offerings with new features and integrations. The
current pricing and plans.
le feature or template option. Since Squarespace regularly
ledge base documentation has the most current information
of this book is to teach you the bigger picture of how to think
. This will empower you to use the full scope of the current
hat are released in the future.

e template includes the general layout of the website, colors,
plate uses the same Page Editor and Layout Engine. Squarespace
. Users with coding knowledge can also create their own

layout and design styles. Every template has the same core
ditional specialized features or layout options. Templates for
styling, shopping cart display, and checkout page styling.
blogging. The templates are all very flexible and all include the
emplates on their website, but don't feel limited to a particular
onality of the template matches the functionality needs you

tor for which template to use. Parallax scrolling is a visual effect
erent rate than the content around it. It is often used to immerse
a site visitor in the experience. Parallax scrolling can be turned on or off in the Style Editor. Some templates

© Sarah Martin 2017
S. Martin, *The Definitive Guide to Squarespace*, https://doi.org/10.1007/978-1-4842-2937-8_1

include Parallax Scrolling where others do not. If a template does not include parallax, it can be added but is difficult. The better option is to choose a template that includes it. Figure 1-1 illustrates how the different parts of a parallax index work together.

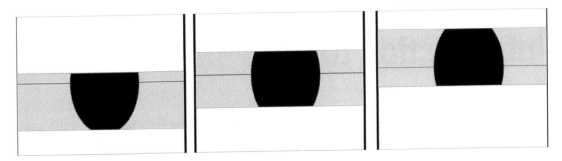

Figure 1-1. *Parallax Scrolling effect*

Index Pages are another deciding factor in template selection. Index Pages group a number of regular pages into a single collection. There are different Index Page layouts. A stacked layout stacks the pages in the collection in order. The stacked pages are all full width. The grid index layout stacks them in a grid format with equal rows and columns. Some index grid layouts allow you to select how many pages appear in each row of the grid. Figure 1-2 illustrates the two different types of index layouts.

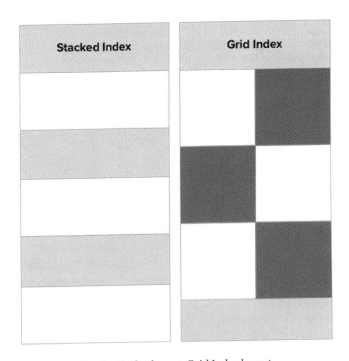

Figure 1-2. *Stacked Index layout, Grid Index layout*

Some templates offer masonry layouts for blog pages or galleries. A masonry layout is similar to a grid in that there are equal size rows or columns. The big difference is that the other dimension is not equal in size. This gives the layout the look of stone masonry. A typical use is a vertical masonry layout, in which the columns are equal width but the items vary in height. Figure 1-3 illustrates the difference between a grid layout and a masonry layout. The layout on the right shows a vertical masonry layout with equal size columns.

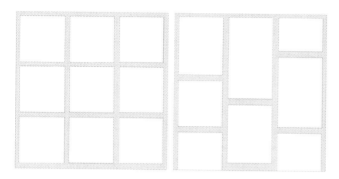

Figure 1-3. *Left - Grid layout with equal size square tiles. Right – Masonry layout with equal width columns and varying height tiles*

Squarespace templates do not allow per-page style customization. Any changes made in the Style Editor will affect all pages in the site. In the case of page type styles, like Blog styles, they will affect every Blog within the site. This restriction is to help DIY website builders ensure that their website has a cohesive design. As a web professional, I find this restrictive given my client's needs. This is where custom coding becomes necessary. With custom CSS, HTML, and JavaScript code injections extensive per-page style customizations can be achieved. We will explore the various code injection techniques and best practices later on in this book.

Template Families

Squarespace templates are also a part of template families. Template families are templates that all share the exact same functionality, but the Style Editor options and demo content are different. For example in Figure 1-4 you can see the Brine, Clay, and Rally templates. Even though these templates look different they are all part of the Brine template family. The first template families we will cover are the new style template families. These templates are designed with more flexibility and features, making them flexible frameworks to build a site on.

Figure 1-4. *Brine, Clay, and Rally template preview images*

Brine Template Family

The Brine template family has over 30 variations available to choose from. The Brine template was the first one released on this framework, hence why the entire family is refered to by this name. Squarespace is regularly adding more templates to this family. A full list of Brine family templates can be found in the Squarespace Knowledge Base https://support.squarespace.com/hc/en-us/articles/212512738-Using-the-Brine-template. It is the largest template family and has the most layout flexibility. The Brine family was created with advanced e-commerce options including checkout page style options. The Brine demo site can be viewed at https://brine-demo.squarespace.com/.

The notable qualities of the Brine template family include index page layouts, parallax scrolling, advanced e-commerce styling options, and full-page background images. The advanced e-commerce options include a product Quick View, zoom, and hover effects. This makes the template an excellent choice for any website that will include a store. The stacked Index Page layout includes parallax scrolling.

Other options included as part of the Brine family include full-page background images and a grid style blog layout. These features make it a great choice for non-e-commerce websites as well. One weakness of the Brine template is that there is not the option to add a sidebar to the individual blog posts. For a website that needs a sidebar as part of the blog posts, a different template must be chosen.

The Brine family also has multiple navigation menu areas. This is one of the notable differences between Brine and other template families. The Brine family template easily allows left, right, or split main header navigation. It also allows for a main navigation and a secondary navigation. The Brine family also has more options for styling the mobile navigation.

The Brine template family is the only template family with parallax functionality built in. The Brine template family allows for multiple content blocks to be added to an index section. It also calculates the position of the parallax image using a vertical and horizontal focal point. This allows great flexibility for different amounts of content to appear over a parallax banner image.

The Brine template family has two parallax image cropping options. The original option and the new Smart Crop option can be selected in the Style Editor. The original parallax code calculates the image size so that it overflows the content section by 500px on every side. This value, 500px, is known as the parallax offset. Figure 1-5 illustrates how the image is scaled relative to the parallax content container. For landscape orientation the image is scaled up to have 500px more width than the parallax content container. For portrait orientation the scaling and cropping is more significant. In Figure 1-5 portrait view the calculation ensures that the vertical height of the image is 500px greater than the height of the parallax content container. This results in a majority of the image being cut off.

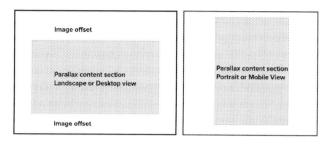

Figure 1-5. *Brine template family parallax image calculation*

The Smart Crop option is the same parallax calculation that was used in the discontinued Marquee template family. Smart Crop images are not cropped if the background image is larger or the same size as the container. If the background image is smaller than the container it is scaled up and cropped only enough to create the parallax image effect. Figure 1-6 illustrates the Smart Crop calculations. For landscape orientations there is no left and right image offset unless the image is too short for the container. For portrait orientation the image is scaled enough to have a small top and bottom image offset. The top and bottom image offset are significantly smaller when using the Smart Crop calculation.

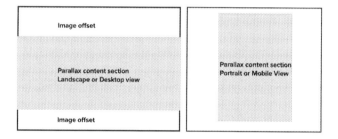

Figure 1-6. *Parallax Smart Crop landscape and portrait parallax calculation*

Tremont Template Family

The newest Squarespace template family is the Tremont family. It currently has four template variations: Tremont, Camino, Carson, and Henson. The Tremont demo site can be found at http://tremont-demo. squarespace.com/. Figure 1-7 shows the preview images for the Tremont family templates. Since this is a new template family I wouldn't be surprised if Squarespace releases more variations in the near future.

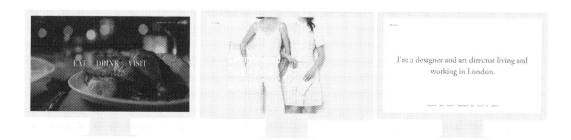

Figure 1-7. *Preview images for Tremont, Carson, and Henson templates*

The Tremont template family focuses on full-bleed images and dynamic overlay effects. The main distinguishing feature of the Tremont template is the Index Page layout, which functions as a portfolio. The Index Page displays each portfolio project page as a full-screen preview image. The Index Page allows the projects previews to be navigated through or transition automatically. The user can also get to the individual project pages.

The gallery pages have three unique layout options in the Tremont template family. There are also full-page color overlays that can be added. The color overlay is semi-transparent and can be customized with blend modes and color selections. Again, this is ideal for portfolio style websites or businesses in a creative field.

A feature of the Tremont template is the scaling font size. This means that the font size scales dynamically with the size of the browser window. Typically websites have the font size set for desktop size screens and mobile screens. There is a mobile "break point" where the website switches from desktop view to mobile view. This is not the case in the Tremont family templates. The fonts scale smaller in relation to the browser size. The Style Editor allows you to set minimum font sizes to ensure the font doesn't get too small. I expect this new approach to font sizing will grow in popularity since it preserves the feel of the site across screen sizes.

York Template Family

The York template family was released in the spring of 2016. It has eight variations: York, Artesia, Flores, Harris, Jasper, Jones, Lange, and Shibori. In Figure 1-8 you can see the preview images for York and Lange. The York family was designed with advanced portfolio features to showcase the work of photographers, graphic designers, illustrators, and creative agencies. The template has a Project Page type that is not available in other templates. The Project Page type has a header area and footer area for customized content. The body of the Project Page displays a mix of text and images. For a project consisting of just images the regular gallery page is still available. The content of the York template appears to slide up from the bottom. This feature can be turned on or off in the Style Editor.

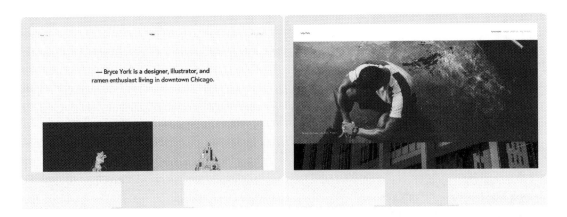

Figure 1-8. *York and Lange preview images*

Another strong feature of the York family templates is the Index Page. The Index Page has the capability to display projects in either a stacked or grid configuration. The York demo site, http://york-demo.squarespace.com/, shows the Index Page with a mix of grid and banner layouts. The Lange demo site, http://lange-demo.squarespace.com/, shows the Index Page with just a stacked layout. The different sections of the Index Page act as links to the project pages. This is different from the regular Index Pages that display all the content from the containing page.

The York template family also has dynamic font sizing like the Tremont family of templates. The template also offers page header banner images and background videos. The Style Editor selections also make the York family templates very flexible overall. The Style Editor also has additional mobile style options giving you more control over the mobile layout. One drawback to the York family is that there is not the option for a blog sidebar or a regular page sidebar.

Skye Template Family

The Skye template family consists of Skye, Foundry, Indigo, Ready, and Tudor templates. The Skye template family was designed for bloggers, magazines, reviewers, or anyone who would like a blog landing page for the homepage of the site. These templates don't require that the blog landing page be the homepage, they were just designed with it in mind. I have seen this template family used to feature rental properties as well.

The blog landing page features a grid of tiles each linking to a blog post. The grid can be configured to show a thumbnail image, title, date, excerpt, and categories. There are multiple design options for the grid tiles. Figure 1-9 shows the preview images for Skye, Tudor, and Foundry. The Skye template demonstrates the grid as a true grid layout. The Tudor template is demonstrating a vertical masonry style layout. The Style Editor has the options to switch between aligning the grid at the top of the tile, the baseline of the tile, or as a masonry layout.

Figure 1-9. *Skye, Tudor, and Foundry template preview images*

The Blog Landing Page also has multiple loading options. The Blog Landing Page can display a set number of posts with a "Load More" button to allow site visitors to view more posts. The "Load More" button can be seen on the Tudor demo site at `http://tudor-demo.squarespace.com/`. The Blog Landing Page can also be set to Infinite Scroll, which loads new posts automatically when the user has reached the bottom of the page. The Skye template demonstrates the Infinite Scroll option `http://skye-demo.squarespace.com`.

Additional blog features include an optional sidebar on the blog post pages, author profiles, and page position indicator. The next and previous post arrows, when hovered over, will display a thumbnail, blog post title, and date. Related posts can be displayed at the bottom of the page and turned on or off in the Blog Page Settings. The navigation icon, also known as a hamburger icon because of the three horizontal lines, opens up a navigation menu overlay. Figure 1-13 shows the navigation overlay when it is open. There are two sections where content blocks can be added. The first is at the bottom of the left-hand column. This section could be used to add additional sharing icons, text, or images. The right-hand column, called the sidetray, can be displayed or hidden using a Style Editor option. The sidetray can be used to highlight the author's information as seen in Figure 1-10 although there are many possible uses.

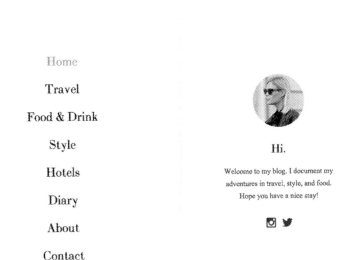

Figure 1-10. *Skye template family navigation menu*

It is important to note that the Skye template family does not have an Index Page option or a traditional navigation menu option. It only has the hamburger icon that opens the menu overlay. The hamburger icon can be confusing for some website visitors, particularly if they are not familiar with mobile devices. If this is the case for your website visitors, there are a couple of options. One option is to use a template with a traditional menu. The other option is to add the word "Menu" next to the hamburger icon with custom code or switch the hamburger icon out for just the word "Menu." Several fellow web designers have found that just switching to the word Menu provided enough clarity for their website visitors. We will go over the CSS needed to switch the hamburger icon to the word "Menu" later on in this book.

Farro Template Family

The Farro template family consists of the Farro and Haute templates. This is another template family designed for bloggers or anyone who publishes a large amount of content. The Blog landing page is the standout feature of this blog. The Blog Page has a number of layout options that can be selected using the Style Editor. The layout options include the traditional Stacked layout and Grid layout. A Split layout intersperses rows of two or three tiles among the stacked tiles. The Packed layout has two columns and allows multiple tiles to be stacked next to a single tile as illustrated in the Farro preview image in Figure 1-11. The Feature layout displays the first post and every fourth post and blog width. The shape of the thumbnail images can be adjusted with the Aspect Ratio option in the Style Editor.

Figure 1-11. Farro and Haute template preview images

The Gallery, Album, Events, and Products Pages all have a special hear area below the site header for intro content. Text, images, and video can all go in the Intro area. The ability to add intro on a Product Page and an Event page is particularly useful. This type of intro content can be added to other sites but it requires custom CSS and JavaScript. If your website needs this type of intro content, then seriously consider using a Farro or Haute.

Like the Skye template family the Farro template family also has a related post feature at the bottom of each blog post, author profiles, and interactive navigation. Also like Skye the Farro template family does not have an Index Page. The Farro template family also has many of the e-commerce style options found in the Brine template family. This makes the Farro template family a very flexible and useful template. However, if you need an Index Page then a Brine family template would be a better choice.

Old Style Template Families

This next section will cover the old style template families. These templates have significantly fewer Style Editor options. This often requires a lot of custom code to create options that are included in the Style Editor of new style templates. Squarespace is looking to phase out all of the old style templates. It is more efficient for Squarespace to maintain a smaller number of very flexible template families than to maintain dozens of restrictive template families. Consolidating the template options into flexible frameworks will allow them to develop new features faster.

For new websites that I am building today I intentionally choose from the new style templates. I want to align my work with the direction that Squarespace is setting. However there are thousands of existing sites using the old style templates. As a Squarespace web professional it is good to understand these old style template families. We will cover the most popular template families first.

Bedford Template Family

The Bedford template family is one of the most popular old style templates. This family has four variations: Bedford, Anya, Bryant, and Hayden. Figure 1-12 has the preview images for the Bedford and Hayden variations. The Bedford template was originally released with Squarespace 6. Squarespace updated their system to Squarespace 7 in October of 2014. This template family has been updated since the release of Squarespace 7. The most recent update added the ability to have background videos in additional to background images. Squarespace probably won't release any more variations of this template.

Figure 1-12. Bedford and Hayden template preview images

The Bedford template family is the most flexible of the old style templates. This flexibility has made it very popular with businesses. The multiple navigation options include sidebar navigation, product category navigation, and footer navigation. The main navigation has the option for drop-down menus and to turn the last menu item into a button. Many businesses have the Contact Us page as the last menu option and set it to be a button. This creates a visually distinct Call To Action in the header. The blog pages can also have a sidebar content area. The Bedford template family has a stacked Index Page layout.

The standout feature of the Bedford template is the special banners area at the top of the site. The special banners area can be a slideshow. Adding a gallery slideshow block to the top of a page will automatically turn it into a banner area slideshow. The banner areas can have an overlay with header text, description, and a button. The header at the top of the page can be transparent over the banner image. The text overlay and transparent header can be accomplished with other templates; however, the slideshow banner is unique to the Bedford and Brine template families.

Marquee Template Family

The Marquee template family consists of seven variations: Marquee, Adversary, Alex, Eamon, Ginger, Mint, and Shift. The Marquee template family has been discontinued. This means no new websites can be built using the template family. However, sites that currently use it can keep their template. This means as a web professional, we will likely encounter websites built using the template for at least the next couple years. The Marquee template family was the first template released with parallax scrolling. The parallax scrolling effect is part of the Marquee's stacked Index Page. Figure 1-13 shows the Marquee, Adversary, and Alex template preview images.

Figure 1-13. Marquee, Adversary, and Alex template preview images

The Marquee template family limits the amount of text that can be added to overlay a parallax image. It is limited to customizing the Page Title and Page Description fields to add a header, description, and button to a parallax content section. This differs from the Brine template family, which allows any type of content block and any amount of content over the parallax image. A common request is to add a single image over the parallax image. Examples include a call to action image or a business logo. The Brine template family can easily do this.

Another feature of the Marquee template family is that the Style Editor has the option for a fixed header. A fixed header is one where the header of the page stays "fixed" or attached to the top of the browser window. This is sometimes called a sticky header. Brine family templates can have a fixed header using custom code; however, the custom code requires JavaScript and CSS to ensure that the fixed header and Announcement Bar don't conflict.

Pacific Template Family

The Pacific template family has six variations: Pacific, Charlotte, Fulton, Horizon, and Naomi. It was designed to be a single-page website template with a stacked Index Page as the entire site. The Index Page is full-bleed meaning that images extend all the way to the browser edge. The Index Page also features a show on scroll navigation bar. This means when a user scrolls down on the homepage, the original header will scroll off the page with the content. Then when the user has scrolled to the second section of the Index Page, a new navigation bar will appear as a fixed navigation for the remainder of the Index Page. The show on scroll navigation can be turned on or off in the Style Editor. The Pacific demo site, http://pacific-demo.squarespace.com/, has the show on scroll navigation enabled. Figure 1-14 shows the Preview images for Pacific, Fulton, and Horizon.

Figure 1-14. *Pacific, Fulton, and Horizon template preview images*

One of the defining characteristics of the Pacific template family is allowing the main navigation to be split evenly on either side of the logo and centered. Some template families can mimic this effect by using two separate menu sections to the left and right of a centered logo, but only the Pacific template family can do it with a single menu. Some of the templates can achieve the look with CSS but the CSS will need to be updated every time a menu item is added or removed.

Since the Pacific template family features a full-bleed Index Page this allows you to include a full-bleed slideshow using the gallery block. Most templates have padding around the content within sections of an index page or a regular page that prevent the gallery blocks from being full-bleed without custom code. The Brine template family also allows for full-bleed gallery slideshows. However, the Brine template allows it by adding a gallery section to an Index Page.

Montauk Template Family

The Montauk template family has four variations: Montauk, Julia, Kent, and Om. The preview images for Montauk, Julia, and Om can be found in Figure 1-15. The Montauk template family features a special grid Index Page layout designed as a project portfolio. The thumbnails in the index grid are navigation to each section of the index. The content sections can be Regular Pages, Gallery Pages, Blog Pages, Event Pages, Product Pages, and Album Pages. When a user clicks on a thumbnail the page content is added at the top of the screen below the header, and the rest of the index grid slides down and displays below the page content. You can see this effect on the Montauk demo site at `https://montauk-demo.squarespace.com/artists-montauk/`.

Figure 1-15. *Montauk, Julia, and Om, template preview images*

The Montauk template also has additional header and footer areas. The additional site header area can contain business information, tag line, or other custom text. The additional footer areas include a page-specific footer area and two site-wide areas. The page-specific footer area for Regular Pages and Gallery Pages does not display if the page is being viewed within an Index Page. The Montauk template family also supports banner images and background videos on Regular, Blog, and Event pages.

Aviator Template Family

The Aviator template family consists of three variations: Aviator, Aubrey, and Encore. It was designed to welcome visitors to a site via a homepage that acts as a simple landing page with a full-bleed background image. In Figure 1-16 you can see how this concept is used in all three of the demo sites. The homepage landing page concept was unique when this template family was first released. However, when Squarespace launched Cover Pages this feature became obsolete. Cover Pages now allow a homepage landing page on any website and offer multiple different options to choose from. There are no unique features for this template family.

Figure 1-16. *Aviator, Aubrey, and Encore template preview images*

Other Templates

There are currently 12 other templates that are not a part of a template family. These templates are Adirondack, Avenue, Five, Flatiron, Forte, Galapagos, Ishimoto, Momentum, Native, Supply, Wells, and Wexley. Figure 1-17 shows the preview images for Flatiron, Native, and Wells. These templates were all released for Squarespace 6 and have limited customization. The Style Editor options offer little to no control over the mobile view.

Figure 1-17. *Flatiron, Native, and Wells template preview images*

Each of these templates met a specific design need when the old style templates were the only option. The Flatiron template is still very popular because it is a unique portfolio layout. Five has a number of page layout options making it popular. However all of these templates are very likely to be discontinued in the near future.

Starting a Site

Once you have selected the template that you want to use you can start your website. From the template's overview screen, select the "Start with Template Name" button. In Figure 1-18 you will see the overview screen for the Brine template. Start a site with the Brine template by selecting the "Start with Brine" button. Most of the examples in this book are going to use the Brine template. I am using the Brine template as a starting point since it is the largest template family and includes advanced e-commerce features.

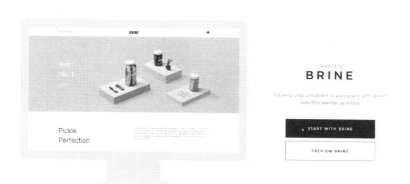

Figure 1-18. *Brine template overview screen*

Logging In

After clicking the Start button, you will be prompted to create a new account or to log in with an existing account. Squarespace accounts are unique to an email address. The email address becomes the username used to log in to Squarespace. Each person can associate their account with multiple websites. For example my email address and password allow me to log in to my personal Squarespace websites as well as my clients' sites. The billing for each Squarespace website is set on a per-site basis and not directly associated with a user account. That way I can have administrator access to my clients' websites without being responsible for Squarespace subscription payments.

If you do not have a Squarespace account then you need to create one. Figure 1-19 shows the prompt screen for creating a new account. The account creation page will create a new website based on your template selection. It will also create a user account for your email address. Creating a user account does not require a credit card, and the template selection can be changed once you are logged into the site.

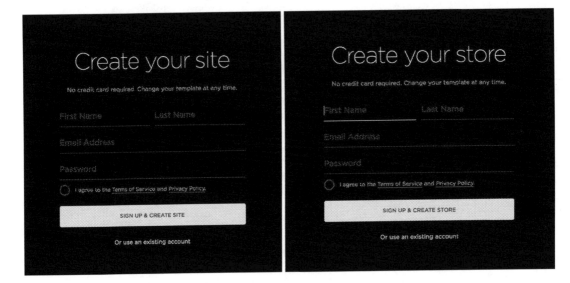

Figure 1-19. *Create a new Squarespace account*

The prompt screen text varies slightly depending on the template. The text uses the word "store" instead of "site" for templates that are categorized as "Online Stores" in the template list at http://www.squarespace.com/templates. Templates within the same family can exhibit this variation. For example, the Brine template uses "Store" while the Mercer template, part of the Brine template family, uses "Site."

If you already have a Squarespace user account, then you would select "Or use an existing account" found underneath the sign-up button in Figure 1-19. Figure 1-20 shows the "Create your site" screen for using an existing login. The major difference between this screen and the previous one is that it only creates a new website. This form will not create a new login.

Create your store

No credit card required. Change your template at any time.

Email Address

Password   Forgot?

SIGN IN & CREATE STORE

Don't have an account? Sign up & create store

Create your site

No credit card required. Change your template at any time.

Email Address

Password   Forgot?

SIGN IN & CREATE SITE

Don't have an account? Sign up & create site

Figure 1-20. *Create Site with Existing Login*

Getting Started with a New Website

When you log in to a brand new website there are a series of prompts that come up. These prompts are for Squarespace to collect user information. The prompts vary for templates categorized as "Online Store." Squarespace also regularly updates the prompts. The images in Figure 1-21 are the Welcome screens that start the series of prompts. To start filling out the prompts click the "Start" button at the bottom of the prompt.

Figure 1-21. *Welcome screen starting prompt*

The prompts will have required fields. For example, if you are starting an online store you will have to enter a physical address. This starting information will also be entered into the website account information section as well as being sent to Squarespace. Any information entered in the prompts can be changed later on in the Squarespace system.

Trial Account Website

All new sites start as trial account websites. Trial account sites have full access to all the Squarespace features but require a login before a user can access the site. This is to ensure that the general public and search engines do not find the website before you are ready. Figure 1-22 shows the trial account prompt that appears when a user goes to the URL of a trial site. The website visitor is asked to log in using a Squarespace user account or continue as a visitor. Visitors need to enter a series of letters shown in the prompt in order to access the site. The visitor access screen in Figure 1-22 shows the prompt. The letters of the visitor access prompt are different every time the website is visited.

Figure 1-22. *Squarespace Trial mode dialog and Visitor Access prompt*

Trial sites also have an expiration date. The standard expiration date is 14 days. Squarespace Circle Members have six-month free trials for all websites. For more information on the Squarespace Circle program visit http://circle.squarespace.com/. Figure 1-23 shows the trial site banner that will appear at the bottom of any trial website when the user is logged in. The trial banner states how many days are left in the free trial.

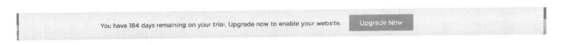

Figure 1-23. *Trial site banner*

When a trial website expires, visitors are no longer able to view the site. Figure 1-24 shows the screen a visitor would see for an expired trial site. The site still exists but the pages and content cannot be accessed until a paid subscription is started. An expired trial site can also be deleted from your user profile screen. I will cover launching a site and changing it from trial to active later in Chapter 4, "Site Settings and Best Practices."

Figure 1-24. *Expired site screen*

Squarespace Menus

Once logged in, you will see the Squarespace interface and option menu for the site. The menu is referred to as the Home menu. The Home menu appears along the left-hand side of the browser window. There are two configurations for the Home menu: the default view and the commerce view. Figure 1-25 shows both versions of the Home menu. The difference between these two menus is that the commerce view has been optimized for an online store website. The Order, Inventory, Customers, and Discounts menu settings have been moved from a sub-menu item of the Commerce menu option to the home menu. All templates can switch between these two menu options in the Settings section.

Figure 1-25. *Default Home menu configuration and Commerce Home menu configuration*

The first menu option is the Pages panel. The Pages panel contains all the pages and navigation menus for a site. There are two portions to the pages panel. The first section contains the menu options that are coded into the template. Some templates only have a Main Navigation section. The Brine template has three navigation sections: main navigation, secondary navigation, and footer navigation as seen in Figure 1-26.

Any items that are added to the menu sections will appear in the navigation for the website. The second section of the Pages panel is the Not Linked section. Pages and items in the Not Linked section are a part of the website but they are not a part of any of the navigation menus.

Figure 1-26. *Main Navigation, Secondary Navigation, Footer Navigation, and Not Linked sections*

The Design Panel contains all the style settings for the website. Figure 1-27 shows the Design Panel options. The template, logo, and title are all set from the Design panel. The Style Editor in the Design panel contains the built-in styling tools for the site. We will cover the Style Editor in depth later. The Checkout Page Style Editor is available in the e-commerce website templates. The Lock Screen has the settings for putting up a password protected Lock screen on the site. This is useful for sites that are active but still under construction. The Announcement Bar can be turned on or off and is a banner that appears across the top of the site. The Mobile Information Bar option contains the settings for enabling the Mobile Information Bar feature and configuring the content. The Squarespace Badge option enables the Squarespace Badge and has configuration settings. The Custom CSS option opens the Custom CSS editor, which we will cover in depth later in this book. The Advanced option allows you to add a Typekit ID to the site to use other Typekit web fonts that aren't already included in the site.

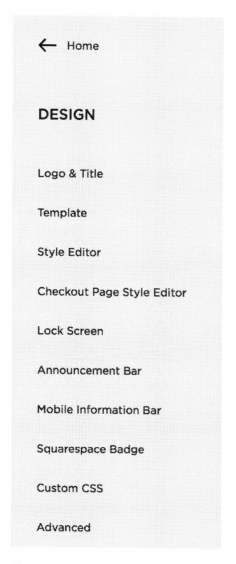

Figure 1-27. *Design Panel options*

The Commerce Panel contains all the online store information. The Order option shows the existing orders and their status. Orders can be edited from the Order option. The Inventory option is where the online store inventory is controlled. The Discounts option is where all discounts are controlled. Discounts can be set on a product, category, or storewide basis. Squarespace is regularly updating its store capabilities. Orders, Inventory, and Discounts all appear in the Home menu for Commerce sites. Commerce plan sites also have a Customers option. This is where customer information is stored and managed. Figure 1-28 shows the Commerce Panel for the default view Home menu.

Figure 1-28. *Commerce Panel for default Home Menu*

The Analytics Panel option contains all the data for the site. You can view Traffic Overview information and Mobile Usage. If your site has an RSS feed you can also track the number of RSS Subscribers. The Referrers option tracks the websites that send traffic to your website. The Popular Content option takes a look at what users are looking at most often. The Search Engine Queries option reports on the search terms users are typing into your site's search boxes. There are also Activity Log and Sales Overview options. Figure 1-29 shows the Analytics Panel. Squarespace is continuing to expand on their Analytics capabilities. At this time it is also recommended to add Google Analytics to your website to supplement the Squarespace analytics. We will cover adding Google Analytics later in the book.

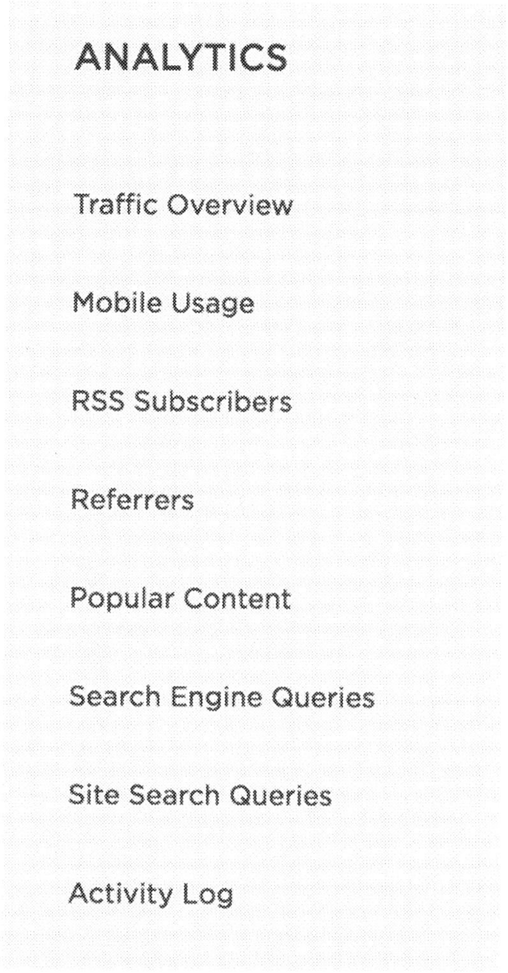

ANALYTICS

Traffic Overview

Mobile Usage

RSS Subscribers

Referrers

Popular Content

Search Engine Queries

Site Search Queries

Activity Log

Figure 1-29. *Analytics Panel options*

The Settings Panel has three different sections of settings. Figure 1-30 shows the Settings Panel. The first section is the General section. These are the general website account settings. The Permissions option is where additional users can be invited to contribute to the website. The Billing & Account information is where the website account subscription and billing information can be changed. The second section is the Website settings section. This contains the basic website information, settings to connect other accounts and advanced settings. Most of these we will go over in depth later in the book. The third section of the Settings Panel is the Commerce section. The commerce settings control the payment options, checkout configuration, shipping, taxes, and notifications for an online store.

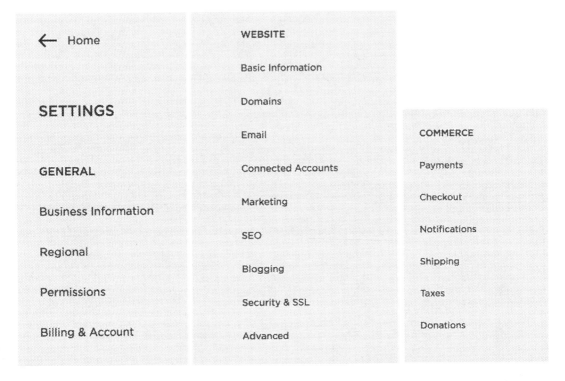

Figure 1-30. *Settings Panel General, Website, and Commerce sections*

The Help Home menu option links to the Squarespace Knowledge Base. The final portion of the Home menu is the profile section. It appears at the very bottom of the Home menu. Figure 1-31 shows my profile. I have added a profile picture and suggest that you do as well. Clicking the profile picture opens up the User Account panel. There are preview images and links to every Squarespace site that your user account is connected to. As you can see in Figure 1-32 my business website and my client websites appear in this section. There is also the option to "Edit Profile" where you can control your notification subscriptions for each website.

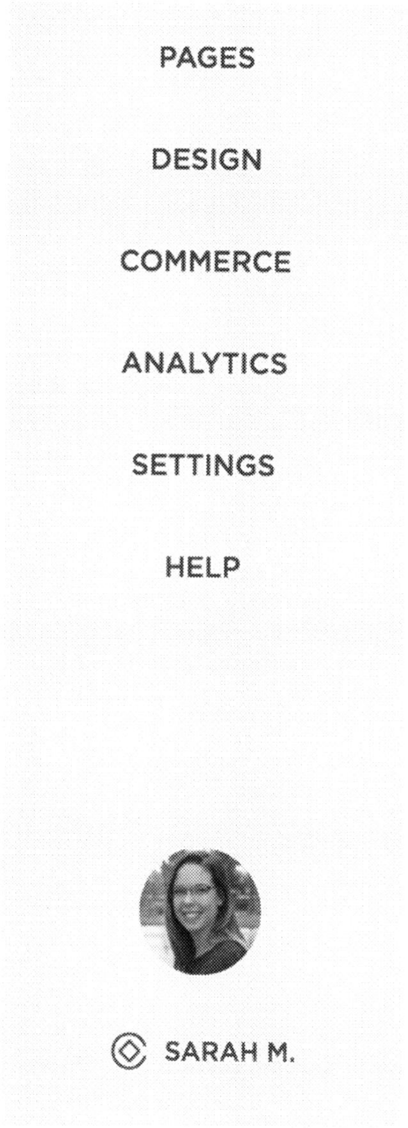

PAGES

DESIGN

COMMERCE

ANALYTICS

SETTINGS

HELP

◇ SARAH M.

Figure 1-31. *Profile in Home menu*

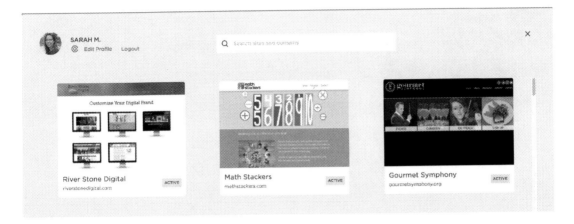

Figure 1-32. *User Account panel*

Squarespace Preview Panel

The other part of the browser window contains the preview panel. This is where you can edit the content of your site and view it in desktop, tablet, and mobile sizes. At the very top of the preview panel in the center there is a gray line. When you hover over the line it turns into a down arrow. You can see these icons in Figure 1-33. When the down arrow is clicked the screen size preview options appear. The preview options are mobile, tablet, and desktop size. When you select one it changes the size of the preview window.

Figure 1-33. *Gray line, down arrow, and preview size icons*

The mobile phone and tablet size screens will show an outline of the device that is being previewed. Figure 1-34 shows the preview panel set to mobile size. The preview panel sizes are great for checking the general layout while you are working on your site. I highly recommend also checking your website on actual mobile and tablet devices when you are nearing the end of the project. While the preview window does a very good job mimicking mobile and tablet devices, it is not perfect.

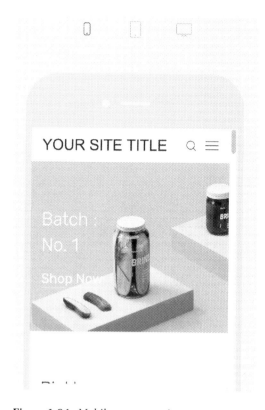

Figure 1-34. *Mobile screen preview*

The preview panel also has an expand arrow in the top left corner. It only appears on hover. When the expand arrow is clicked it hides the Squarespace menu panel on the left allowing for a full-screen preview of the website. Once in full-screen preview the collapse arrow will appear in the top left corner on hover. The collapse arrow when clicked returns the preview panel to its original state and the Squarespace menus are again visible on the left-hand side. Figure 1-35 has the expand arrow, the collapse arrow, and a screenshot to see the arrows in context.

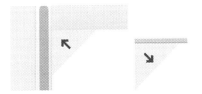

Figure 1-35. *Expand arrow, collapse arrow, and arrow in context*

Introduction to Squarespace Wrap-Up

You should now be familiar with Squarespace and feel comfortable selecting a template and starting a website. Once logged into the site you should have a general understanding of the menus and feel confident exploring your new site. In the following chapters we will look at all the tools available to add content to your website. In Chapter 3 we will take a look at how to style your new website. In Chapter 4 we will go over the general site settings and best practices. The second part of this book, Chapters 5-11, will cover in depth all the ways to customize a Squarespace website.

CHAPTER 2

■ ■ ■

Getting Started on Your Site

In this chapter we will begin putting content into the website that we created in Chapter 1. For all my website projects I put together a sitemap and an overview of what content goes on each page prior to designing the site. This helps me ensure that the design takes into account all of the content. For the book's example website, we will work through creating a site for a Houston, Texas, area organization: PAWsitive Connections TX. PAWsitive Connections seeks to connect homeless pets with new owners and provide pet owners with resources to care for their animals. Figure 2-1 shows the sitemap that was created for the PAWsitive Connections TX site website.

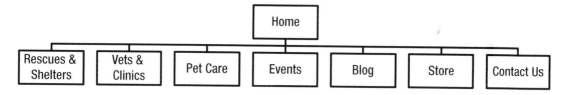

Figure 2-1. *PAWsitive Connections TX sitemap*

In addition to a sitemap, wireframes are another tool for planning content. A wireframe is a draft of the layout for a webpage without any of the styling elements. For a typical project I will put together a wireframe for the homepage, mobile view of the homepage, and any other unique pages. Wireframes help in planning the site content without the distraction of specific pictures, fonts, and colors. Wireframes can be created in Sketch, Photoshop, and many other programs. My preferred method for creating wireframes for Squarespace websites is to use the Starter Page Layouts and demo content to create a live and clickable wireframe.

Demo Pages

When you first log into your new website the Pages panel will have demo pages for all content that is included in the template's demo website. Figure 2-2 shows the demo pages having "DEMO" after the page name. There are a few ways to handle these demo pages. Depending on your personal preference you can delete them, move them to the "Not Linked" section to save as a reference, or use them as the basis for a page. I will typically delete all the pages that I definitely won't need and use some as a starting point for my wireframes.

© Sarah Martin 2017
S. Martin, *The Definitive Guide to Squarespace*, https://doi.org/10.1007/978-1-4842-2937-8_2

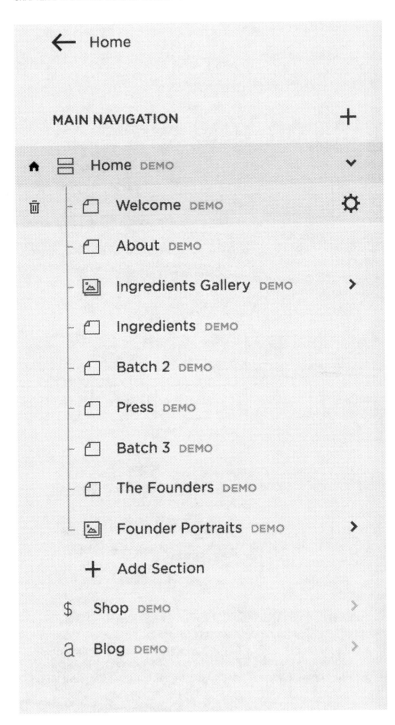

Figure 2-2. Brine template demo pages

To delete the demo pages, hover over the name of the page and a trashcan icon will appear on the left side. Click on the trashcan to delete the page. Figure 2-3 shows the trashcan icon. Once clicking the trashcan, a confirmation message will appear ensuring that pages aren't accidentally deleted. The icon directly to the left of the page name indicates the type of page that it is, in this case a regular page. The gear icon on the right opens up the settings panel for each page type. We will explore these features later in this chapter.

Figure 2-3. *Page Controls and icons*

To use a page as a starting point for a wireframe click on the demo page name and a prompt will appear asking you to delete the demo page or create a page like it. Figure 2-4 shows the prompt for a Regular Page as well as a Blog. The prompt will be slightly different depending on the demo page type. To keep a demo page for future reference you can click on the page name and drag it down to the Not Linked section of the Pages panel. This will allow the page to exist in your site but not appear in any of the navigation menus.

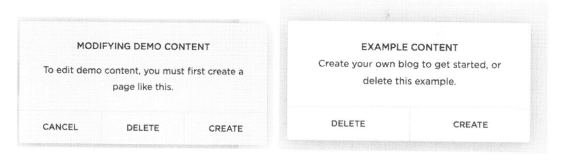

Figure 2-4. *Regular Page and Blog demo content prompt*

For this example I will keep the Contact page demo for the PAWsitive Connections TX website since we included a contact page in the sitemap. The Contact page contains all of the filler content and some of the content blocks already. Figure 2-5 shows the wireframe content for the Contact page. I will keep the Shop, Blog, and Contact pages for use in the PAWsitive Connection TX site.

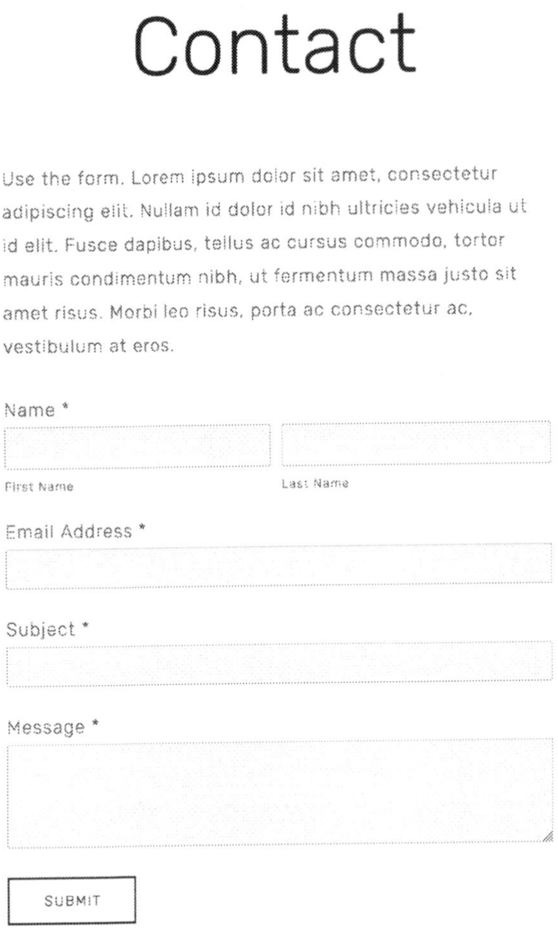

Contact

Use the form. Lorem ipsum dolor sit amet, consectetur adipiscing elit. Nullam id dolor id nibh ultricies vehicula ut id elit. Fusce dapibus, tellus ac cursus commodo, tortor mauris condimentum nibh, ut fermentum massa justo sit amet risus. Morbi leo risus, porta ac consectetur ac, vestibulum at eros.

Name *

First Name   Last Name

Email Address *

Subject *

Message *

SUBMIT

Figure 2-5. *Contact page wireframe content*

For this site I want to start with my own homepage rather than using the demo homepage. The demo homepage is indicated with a house icon next to the page type. However, when I go to delete the demo homepage, I get a prompt telling me that I cannot delete the homepage. A new homepage needs to be assigned before deleting the demo homepage. Figure 2-6 shows the home icon and the Cannot Delete Homepage message.

Figure 2-6. *Home icon and Cannot Delete Homepage prompt*

Adding Pages

In order to delete the demo homepage we will first need to create a new homepage and assign it as the homepage. To create a new page, click on the + sign to the right of the section name. In this instance we want to add a page to the Main Navigation. The Create New Page menu will appear with all of the options for creating a new page. These new pages are not limited to a page in the traditional sense of the word. The Create New Page options include Page (Regular Page), Products, Cover Page, Folder, Album, Blog, Events, Gallery, Link, and some template-specific page types. Figure 2-7 shows the + sign next to the Main Navigation section as well as the Create New Page prompt.

Figure 2-7. *Add new page + icon and Create New Page menu*

We will go through the different page types later in this chapter, but for now I will select Index since that is the same page type as the demo homepage. I will name it "Home" and then open the Page Settings menu by clicking on the gear icon. Figure 2-8 shows the prompt to name the new page and the Page Settings gear icon.

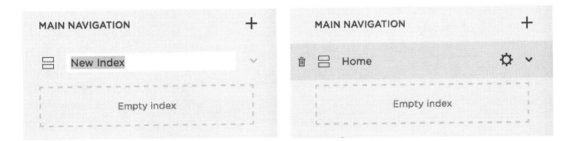

Figure 2-8. *New page name prompt and Page Settings gear icon*

Inside the Page Settings menu there are three menus of page settings. The options are Basic, Media, and Advanced. Scroll down to the bottom of the Basic menu and there is a button that says "Set As Homepage." Select this button and then hit save. Now when we go back to the Pages menu we see that the home icon is now next to our new Home index page. Figure 2-9 has the Basic page settings menu, the scrolled down view of the Basic menu, and the home icon next to our new Home page. The demo page named Home can now be deleted.

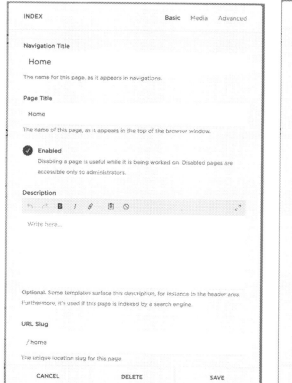

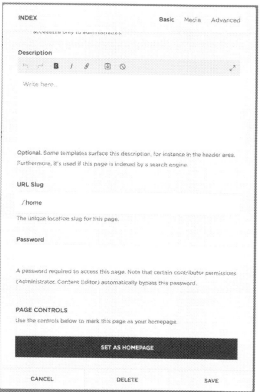

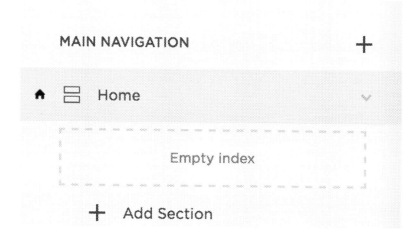

Figure 2-9. *Basic Page Settings menu, scrolled down view of Basic Page Settings menu, and newly set homepage with icon*

Page Settings

The first menu screen in the Page Settings is the Basic menu, as shown in Figure 2-9. The Navigation Title is the way that the page appears in the navigation menu for the site. The Navigation Title is also how the page appears in the Pages menu. The Page Title is the actual title of the page. For all templates the Page Title appears at the top of the browser window or tab. On some templates the Page Title is also displayed as text in the header area of the page layout. Search engines index the Page Title. The next setting in the Basic Page Settings menu is the Enabled button. If a page is Enabled it can be viewed by everyone. A disabled page is only accessible to site administrators. Search engines use the Description as the meta description for the page. It is also displayed on some templates in the banner area. The URL Slug sets the URL for the page. It is the portion of the URL that comes after the main domain of the site. The Password field allows you to set a password for a specific page. This is useful for providing clients with a page for their specific content.

The Media menu is the second menu option in Page Settings. This is where a banner or thumbnail image is uploaded for a specific page. For templates that support video backgrounds, YouTube and Vimeo videos can be added here as well. The third menu option in Page Settings is the Advanced menu. This is where you can add and manage Tags and Categories. For collections like a Blog, Tags and Categories will include all tags and categories used within the collection. The Page Header Code Injection is where custom code can be added to that specific page. We will explore all of the Code Injections later in this book. Figure 2-10 shows the Media menu and the Advanced menu.

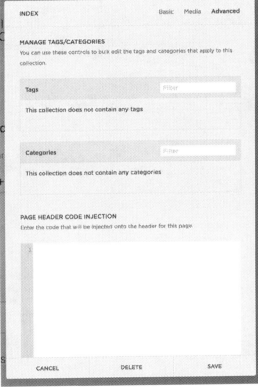

Figure 2-10. Page Settings Media menu and Advanced menu

Types of Pages

A Regular Page is the basic page type of the site. A Regular Page has a header area, content area, and footer area. The header and footer areas are global, meaning they appear the same on all pages. Changes made to the footer of one page will make the change on all pages. According to the sitemap we need a page for the local Rescues and Shelters listing. I will click the + icon opening up the New Page menu and select a Page.

The Create New Page menu asks me to give the page a Page Title and provides options for a Starter Layout. Starter Layouts populate the page with an initial set of Squarespace blocks with filler content. This is great for visualizing a page layout as a clickable wireframe. For the Rescues and Shelters page, I will select the Details 1 Starter Layout and click the Start Editing button. Figure 2-11 shows the Starter Layout menu screen and some of the layout options.

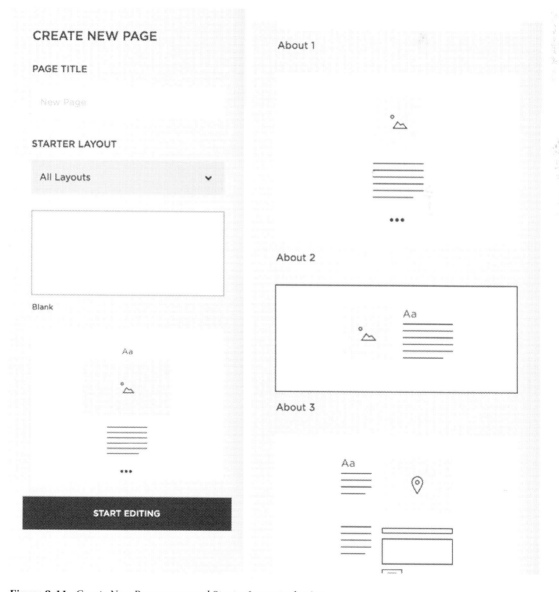

Figure 2-11. *Create New Page menu and Starter Layout selection*

Cover Pages are special page layouts and do not have the header or footer of the rest of the site. Cover Pages can be used as a splash page to put up while you work on the rest of the site or as a landing page for a particular campaign. Like a Regular Page with Starter Layouts, Cover Pages have a number of layouts to choose from. Figure 2-12 shows the Cover Page layout menu. Unlike other page types, you cannot add or remove content blocks from Cover Pages. Each cover page has specific fields for entering content into the Cover Page and a dedicated style editor that has Cover Page only styles. Additional content and styles can be added to a Cover Page but it has to be done through Code Injection.

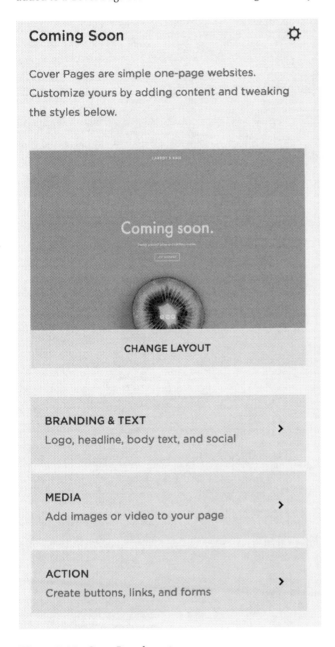

Figure 2-12. *Cover Page layout menu*

Albums are a special type of page for adding audio files to the site. They would typically be used for a CD or other collection of songs. An Album Page is very similar to the Record Cover Page. Like the Record Cover Page, additional blocks of content cannot be added to the Album Page. The main difference is that the Album Page will display the regular site header and footer where the Record Cover Page does not.

Folders are a non-content type of item that can be added to the site. Folders can contain any of the other page types. A folder in the navigation will create a sub-navigation section. Folders can also be used to organize your content. When a folder is added it has a section underneath that says + Add Page. Clicking on + Add Page will bring up the regular Create New Page menu and allow you to add any type of page to the folder. Figure 2-13 shows a Folder and the + Add Page section. It also has an example of a page having already been added to the folder. The example Test Page would appear in the sub-navigation for this Folder. The sub-navigation takes a different form depending on the template. Most templates have drop-down menus that appear under the main navigation item for Desktop view. For mobile view the sub-navigation is often an accordion that expands or another overlay panel that slides onto the screen.

Figure 2-13. *Folder and new page within the Folder*

Links are another type of non-content item. Links can be a Content link, File link, or External link. Content links are links to other pages within the website. File links are links to a PDF or other file that is stored in the Files section of the site. External links are links to other websites. It is always recommended to open external links in a new window. When adding a link in the Pages menu the Configure Link panel opens and asks you for the Link Title and the Link itself. Figure 2-14 shows the Configure Link panel and the Content link, File link, and External link options.

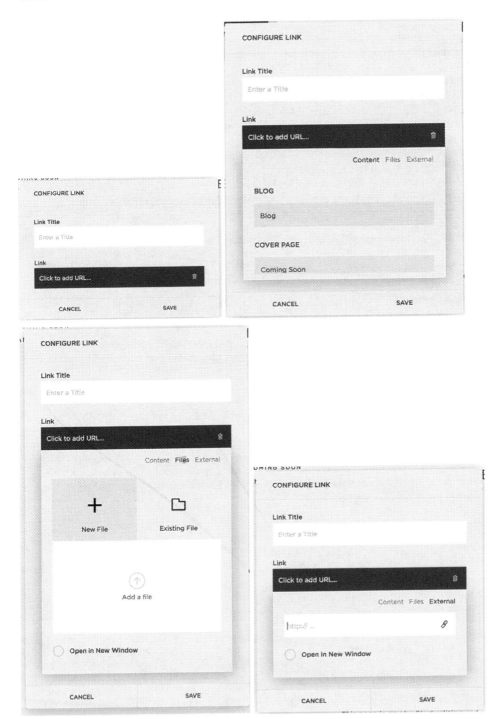

Figure 2-14. *Configure Link menu, Content, Files, and External links options*

Squarespace Collections

Collection is the term used by Squarespace to reference a group of items. There are a number of page types that are collections. Index Page, Gallery, Blog, Events, and Products are all types of Collections in Squarespace. Some templates have additional specialized Collections. It is also possible to create a custom collection with Developer Mode.

Earlier I created an Index Page for the Home page of the example site. An Index Page is a collection of Regular Pages. The Index Page groups Pages together and uses them as sections in the layout. In the Brine template the Index Page is a Stacked Index where each is Page a full-width panel in the Index. As you can see in Figure 2-9 the empty Home index has a + Add Section option to add sections to the Index. For the Brine family template the Index can contain Page and Gallery sections. Some templates have special page types that can also be added to the Index. Index Pages pull the content of the Regular Pages, and not the entire Regular Page; therefore it is not possible to password protect a single page within an Index. The entire Index can be password protected in the Index Page's Settings.

Gallery Page

Gallery Pages are used for displaying a group of images or videos. Most templates use the standard Gallery Page, which displays the images or videos in a slideshow or a grid. Some templates have special Gallery Pages with additional features or layouts. In the example site I will create a Gallery Page named Furry Friends and add pictures of animals that have been helped by PAWsitive Connections TX. The Gallery Page initially begins empty. Click the + sign to add items to the gallery. A menu appears with the items that can be added to the gallery. The options are an Image, Video, or a Getty library image. Figure 2-15 shows the empty gallery and the menu for adding items to the gallery.

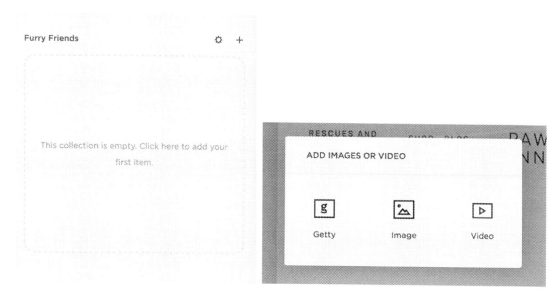

Figure 2-15. *An Empty Gallery Page named Furry Friends and the options for adding items to the gallery*

After the type of item to add to the Gallery is selected the item's settings appear. There are four pages of options for a Gallery item. The Content menu is where the actual image is uploaded and the Title for the item is entered. The text editor area adds a description to the item. Other controls like Tags, Categories, Comments and publishing are also part of the Content menu. Gallery items can be published immediately, scheduled to publish in the future, marked as needing to be reviewed, and marked as a draft. Figure 2-16 shows the Content menu and the publishing options.

Figure 2-16. *Content menu and publishing options*

The Options menu contains the Image URL, Author information, and the ability to select the image as a Featured Image. The Source URL provides a source for the item or a reference link for further reading. The Source URL is often displayed below the image. A Clickthrough URL allows the gallery item to link to another webpage.

The Location Menu sets a specific location for that gallery item. The Social menu allows the gallery to be connected to social media accounts. Figure 2-17 shows the Options, Location, and Social menus.

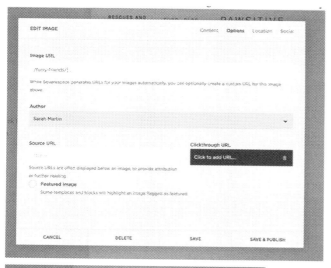

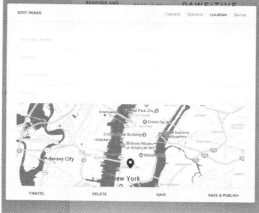

Figure 2-17. *Options, Location, and Social item menus*

Once items have been added into a Gallery Page it no longer appears empty. Thumbnails of the Gallery items now appear as shown in Figure 2-18. Adding a Video to the Gallery Page is the same process as adding an image. The Video item has an additional field to enter the embeddable URL of the video. There is also a Use Thumbnail option that will display the video thumbnail image rather than the videos default preview image. The video Content option is also shown in Figure 2-18.

Figure 2-18. *Gallery with two image items and Video item Content options*

Blog

The Blog, or blog list, is another type of Collection that contains blog posts. The Blog displays the blog posts in a list or grid, depending on the template. The Page Settings for the Blog contain additional blog-specific settings. In the Page Settings Basic menu there is a Posts Per Page setting that determines the number of Posts to display on the Blog page. The Features menu determines if the Full blog post text or the Excerpt is displayed on the blog list. The Syndication menu allows the blog to connect to podcasting and RSS feeds. The Advanced menu has an additional code injection called Post Blog Item Code Injection. Figure 2-19 shows the Basic, Advanced, Syndication, and Features menu options.

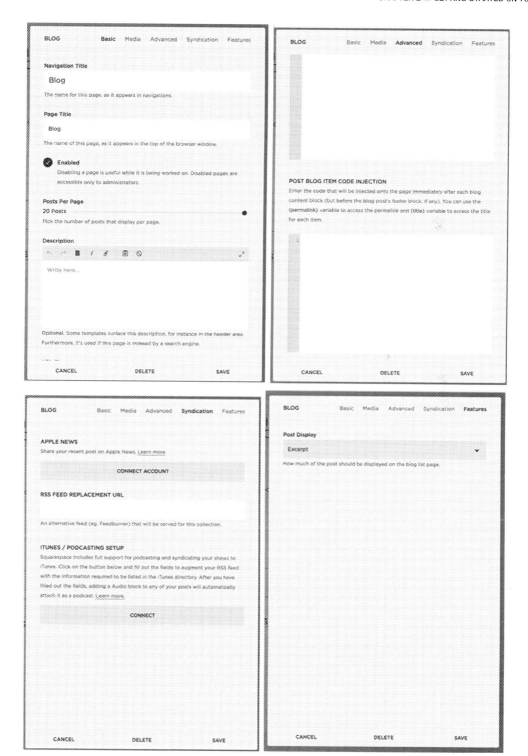

Figure 2-19. *Blog Settings Basic, Advanced, Syndication, and Features menu*

The Blog Post Editor opens when the + sign is clicked to add a new post. The Blog Post Editor has Content, Options, Location, and Social sections. The Content section is where the actual content for the post can be added. It contains a section for the post title, the content for the title, Tags, Categories, Comments and publishing settings. Once a blog post is created the content can also be edited in the page editor. The Options section is where a thumbnail image can be uploaded. Some templates display the post's thumbnail as a banner image on the individual post page. Other templates use it as the image in the blog list grid. The Options section also includes settings for Post URL, Author, Source URL, Excerpt, and Featured Post. Some templates and blocks will highlight a Featured Post with additional styling or layout changes. Figure 2-20 shows the Blog Post Editor Content and Options menus.

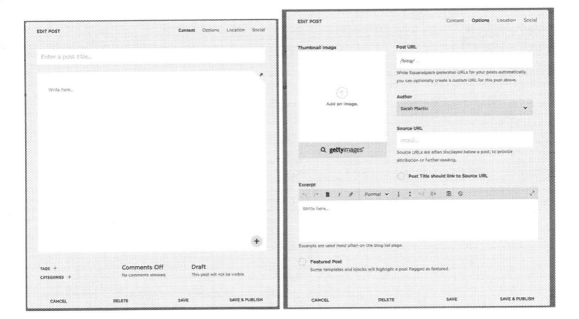

Figure 2-20. *Blog Post Editor, Content, and Options sections*

Events

The Events Page is a Collection of individual Event items. In the Events Page's Basic menu there is a select field to choose the Default Event View. The options are a list or calendar layout. Figure 2-21 shows the Default Event View in the Basic menu. The major limitation with the Squarespace Events Page is that there is no support for recurring events. This means that weekly or other recurring events have to be repeatedly duplicated. Recurring events is an often-requested feature. Squarespace has indicated that recurring events is on the road map for development. In the meantime if a client needs easy recurring events, or has a large number of events, there are other calendar tools that can be added to the Squarespace site via a Code Block.

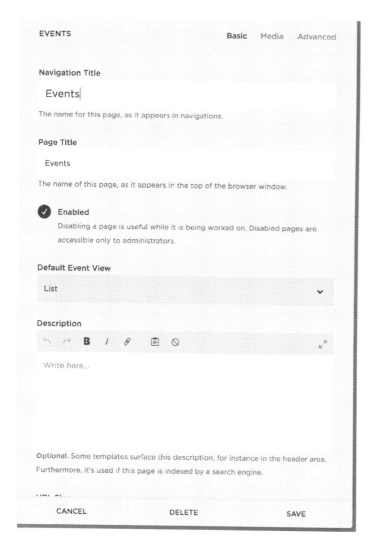

Figure 2-21. Events Page Settings Basic menu

The Event Editor opens when a new Event is added and is very similar to the Blog Post Editor. The Content menu contains the settings for event title, content, Tag, Categories, Comments and publishing. The Event Editor Content menu also includes fields to set the start and end times for the event. Event items can last for a single day or span several days. A date and time must be set for each Event item. An Event item cannot be set as an all day event; it must have a start and end time. The Event Editor Options menu contains the settings for Event URL, Author, Source URL, Excerpt, Featured Event, and the Thumbnail Image. Depending on the template the thumbnail image may appear only in the Events list or it may also appear on the Event item page. Figure 2-22 shows the Event Editor Content and Options menus.

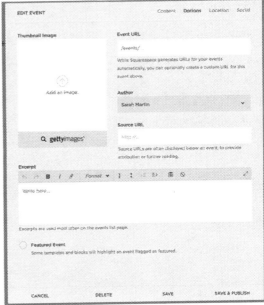

Figure 2-22. *Event Editor Content and Options menus*

Products

The Products Page is the online store. It is a Collection that contains all the items for sale in the store. Some templates have advanced features including additional category and display options. This section will only go over the basic settings and features available in every template. Squarespace supports three types of products: digital, service, and physical. Digital products are purchased and then downloaded. The customer receives the download link in the purchase confirmation email. The download link will expire after 24 hours. Service products are for services provided by a person. Service products are not shipped and therefore do not include shipping information in the checkout process. Service products also don't require sales tax. Physical products are products that are shipped to a customer or require the collection of sales tax. Figure 2-23 shows the new product menu with the three types of product selections.

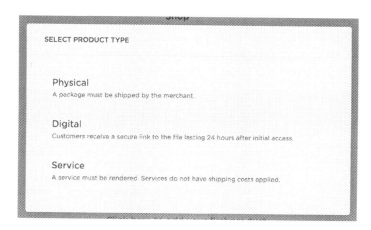

Figure 2-23. *Product type, Physical, Digital, and Service*

Squarespace is actively improving their e-commerce offerings with new features being released regularly. It is important to understand that there is very little about online stores that can be customized outside of the Squarespace interface. All transactions are processed on separate secure Squarespace servers. This is fantastic for protecting a customer's privacy and personal information, but it makes it very difficult to change the checkout process. It is important to check the Squarespace documentation to ensure that all your client's needs are met before starting a Squarespace e-commerce site. It is especially important to ensure that Squarespace can meet the shipping, tax, and discount code needs.

Each item for sale will be a Product in a Products collection. Each Product has a number of settings in the Product Editor. The menus in the Product Editor include Item, Pricing & Variants, Additional Info, Form, Options, and Social. The Item menu has settings for product name, description, thumbnail image, tags, categories, and publishing status. The Pricing & Variants field opens the Pricing & Variants menu. Settings in the Pricing & Variants menu include the SKU, Price, Stock, Weight, Dimensions and custom fields. Figure 2-24 shows the Item and Pricing & Variants menus.

Figure 2-24. *Product Editor Item and Pricing & Variants menus*

The Additional Info menu contains the main content for the item. This is where any content Blocks can be added. The content in the Additional Info section typically appears underneath the product thumbnails, name, description, and add to cart button. If you are duplicating products the Additional Info section is not duplicated into the new product. The Form menu allows a custom form to be added to the product. This is useful if additional information needs to be collected from the user to customize their purchase. For example, if the product were a mug with a custom message, the custom form would be used to collect the message. Figure 2-25 shows the Additional Info and Form menus.

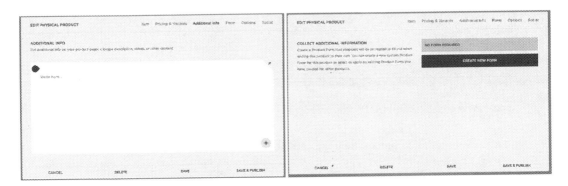

Figure 2-25. Product Editor Additional Info and Form menus

The Service and Digital products have similar Product Editors. The Digital Product Editor has an additional field to upload the digital file. The Services Product Editor doesn't have the weight or dimensions of the product since that isn't necessary for Service products. Please refer to the Squarespace documentation for detailed descriptions of all the Product settings.

Setting Up Navigation Menus

Once pages have been added to the site they need to be organized into menus. Every template has a Main Navigation menu area and a Not Linked area. Some templates have additional menu areas. The Brine template has three menu areas: Main Navigation, Secondary Navigation, and Footer Main Navigation. I would like the header navigation to appear on the left and right around the site's logo. I will use the Main Navigation on the left of the logo and the Secondary Navigation on the right. I will also move the Home index out of the Main Navigation and down to the Not Linked section. If the homepage is in the Not Linked section it won't appear in the navigation menus, but the site's logo or site title will link to the homepage. Figure 2-26 shows the Main Navigation and Secondary Navigation set up and the Not Linked section containing the Home index. An existing page can be clicked and dragged within a menu section, or between menu sections, to reorder the navigation.

Figure 2-26. *Main Navigation, Secondary Navigation, Not Linked menus for PAWsitive Connections TX website*

Adding Content Using Blocks

Squarespace Blocks are used to add content to the website. The main content area of each page or post accepts content Blocks. Blocks can also be added to the footer area of most templates. Some templates have special regions for adding Blocks to a sidebar or navigation menu area. There are many different types of Blocks and Squarespace is regularly adding Blocks to the platform. This section will discuss some of the core blocks but there are many more. There are Blocks for specific services, filtering options, calendars, and many more. Please refer to the Squarespace documentation for a list of all Blocks and their functionality.

The Text Block allows you to add a section of text. The Text Block has a basic text editor controls, bold, italic, ordered list, bulleted list, tabs, text alignment, and text style selection. The text style is limited to Normal, Heading 1, Heading 2, Heading 3, Quote, and Code. This limitation can be frustrating but exists to help users keep a consistent look and feel to their website. If text needs a special style this can be accomplished with a code block. Text Blocks also have the ability to add a link. This is especially important to note because this is the easiest way to add files to the file management system. I typically create a Text Block and start to make a link. Then I upload files and delete the Text Block. The files will stay stored in the file management system even when the Text Block is deleted. Any item added to the file management system will have a URL of '/s/filename.pdf'. When customizing a site I will often use this technique to add an image or file to the file management system to be used in my custom code. Figure 2-27 shows the editor for a Text Block.

Testing!|

Figure 2-27. *Text Block Editor*

The Image Block is another core block. The Image Block is for adding a single image to a section of the site. The Image Block has a content menu to upload an image and the Design menu to style the Image Block. Image Blocks on Regular Pages have six different layouts to choose from. Other types of pages have only the Inline layout. The Inline layout has style options for caption placement, opening the image in a lightbox, and adding a clickthrough URL. Figure 2-28 shows the Image Block Content and Design menus.

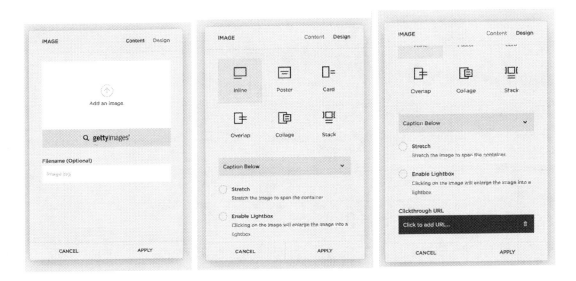

Figure 2-28. *Image Block Content and Design menus*

Gallery Blocks add a collection of images to the page. Gallery Blocks have four different layouts: Slideshow, Carousel, Grid, and Stack. Images can be added directly to a Gallery Block or an existing Gallery Page can be selected to use in the Gallery Block. Gallery Blocks can display the image and the image's title and description. The Content menu is where the images are uploaded or a Gallery Page is selected. The Design menu lists the four layout options and the controls for each option. Figure 2-29 shows the Gallery Block Content and Design menus. Later in the book we will use custom code to add cool hover effects to a Grid Gallery Block.

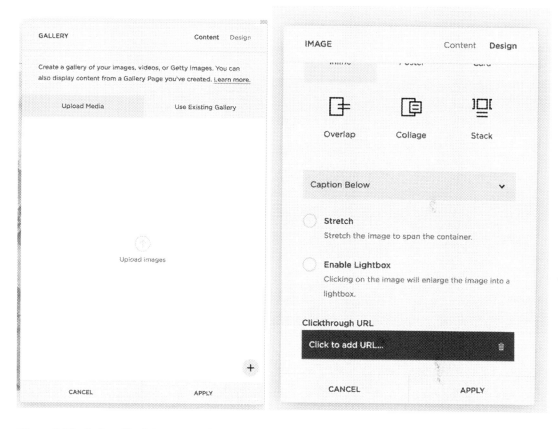

Figure 2-29. *Gallery Block Content and Design menus*

Summary Blocks are similar to Gallery Blocks in that they display a group of information. Summary Blocks can only be used with Product, Event, Blog, and Gallery Collections. The Summary Block has four layout options: Wall, Carousel, List, and Grid. Summary Blocks can display the item's title, thumbnail, excerpt, and metadata. Since the Summary Block can display so much information it is great to highlight blog posts and events across the site.

The Code Block is another extremely useful block that we will use in the example website. Code Blocks can accept HTML, CSS, and JavaScript code. Code Blocks are used for adding third-party plug-ins to the site as well as creating custom features not already included in Squarespace.

Arranging Blocks

Any section where Blocks can be added uses a 12-column grid. The columns make it easy to add rows and columns of Blocks. It's easy to make block 1/2, 1/3, 1/4, and 1/6 the width of the grid. It also allows for columns of 1/3 and 1/4 with the rest of the content spanning 2/3 or 3/4 of the page respectively. Figure 2-30 shows a 12-column grid with various size blocks to illustrate some of the possible layouts. There are limitations with the 12-column grid. The Blocks can't span part of a column. For example, the 12-column layout also doesn't allow for 5 equally sized items in a row since 5 cannot equally divide 12. Five items in a row can be done within some of the Block settings but the Block itself must span whole columns. The other scenario I have run into problems with the 12-column grid is adding sponsor logos. Using an image block to add a sponsor logo has occasionally resulted in a logo that is too big or too small, depending on the number of columns it spans. In this case I have sometimes created a gallery for the logos as a workaround.

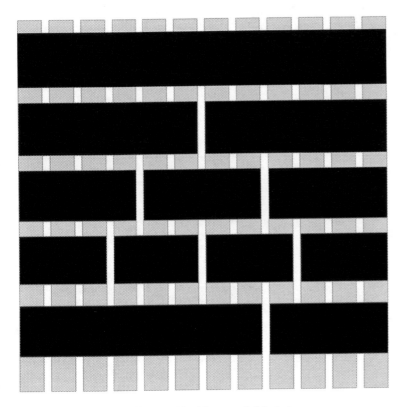

Figure 2-30. *Twelve-Column grid with example block sizes*

When working in the 12-column grid, teardrop-shaped insertion markers appear indicating where another Block can be added. Clicking on the insertion marker will open the new Block menu. Guidelines also appear indicating where the new block will be placed. If the guideline spans the full width of the grid then it will create a new row. If the guideline spans the full height of the page then it will create a new column. Figure 2-31 shows the teardrop insertion marker and a full-width row guideline.

Contact

Use the form. Lorem ipsum dolor sit amet, consectetur adipiscing elit. Nullam id dolor id nibh ultricies vehicula ut id elit. Fusce dapibus, tellus ac cursus commodo, tortor mauris condimentum nibh, ut fermentum massa justo sit amet risus. Morbi leo risus, porta ac consectetur ac, vestibulum at eros.

Figure 2-31. Teardrop insert marker and insert marker with new row guideline

Squarespace automatically wraps all blocks into a single column for mobile size screens. Rows wrap from left to right into a single column. Columns stack from left to right. To get the desired mobile layout the blocks must be added in the correct place. A typical scenario is three columns of images and a paragraph of text under the image. For desktop view the images appear in a row and the text appears in a row under the images. However for mobile view the text needs to appear directly below its associated image. Figure 2-32 shows how the guidelines could appear when adding the blocks and the corresponding mobile view. The image blocks were all added first and a new row was created for the text blocks. Following the Squarespace layout rules the first row of images wraps into a single column and then the next row. This results in the mobile view showing three images and then three text blocks.

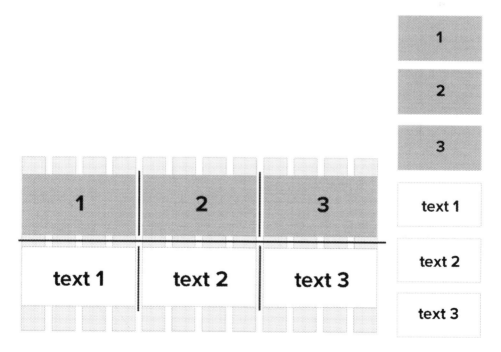

Figure 2-32. Layout option 1 with corresponding mobile view

The layout can be adjusted to appear correctly on mobile view by having the image and text be contained in the same row. This is accomplished by using the guidelines to "stick" the text block to the bottom of the image block. This ensures that the text blocks are part of the same column and outer row as the image blocks. Figure 2-33 shows the guidelines for laying the blocks out correctly. I would first add the three image blocks and then add each text block ensuring that the guideline for inserting it is only as wide as the image block. This creates three columns of images with a second row of text within each column. Then when the layout wraps for mobile view the image / text sections wrap together creating the desired layout.

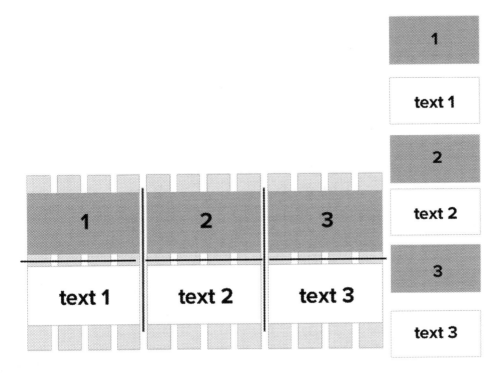

Figure 2-33. *Layout version 2 with corresponding mobile view*

There are some scenarios where the desired desktop layout does not wrap to the desired mobile view. There are ways to use custom code to force the blocks to wrap to the desired mobile view. However, it is best practices to always get the layout as close as possible using the built-in Squarespace layout tools.

Wrap-Up

You should now feel comfortable adding pages and content to your site. A strong understanding of the 12-column grid layout will aid in the design of the site. I recommend overlaying a 12-column layout when working on the design files to ensure that the website can match the approved client design. The next chapter will start exploring the Style Editor and other style settings for the site.

CHAPTER 3

■ ■ ■

Styling Your Site

In this chapter we will explore the built-in styling tools that Squarespace offers. These tools are user friendly and require no custom coding. The styling tools are all found in the Design panel. The main style tool is the Style Editor. The Style Editor contains different settings based on the template. Each of these settings is called a Tweak. Tweaks can be anything from layout options to colors and fonts. The newer template families have more Tweaks than the older templates. Older templates can usually achieve the same style customization using CSS if the template lacks a Style Editor Tweak. We will discuss customizing the site using CSS later in this book.

Logo & Title

The first Design panel option is called Logo & Title. This is where the Site Title and optional Tag Line are set and where a Logo can be uploaded. The Site Title is the name of the website and is usually the business or organization's name. The Site Title can appear in multiple places on the website. The Tag Line is an option that appears on some templates but not others. If a Logo is added to the site then the logo is displayed in place of the Site Title. Some templates have Style Editor Tweaks to change this behavior. Figure 3-1 shows the Site Title / Tag Line and Logo Image settings. The Site Title and Tag Line are just typed into the corresponding boxes. To add a logo, click the upload arrow and select a logo file from your computer.

© Sarah Martin 2017
S. Martin, *The Definitive Guide to Squarespace*, https://doi.org/10.1007/978-1-4842-2937-8_3

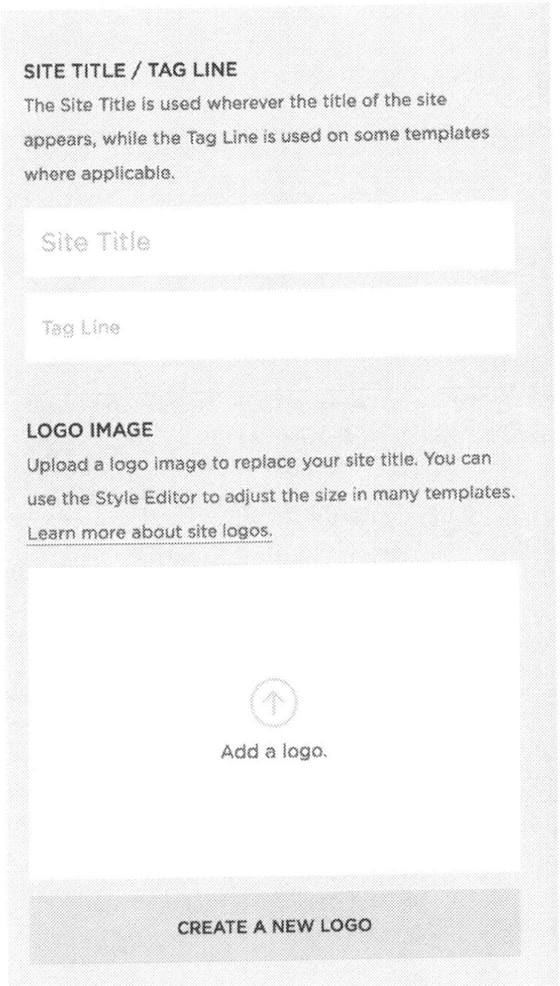

SITE TITLE / TAG LINE

The Site Title is used wherever the title of the site appears, while the Tag Line is used on some templates where applicable.

Site Title

Tag Line

LOGO IMAGE

Upload a logo image to replace your site title. You can use the Style Editor to adjust the size in many templates. Learn more about site logos.

↑

Add a logo.

CREATE A NEW LOGO

Figure 3-1. Site Title, Tag Line, and Logo settings

The Logo & Title section also has the option to add a Browser Icon (Favicon) and a Social Sharing Logo. If you do not add a Browser Icon then the default Squarespace icon will display. Figure 3-2 shows the default Browser Icon and the Browser Icon and Social Sharing Logo input areas. It is important to note the information above the Social Sharing Logo (Optional) input. The Social Sharing Logo will be used as the sharing preview image for all non-collection pages. This includes Regular Pages and Index Pages. For Collection items (like blog posts and events) the thumbnail image for the item will be used for sharing. It isn't possible to add individual sharing images to specific Regular Pages. If you do not include a Social Sharing Logo then the social site will take its best guess at what image to use.

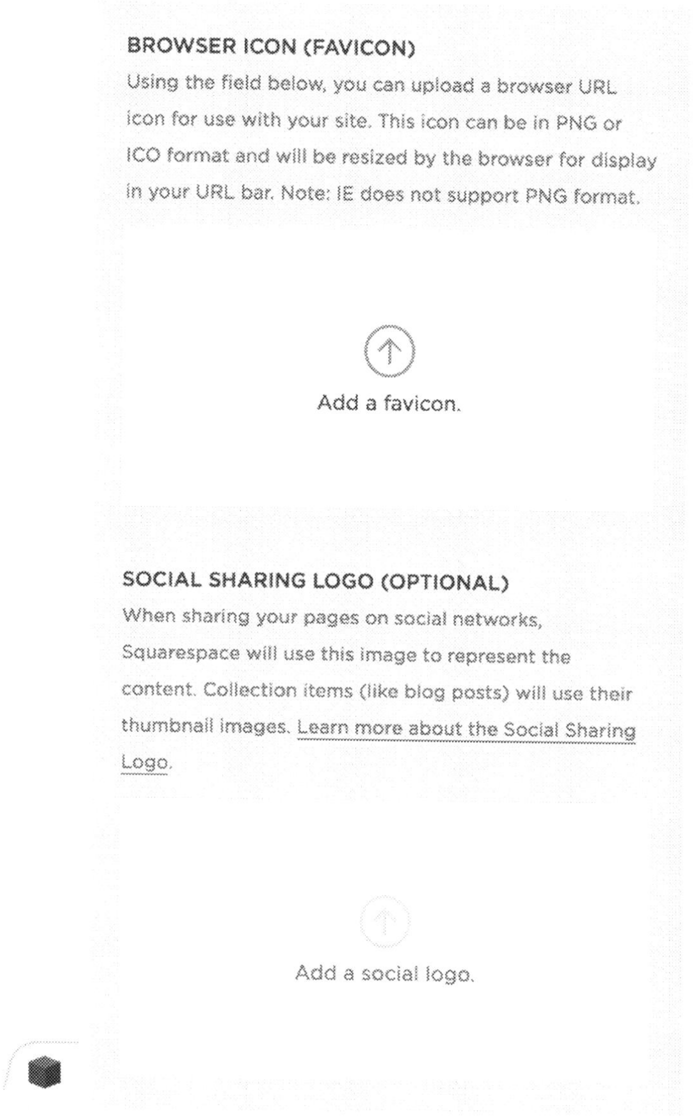

BROWSER ICON (FAVICON)

Using the field below, you can upload a browser URL
icon for use with your site. This icon can be in PNG or
ICO format and will be resized by the browser for display
in your URL bar. Note: IE does not support PNG format.

Add a favicon.

SOCIAL SHARING LOGO (OPTIONAL)

When sharing your pages on social networks,
Squarespace will use this image to represent the
content. Collection items (like blog posts) will use their
thumbnail images. Learn more about the Social Sharing
Logo.

Add a social logo.

Figure 3-2. *Default Browser Icon and Browser Icon and Social Sharing Logo input sections*

Template Selector

The Template selection area is where the template for the website can be changed. The site's current template is listed and marked as "LIVE." Figure 3-3 shows the Brine template marked as "live." Select the Install New Template button to view the overview of templates. The template selection process is the exact same as it is for starting a site. The overview of Templates is displayed and you can navigate between them to view the template options. When viewing a particular template, the Preview button will open the demo site for the template. When adding a template from the Template Selector, the Start button installs the template into your existing site account rather than starting a new website. Figure 3-3 shows the Start and Preview buttons for the Farro template.

Figure 3-3. Brine template marked as "live," Start, and Preview buttons for Farro template

The newly installed template will display in the Template menu section of your site. Figure 3-4 shows where the Farro template was added to the example website. The Brine template is still marked as "live" and the Farro template now appears below it. Hovering over the template will display the options to preview the template or uninstall it. Previewing the template will change the template only inside the Squarespace interface. This allows you to update and style the site while the original site continues to be live. It is possible for some adjustments to appear on the live site. If both templates have the same tweak, or if you remove background images, the changes will appear on the live site. I recently completed a project moving a site from the Marquee template to the Brine template. For these types of conflicting changes, I kept a list and made the changes right before making the new template live. Figure 3-4 also shows the Preview and Uninstall buttons.

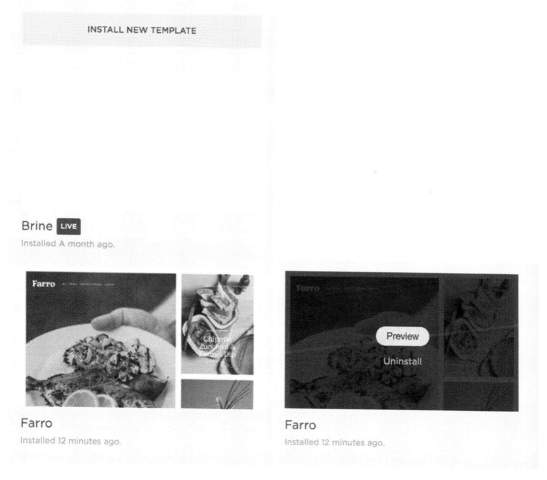

Figure 3-4. Installed template listing, and Preview and Uninstall buttons

When previewing a template, a utility bar shows at the bottom of the main section. The utility bar has two buttons: "Cancel Preview" and "Set as Live Template." Choosing "Cancel Preview" will exit preview mode returning you to the live template. Choosing "Set as Live Template" will make the template you are previewing, along with the selected settings, the live template. Figure 3-5 shows the utility bar with buttons. Custom code doesn't always appear or work correctly in preview mode. Previewing custom code will require using a different approach to updating a live site, which we discuss later.

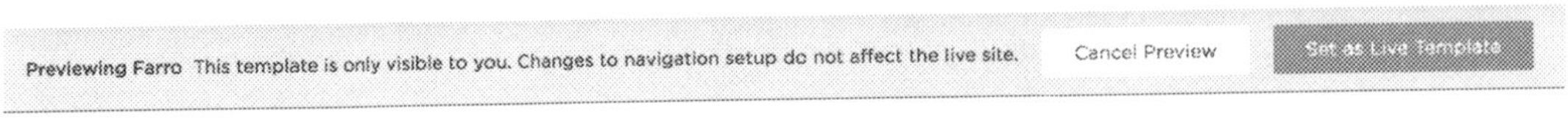

Previewing Farro This template is only visible to you. Changes to navigation setup do not affect the live site.   Cancel Preview   Set as Live Template

Figure 3-5. *Preview template utility bar with Cancel Preview and Set as Live Template buttons*

Style Editor

The Style Editor is where the majority of the site styling is done. Every template within a template family will have the same set of Tweaks. The Tweaks and their names will vary between template families. Some Tweaks will only appear in the Style Editor if you are viewing a page that corresponds to that Tweak. For example, the Blog Tweaks will only appear if you are on a Blog Page.

Finding a Style Tweak

All of the Tweaks in the Style Editor are organized into categories. The categories group the Tweaks by location or purpose to make it easy to find the Tweak you are looking for. For example, in Figure 3-6, the Site category groups together the Tweaks that implement site-wide styles. Areas of the site can also be selected in the right-hand panel to display only the Tweaks related to that area. For example, if I click the logo on the example site then a blue box appears around it and the Tweaks in the Style Editor are filtered to show just the related Tweaks. Figure 3-6 also shows the blue box around the logo and the filtered Tweaks. The filtered tweaks list the positioning options and the Logo Width Tweak.

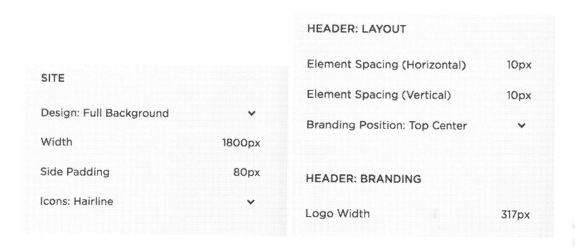

Figure 3-6. *Site category Tweaks, Logo selection, and corresponding filtered Tweaks*

Style Editor Controls

The controls for the Style Editor include Save, Cancel, undo, redo, show all, and recent change indicator dots. Figure 3-7 shows the main controls. Changes to Tweaks are only saved one you click Save. If you click Cancel the Tweak values revert to the last saved version. The undo and redo controls allow you to undo or redo recent changes. If there are no changes to undo or redo then the corresponding indicator is gray instead of black. If you are viewing the filtered Tweak list, a Show All link appears next to "Style." Clicking Show All clears the filter allowing all Tweaks to display. The recent change indicator appears as a dot to the left of the Tweak name. The dot appears next to any Tweak value that has been changed since the last time the Tweaks were saved.

Figure 3-7. *Style Editor controls and recent change indicator dot*

Typography

Font styling, also known as typography, is a common style change. Many businesses have specific fonts they like to use. Font settings also define the personality of the site. Squarespace has a number of Typekit and Google Fonts built in to the Style Editor. Figure 3-8 shows what a couple of the font Tweaks look like in the Brine template family. The first tweak sets the body text for the site. Clicking on the drop-down arrow next to the Body Text tweak causes the Font selection tool to appear. The second image in Figure 3-8 shows the font selection tool. The first drop-down menu allows you to pick the font. The second defines the weight of the font. A font weight is how thick the lines are. For example when a font is bold it has a higher weight value. Some fonts have more weight options than others. The Style drop-down lets you choose between normal and italic. The Size selector allows you to pick the font size. The font size is determined in pixels, which is abbreviated px. Letter Spacing is the amount of space between each letter. Letter spacing is defined in ems. Ems is a unit of measure relative to the current font size. So 2em would be twice the size of the current font. Line height is the space between lines of text and is also defined in ems. If you prefer to use px rather than ems, you can skip using the size slider, click on the value, and type in your new value with px as the unit. The second Tweak sets the color of the font.

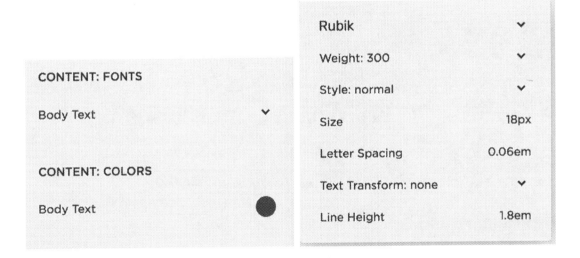

Figure 3-8. Typography options for Body Text Tweaks

Color Selection

The color selection tool is the same for all types of color tweaks. Therefore the process of selecting a background color is the same as selecting a font color. There are four areas to the color selection tool. Figure 3-9 shows the color selection tool. The first area is the rainbow bar across the top. This is a slider that selects the color hue. The second area is a square indicating the different brightness and saturation options. The Third input area is the transparency slider. This is very useful for color overlays and allows you to determine how much of the image underneath should show through the color. The final area is the direct color input area. If you have not put in a color code then this area shows the color code for the current color selection. If you would like to use a specific color, you can enter the color code in RGB, RGBa, HSL, HSLa, HEX, and HTML format.

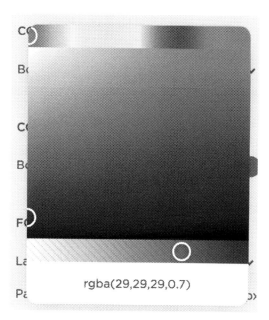

Figure 3-9. *Color Selection tool*

Color codes are different ways of defining color. RGB and RGBa stand for red, green, blue, and opacity. RGB color is referred to as light color. This is how computer screens and stage lights make different colors. This is different than pigment color, like CMYK, which is used for printing. HSL and HSLa is another method for defining color. HSLa stands for hue, saturation, luminosity, and opacity. The Squarespace color selector tool works off of this principle. Hex codes are six-digit codes that define a color. For example, white is #ffffff and black is #000000. Hex codes do not support an opacity value making RGBa and HSLa more robust options. The final type of color code that the color tool accepts is the HTML color code. These are names of colors like 'white', 'red', and 'blue'. There is a limited number of HTML colors and they are not frequently used.

Sizes and Values

The Style Editor offers a slider control to set sizes and values. The slider bar with indicator dot appears when you hover over the Tweak. In addition to dragging the dot, you can click on the number and type in your own value. This is useful if you would like your value to be bigger than the slider bar allows. Even though you can type in a value you cannot change the unit of the number. For example in Figure 3-10 the unit has to stay pixels (px).

Figure 3-10. *Size and Value slider selector*

Background Images

Earlier in Chapter 2 we discussed how to add Background Images to particular pages. Some templates have a Tweak allowing you to set a side-wide background image. Figure 3-11 shows a background image tweak and its image upload tool. Clicking on the Tweak name or circle will open the image upload tool. The image upload tool has four selectors in addition to the actual upload area. The Size setting has options for auto, contain, and cover. Auto allows the background image to default to its actual size. The contain option will ensure the entire photo is visible in the container. This often results in blank areas around the photo. The final option, cover, ensures that the photo covers the container area. Some of the image may be cropped off if the image shape doesn't match the browser window shape.

Figure 3-11. *Background Image Tweak and image upload tool*

The Position option indicates where the photo lies in relation to the container. The first value is the vertical positioning and the second is the horizontal positioning. If the top left is selected then the top left corner of the image will always be visible in the top left corner of the container. The Repeat field indicates if the image should repeat. The options are no-repeat, repeat, repeat-x, and repeat-y. Repeat will repeat the image in a pattern that covers the whole container. Repeat-x and repeat-y allow the image to only repeat in the specified direction. Repeats can be useful for creating a border out of a single small image. The Fix Position: Tweak has the options of fixed and scroll. If fixed is selected then the image will stay in the same place while the content scrolls over it. If scroll is selected then the background image moves along with the content.

Layout Options

Many of the templates have drop-down selectors for different layout options. Figure 3-12 shows some of the layout options for the Brine template family. The Brine template family has six header areas. There are two rows each with a left, center, and right section. The drop-downs provide the option for the branding and navigation menus to be in any of these six areas. Figure 3-12 also shows the example website header with the Logo in the center and navigation on the left and right.

Figure 3-12. Layout Tweaks in Brine template family and example website header

Mobile Styles

The newer templates all include mobile style Tweaks. The older templates have far fewer mobile style options. Since the different template families have different types of mobile navigation, the Mobile Tweaks are very specialized to the template family. There are Tweaks for color, size, and layout. Figure 3-13 shows some of the mobile menu Tweaks for the Brine template family. There is a special Tweak that some templates have called the Mobile Breakpoint. The Mobile Breakpoint is the browser width when the layout switches from the Desktop view to the Mobile view. For example, in Figure 3-13 the Mobile Breakpoint is set to 640px. This means that for browsers larger than 640px wide the Desktop navigation layout will show. For browsers smaller than 640px wide the mobile navigation layout will show. When a site has a large number of navigation menu items, the menu items may wrap to two lines on tablet size screens. If this is happening then the Mobile Breakpoint should be set to a higher value to so that tablets display the mobile navigation.

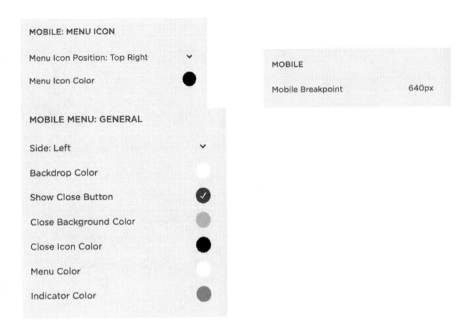

Figure 3-13. *Mobile Tweaks in Brine template family*

Page Specific Styles

The Blog, Event, Gallery, Index, and Product page types all have specific styles that only appear in the Style Editor when viewing one of those pages. For example, Figure 3-14 has some of the Blog Tweaks that appear when viewing a Blog page in the Brine template family. In the Brine template I can select between a grid blog layout and a stacked layout. For the Skye template family this is where the Blog layout can be changed from a grid layout to a masonry layout. There are Tweaks for the location of metadata and different pagination options. The page specific Tweaks are very unique to each template family. You can read more about the Tweaks available for a particular template on the Squarespace website.

Figure 3-14. *Blog Tweaks in Brine template family*

Image Block Example

Like the Blog styles, the style options for the Image Block only appear in the Style Editor on Regular Pages that have an Image Block added. I have added a collage layout Image Block to the example website. Figure 3-15 shows the default styling of the block based on my current Style Editor selections. The title obviously isn't in a good location since it covers the puppy's face.

Figure 3-15. *Default Styling of Collage Image Block*

Now that the image block has been added to the page the Tweak options appear in the Style Editor. Figure 3-16 has the full list of Tweaks for the Collage Image Block. I can use the second Tweak Content Position to move the content to the bottom of the image and off of the puppy's face. I also select a different font, change the size of the image and the text, and update the background color of the text. Figure 3-16 also shows the new Tweak values and the final style of the Image Block.

Figure 3-16. *Updated Image Block, original Tweak values, and updated Tweak values*

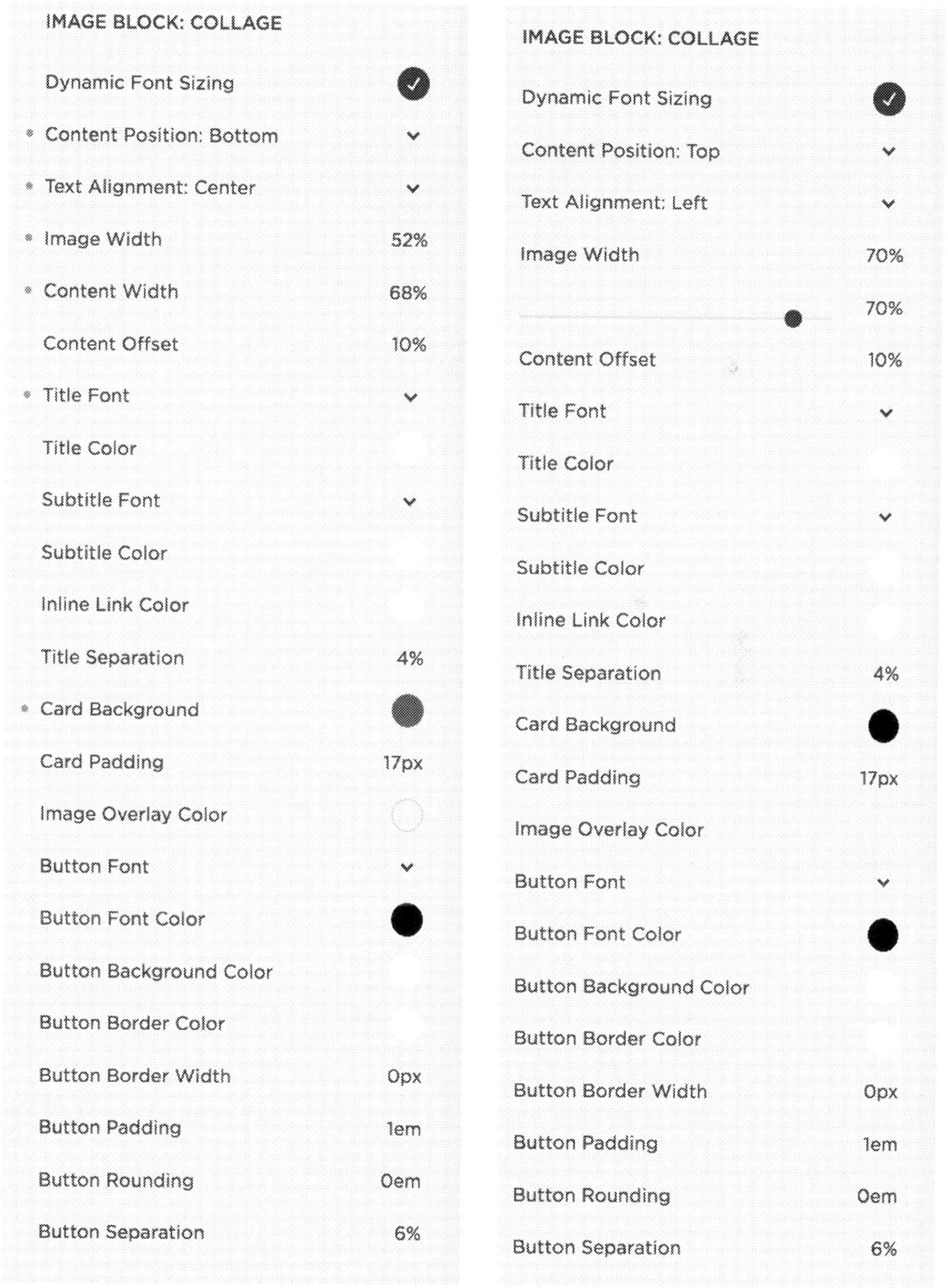

IMAGE BLOCK: COLLAGE

Dynamic Font Sizing	✓
⁕ Content Position: Bottom	⌄
⁕ Text Alignment: Center	⌄
⁕ Image Width	52%
⁕ Content Width	68%
Content Offset	10%
⁕ Title Font	⌄
Title Color	
Subtitle Font	⌄
Subtitle Color	
Inline Link Color	
Title Separation	4%
⁕ Card Background	●
Card Padding	17px
Image Overlay Color	○
Button Font	⌄
Button Font Color	●
Button Background Color	
Button Border Color	
Button Border Width	0px
Button Padding	1em
Button Rounding	0em
Button Separation	6%

IMAGE BLOCK: COLLAGE

Dynamic Font Sizing	✓
Content Position: Top	⌄
Text Alignment: Left	⌄
Image Width	70%
	70%
Content Offset	10%
Title Font	⌄
Title Color	
Subtitle Font	⌄
Subtitle Color	
Inline Link Color	
Title Separation	4%
Card Background	●
Card Padding	17px
Image Overlay Color	
Button Font	⌄
Button Font Color	●
Button Background Color	
Button Border Color	
Button Border Width	0px
Button Padding	1em
Button Rounding	0em
Button Separation	6%

Figure 3-16. (*continued*)

69

Checkout Page Style Editor

The Checkout Page Style Editor is a mini Style Editor for just the checkout page. The checkout page is what the site visitor sees after they click the "checkout" button on the shopping cart page. The checkout page is where the actual payment transaction takes place. Checkout pages run on separate special e-commerce servers. This separation is great for the security and protection of your customer's information. The separate checkout process does mean that there is limited customization available for the checkout transaction. The Tweaks are limited to colors and header alignment. There isn't the option to change the font, layout, or actual text. Figure 3-17 shows the Checkout Page Style Editor menu and the example website's checkout page.

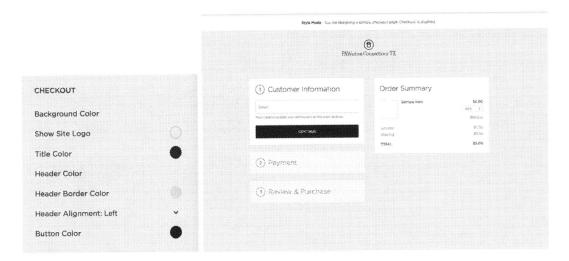

Figure 3-17. *Checkout Page Style Editor and example site Checkout Page*

Lock Screen

The lock screen displays when a website visitor views a password-protected page or website. The Lock Screen option in the Design panel contains the styling options for the lock screen. Like the Cover Page, there are style options and several different layouts to choose from. The lock screen is useful for providing a client or group of people access to private content. A lock screen can also be put up site-wide when a site is under construction. There is only one lock screen, so it cannot be customized on a per-page basis. A password can be added to a particular page in the page's Settings menu. A site-wide password can be set by selecting the Settings panel, clicking Security & SSL in the Website Category, selecting Enable Site-Wide Password, and adding a password. Figure 3-18 shows the Site-Wide Password selection in the Security & SSL section. We will explore these settings further in the next chapter.

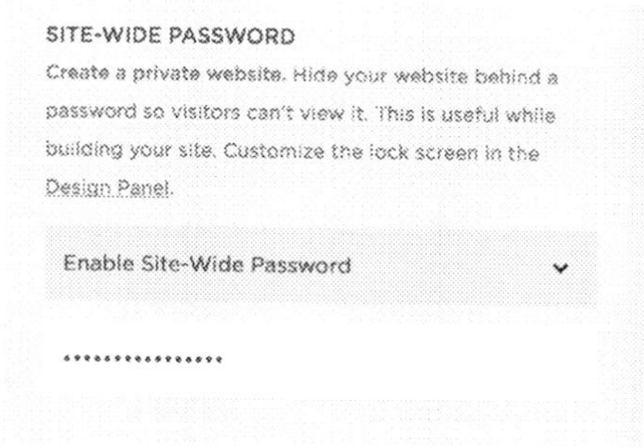

SITE-WIDE PASSWORD

Create a private website. Hide your website behind a password so visitors can't view it. This is useful while building your site. Customize the lock screen in the Design Panel.

Enable Site-Wide Password ⌄

••••••••••••••••

Figure 3-18. Enable Site-Wide Password menu settings

Using a site-wide password and lock screen is a popular method for updating an existing Squarespace website with a new template. If it is possible given the business's needs, then a site-wide password can be added and a lock screen put up while the website is under construction. This allows you full access to the site, including testing any custom code, without the site being available to the public. The final option for updating a site is to create a new website account for the updated website. When the new site is ready, Squarespace customer service can transfer the subscription from the original site to the new site.

In the Lock Screen panel there are four setting menus to choose from. Figure 3-19 shows the Lock Screen menus. Unlike other Squarespace options, the Lock Screen doesn't need to be enabled in order for the menu options to appear. In the case of a photographer, the lock screen can be styled and used as necessary to give clients private access to their photos. A running club could password-protect their routes and training schedule, allowing just their members to access the information.

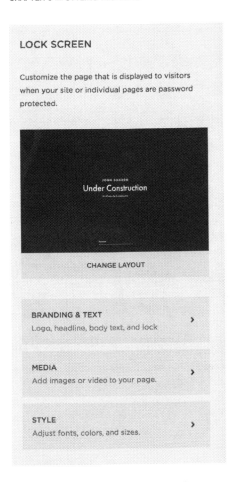

Figure 3-19. *Lock Screen menu options*

Selecting the "Change Layout" menu brings up the lock screen layout options. For the example site, I have chosen to use the "Under Construction" layout for the lock screen. Figure 3-20 shows some of the lock screen layout options. The layouts are all very simple and do not allow for the addition of Blocks. The main difference between the layouts is where the password and content fields are located on the page.

CHANGE LAYOUT

Figure 3-20. *Lock Screen layouts*

Once a layout has been selected, the content can be added in the Branding & Text menu option. The settings include Text or Logo, Headline, Body content, and lock icon option. For the example website I have chosen to go with the Text option for the organization name. If Logo is selected then the input to upload the logo image appears in the menu. The Headline text is typically a single line of text. The Body area can have a little more text with bold, italic, and linked content. The Display Lock Icon selector displays the lock icon if selected.

Figure 3-21 shows the Branding & Text menu.

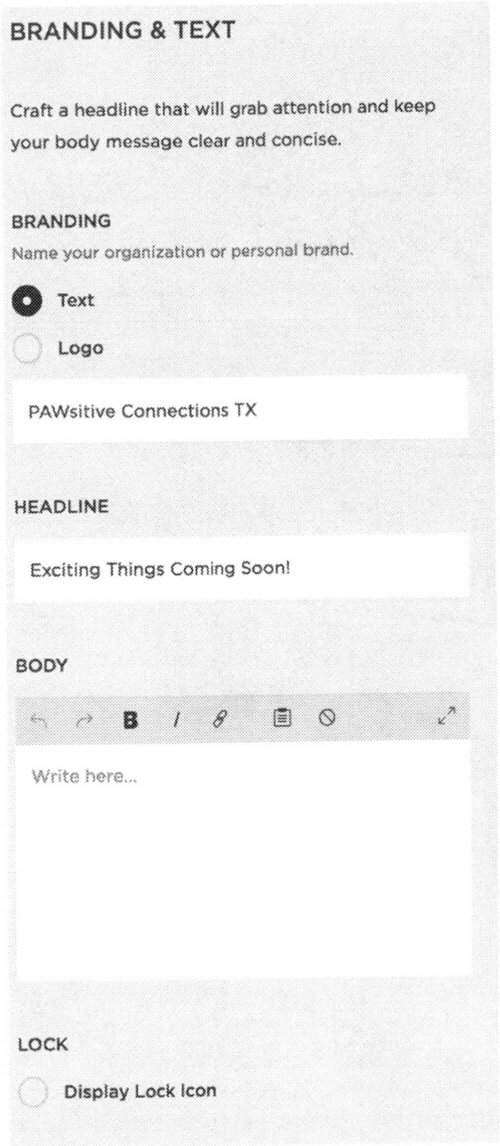

BRANDING & TEXT

Craft a headline that will grab attention and keep your body message clear and concise.

BRANDING
Name your organization or personal brand.

⦿ Text

◯ Logo

> PAWsitive Connections TX

HEADLINE

> Exciting Things Coming Soon!

BODY

> Write here...

LOCK

◯ Display Lock Icon

Figure 3-21. *Branding & Text menu options*

The next menu option is the Media menu. This is where a single image, gallery of images, or a video can be added to the lock screen. For the example website I added the puppy picture as the lock screen background. Adding multiple images creates a slideshow. Figure 3-22 shows the media menu for adding an image or a video. The background video option allows you to add a YouTube or Vimeo background video. There are also settings for filter effects, playback speed, and setting a Mobile Fallback Image. The Mobile Fallback Image displays on mobile devices. Mobile browsers don't support background videos.

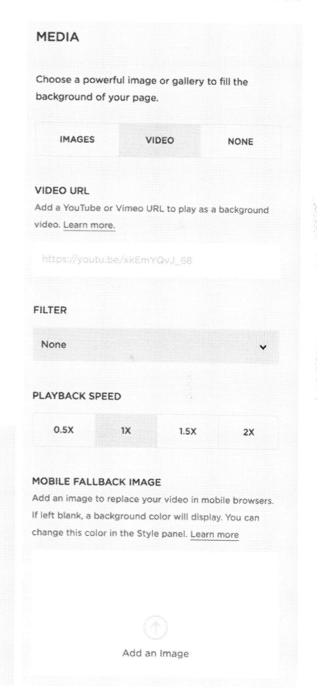

MEDIA

Choose a powerful image or gallery to fill the background of your page.

| IMAGES | VIDEO | NONE |

VIDEO URL
Add a YouTube or Vimeo URL to play as a background video. Learn more.

https://youtu.be/xkEmYQvJ_68

FILTER

None ⌄

PLAYBACK SPEED

| 0.5X | 1X | 1.5X | 2X |

MOBILE FALLBACK IMAGE
Add an image to replace your video in mobile browsers. If left blank, a background color will display. You can change this color in the Style panel. Learn more

↑
Add an Image

MEDIA

Choose a powerful image or gallery to fill the background of your page.

| IMAGES | VIDEO | NONE |

(+)
Add Images

Figure 3-22. *Media menu showing Image and Video options*

75

The final Lock Screen menu is the Style menu. It is a mini Style Editor just for the Lock Page. The style Tweaks include font and color all text, background color, page border, image overlay, and password input styles. The layout selected determines the placement of the text and password input. Therefore there are no layout Tweaks in the Style menu. Figure 3-23 shows the Lock Screen Style menu and the styled Lock Screen for the example website.

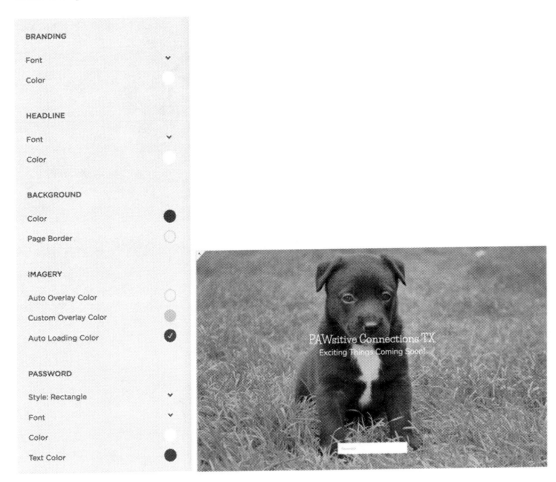

Figure 3-23. *Lock Screen Style menu and example website styled lock screen*

Announcement Bar

The Announcement Bar adds a text banner to the top of the website. This is often used to announce upcoming events, promotions, new releases, or any other type of time-sensitive information. It is important to keep in mind that the Announcement Bar can be closed by website visitors and won't appear repeatedly. The Announcement Bar adds an extra area to the site, drawing attention to the information, without changing the rest of the page layout. When enabled, the Announcement Bar appears at the top of every Page except for Cover Pages. I have seen the Announcement Bar used as a permanent feature of the site. When being used as a permanent design feature custom code was added hide the close button. This prevented the site visitor from closing the Announcement Bar.

The Announcement Bar option is disabled by default. Enabling the Announcement Bar will allow the menu options to appear. Figure 3-24 shows the Announcement Bar menu when it is disabled and enabled. The Announcement Bar allows for text to be added. The text can be bold, italic, and linked. The entire Announcement Bar can be made clickable by adding a link to the Clickthrough URL field. There is also an Announcement Bar Visibility option that appears when you have closed the Announcement Bar. Clicking the Reset Visibility button will allow the Announcement Bar to appear in your browser window. This is useful for testing purposes. The Reset Visibility button does not reset visibility for your website visitors. You can reset the visibility for your visitors by updating the content of the Announcement Bar.

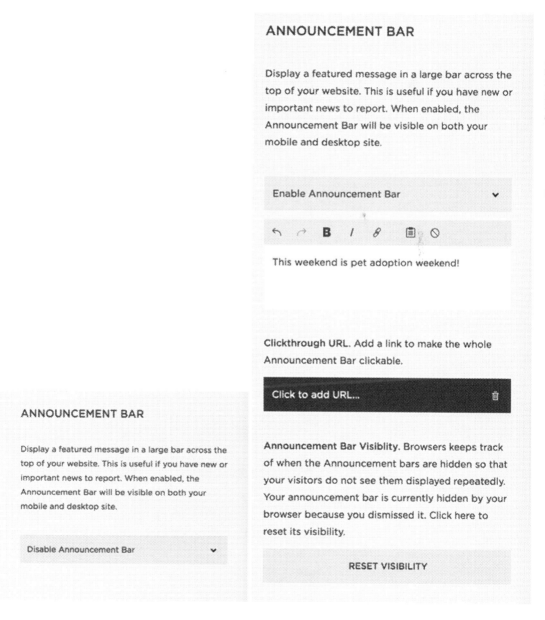

Figure 3-24. *Announcement Bar Disable menu options and Enable menu options. The Announcement Bar Visibility option only appears if you have dismissed the Announcement Bar by closing it.*

The Style Editor Tweaks for the Announcement Bar appear when the bar is enabled. The style options include changing the font, background color, and text color. Figure 3-25 shows the Style Editor Tweaks and the default view of the Announcement Bar for the example website. I want to draw attention to the Announcement Bar text so I update the color to green and change the font to Life Saver. The result is the second screen shot of the Announcement Bar shown in Figure 3-25.

Figure 3-25. *Announcement Bar Style Editor Tweaks, default bar styling, and updated styling*

Mobile Information Bar

The Mobile Information Bar is a great way to give mobile device users quick access to important information. It is disabled by default. When the Mobile Information Bar is enabled, the menu options appear. The Mobile Information Bar can include an email address, phone number, location, and hours. Checking any of the circles adds an icon for that information to the Mobile Information Bar. The actual content for the Mobile Information Bar is added to the Business Information menu under Settings. Figure 3-26 shows the default view for the Mobile Information Bar and the menu when it is enabled. Some templates have their own customizable Mobile Information Bars. The Brine template has two mobile bars, one at the top and one at the bottom of the site. If a template has special mobile bars then the standard Mobile Information Bar won't display.

MOBILE INFORMATION BAR

Show a simple notification tray to visitors on mobile devices. The Mobile Info Bar will appear at the bottom of your mobile site giving visitors quick access to directions, hours, an email address, and phone numbers. The information displayed in the Mobile Info Bar must be added/edited via Settings > Business Information

Enable Mobile Info Bar (Light) ⌄

◯ **Show Email**
info@pawsitiveconnectionstx.org
Edit Email

◯ **Show Phone Number**
555-555-5555
Edit Phone Number

◯ **Show Location**
Add a Location

◯ **Show Business Hours**
Monday: closed
Tuesday: closed
Wednesday: closed
Thursday: closed
Friday: closed
Saturday: closed
Sunday: closed
Edit Business Hours

MOBILE INFORMATION BAR

Show a simple notification tray to visitors on mobile devices. The Mobile Info Bar will appear at the bottom of your mobile site giving visitors quick access to directions, hours, an email address, and phone numbers. The information displayed in the Mobile Info Bar must be added/edited via Settings > Business Information

Disable Mobile Info Bar ⌄

Figure 3-26. *Mobile Information Bar default menu and enabled menu options*

There are two color schemes for the Mobile Information Bar: light and dark. Figure 3-27 shows the light and dark color schemes. The Mobile Information Bar can have any combination of these icons based on the checked options. The icons will always appear in this same order and be centered. The icon order is email, call, map, and hours. There are no Style Editor Tweaks for the Mobile Information Bar. The color and layout can only be changed using custom code.

Figure 3-27. *Mobile Information Bar Light and Dark color schemes*

Squarespace Badge

When starting a site some templates will have a text block with "Powered by Squarespace" in the footer blocks area. This block can be removed or edited just like any other content block. The Squarespace Badge menu provides different options for adding Squarespace recognition to your site. The default setting is Disable Squarespace Badge. The drop-down selector gives the options to add a black or white Squarespace Badge to the site. For the example website I will choose the black badge. Figure 3-28 shows the default view of the Squarespace Badge menu as well as the menu when the black badge option is selected.

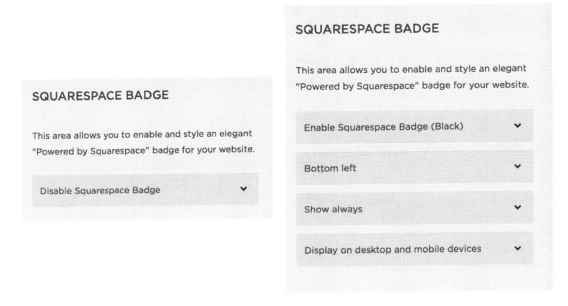

Figure 3-28. *Default menu for Squarespace Badge and menu when Enable Squarespace Badge is selected*

Three style options appear when the option to Enable Squarespace Badge is selected. The first new menu option sets the location of the badge. The badge can be left, center, or right at the top or bottom of the site. The next option allows the badge to always show, known as a fixed position, or only when the web page is scrolled to the bottom. This option only works for the bottom of the page badge locations. The final option allows the badge to display on only desktop devices or on all devices. Figure 3-29 shows the black Squarespace Badge as it appears on the bottom of the example website and its hover effect. The hover effect expands the badge and adds a semi-transparent overlay over the rest of the web page.

Figure 3-29. *Squarespace Badge and hover effect*

Custom CSS & Advanced

The Custom CSS menu option allows you to add CSS code to your site. We will be covering this extensively in future chapters. The Advanced menu option allows you to add a Typekit kit ID to your site. Typekit is a web font service provided by Adobe. Adobe offers a subscription to just Typekit and Typekit is included in the Creative Cloud subscription plan. Squarespace already includes some Typekit fonts. If you have a Typekit subscription and want to use additional Typekit fonts, then you can create a kit in your Typekit account. The kit will have its own ID. This ID is then added to Squarespace in this field. Figure 3-30 shows the Typekit kit ID input field.

Figure 3-30. *Typekit kit ID input area*

Wrap-Up

You should now feel comfortable with all of the built-in styling tools that Squarespace provides. It is very common to develop a favorite template to work with. Different web professionals find that their personal design style fits best with a particular template family. As you get more comfortable with the templates and their Style Editor Tweaks, you may develop a favorite as well. Now that we have covered building and styling the site, we will explore other site settings and best practices in Chapter 4.

CHAPTER 4

■ ■ ■

Site Settings and Best Practices

In this chapter we will explore some additional site settings. We will take a closer look at commerce, analytics, and advanced settings within Squarespace. Then we will explore SEO best practices and security options. Finally, we will wrap up with the process for launching a site. Squarespace is actively updating its commerce options with new capabilities. You can get the latest information and how-to documents on Squarespace's website.

Commerce

As we discussed in Chapter 1, there are four main menu options related to Commerce. The options are Orders, Inventory, Customers, and Discounts. For commerce websites these menu options appear in the Home menu. For all other websites they appear within the Commerce menu. In addition to these four menu options there is another section of commerce settings. These additional settings are found in the Settings menu under the Commerce category.

Orders

The Orders menu brings up a list of all orders placed through the website. Figure 4-1 shows the Orders menu. The orders can be filtered via the drop-down menu by Pending, Fulfilled, and Canceled status. The search bar will search the orders based on order number, email address, or name associated with the order. Exporting the orders as a CSV file allows the information to be uploaded into an inventory management system or other program.

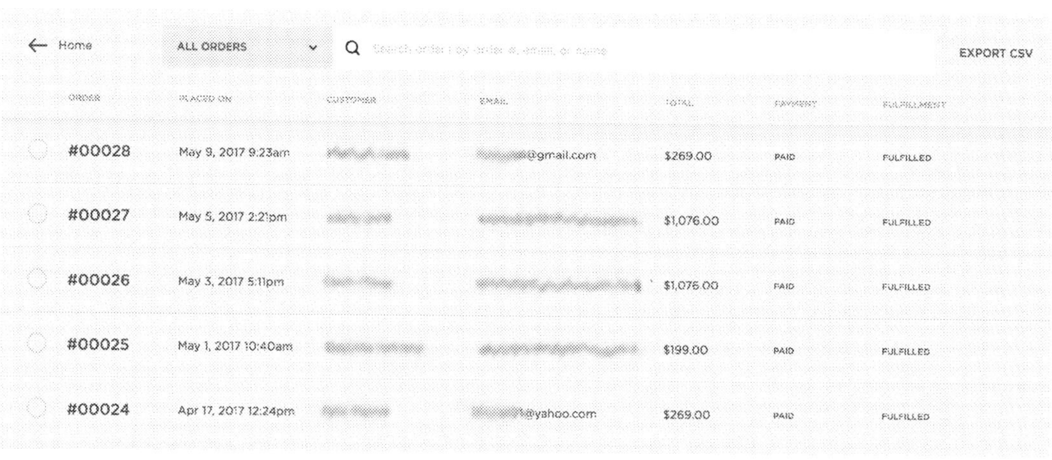

Figure 4-1. *Order list*

© Sarah Martin 2017
S. Martin, *The Definitive Guide to Squarespace*, https://doi.org/10.1007/978-1-4842-2937-8_4

To see the order details, click on the order number. Figure 4-2 shows the order detail screen. From the order detail screen you can print a receipt, issue a refund, or mark the status as pending. It also provides a link to the payment transaction in Stripe or PayPal. Figure 4-2 also shows the Email Notifications panel. The Email Notifications panel is an option in the top order detail menu along with Activity and Internal Notes. From the Email Notifications panel you can resend the order confirmation email or the order fulfilled notification email. The emails can be sent to the original email address, which will automatically populate in the email field, or to a new email address that you add.

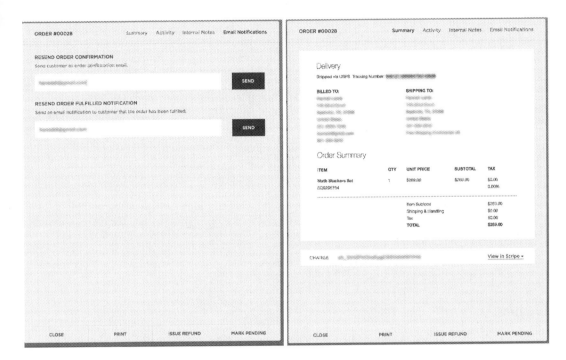

Figure 4-2. *Order detail screen and Email Notifications panel*

Inventory

The Inventory panel shows a list of all products across the website. If the website has multiple Product Pages then the Inventory menu shows all the products from all the Product Pages. Figure 4-3 shows the Inventory panel. In this particular website, there are two stores. One store does not charge sales tax and is used to sell products to schools. The other store charges sales tax, if necessary, and sells primarily to families. The inventory listing shows duplicate products because both stores carry many of the same products. If you click on an inventory item the Product editor opens. This is the same product editor that can be opened from the Products Page. You can also search for a product and add a product from the Inventory panel.

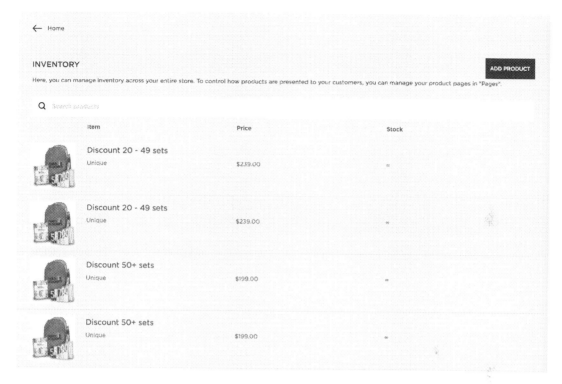

Figure 4-3. *Inventory Panel*

Customers

The Customers menu is only available on the Basic and Advanced Online Store subscription plans. The Personal and Business website plans do not have access to this option. The Customers menu allows for the customers to be filtered by name, email, and tags. It also supports exporting the information as a CSV file. The list of customers can be ordered by name, email address, number of orders, last order, or total amount spent. Figure 4-4 shows a list of customers.

NAME	EMAIL	ORDERS	LAST ORDER	TOTAL SPENT
		1	May 9, 2017	$269.00
		1	May 5, 2017	$1,076.00
		1	May 3, 2017	$1,076.00
		1	May 1, 2017	$199.00
		1	Apr 17, 2017	$269.00
		1	Apr 8, 2017	$269.00
		1	Apr 7, 2017	$239.00

Figure 4-4. *Customer list*

85

Detailed information on each customer can be accessed by clicking on the customer's name. The customer detail page has two sections: the customer profile and the order history. Figure 4-5 shows these panels. In the customer profile you can access contact information and add internal tags and notes pertaining to the customer. The customer order history provides a list of all orders the customer placed along with order number, date, status and total amount of the order.

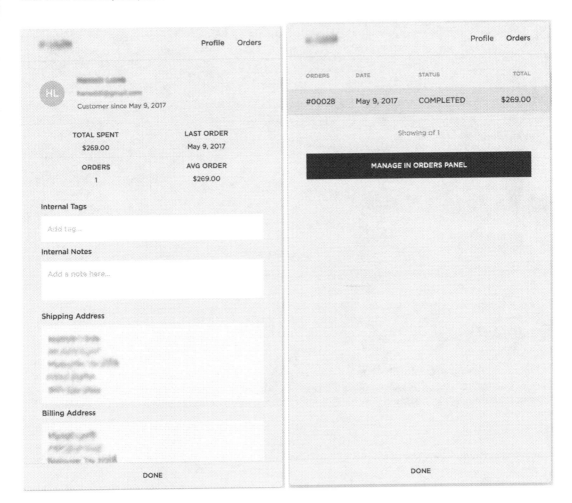

Figure 4-5. Customer profile and order history

Discounts

The Discounts panel allows you to manage all active, scheduled, and expired discounts. Figure 4-6 shows the Discount panel. Clicking the + icon will open the menu to create a new discount. Click on an existing discount to see the discount's details. Figure 4-6 also shows the Discount detail view. There are several types of discounts including a fixed amount off, percentage off, and free shipping. The discount can apply to any order, orders over a certain dollar amount, a single product, or a product category. There is an input for the discount code or you can generate a random one. You can also set the start and expiration dates. There is a check mark to select the discount to never expire. The Automatic Discount feature, where discount is applied automatically at checkout with no code required, is only available with the Advanced Online Store subscription.

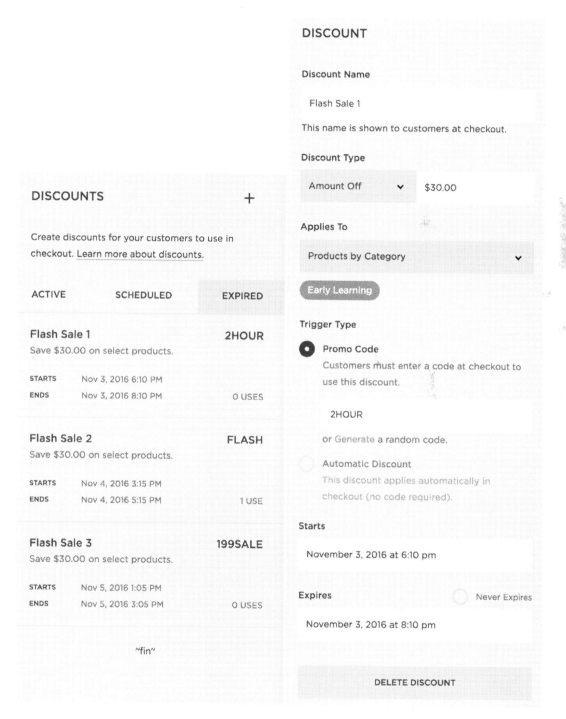

DISCOUNTS   +

Create discounts for your customers to use in checkout. Learn more about discounts.

ACTIVE	SCHEDULED	EXPIRED

Flash Sale 1   2HOUR
Save $30.00 on select products.

STARTS   Nov 3, 2016 6:10 PM
ENDS   Nov 3, 2016 8:10 PM   0 USES

Flash Sale 2   FLASH
Save $30.00 on select products.

STARTS   Nov 4, 2016 3:15 PM
ENDS   Nov 4, 2016 5:15 PM   1 USE

Flash Sale 3   199SALE
Save $30.00 on select products.

STARTS   Nov 5, 2016 1:05 PM
ENDS   Nov 5, 2016 3:05 PM   0 USES

~fin~

DISCOUNT

Discount Name

Flash Sale 1

This name is shown to customers at checkout.

Discount Type

| Amount Off ⌄ | $30.00 |

Applies To

Products by Category   ⌄

Early Learning

Trigger Type

● Promo Code
   Customers must enter a code at checkout to use this discount.

   2HOUR

   or Generate a random code.

○ Automatic Discount
   This discount applies automatically in checkout (no code required).

Starts

November 3, 2016 at 6:10 pm

Expires   ○ Never Expires

November 3, 2016 at 8:10 pm

DELETE DISCOUNT

Figure 4-6. *Discount listing and discount detail view*

Settings Menu, Commerce Category

This group of commerce settings is found by selecting Settings from the Home menu. The Commerce category of settings is found at the bottom of the list, under the General and Website categories.

Payment

There are currently three options in the payments panel as shown in Figure 4-7. As you can see, the first two options are for connecting payment accounts. Stripe is the primary payment option within Squarespace. Stripe can be connected while the store is in trial mode and has a test setting. The test setting allows test purchases to be made without a credit card being charged. PayPal is the secondary payment account option. PayPal cannot be connected to a trial account. The account has to be active before PayPal can be connected. The Store Currency option allows you to choose the currency displayed in the store. At this time the store can only support one currency at a time.

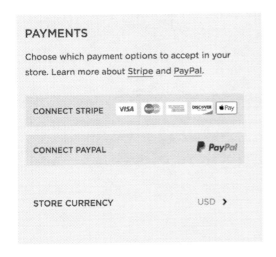

Figure 4-7. Payments panel

Checkout

The Checkout panel contains a number of settings and features related to the checkout process. The first is Checkout On Your Domain. This feature makes the URL on the checkout screen look like your domain instead of the default secure.squarespace.com URL. This feature is only available with Advanced Online Store subscription plans. Abandoned Checkout Recovery is another feature only available with Advanced Online Store plans. If enabled, customers will be sent an email reminder 24 hours after they abandon the checkout process. This leads to recovered sales by prompting the customer to complete their purchase. The newsletter option adds a MailChimp subscription check box to the checkout process. This feature only works with MailChimp and not other email service providers. Figure 4-8 shows these settings in the Checkout panel.

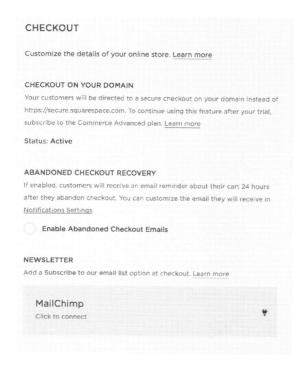

Figure 4-8. *Checkout settings group 1*

The Default Country In Address Fields setting allows you to set the country that is pre-selected for shipping and billing addresses. This should be set to the country where most of your customers live. During the checkout process the customer is given the option to use their shipping address as their billing address. This option is presented as a check box. The Shipping and Billing Address setting allows you to decide if that check box should be checked or unchecked by default. The Express Checkout setting allows the customer to bypass the shopping cart. When this feature is enabled the customer sees a Purchase button rather than an Add to Cart button. When the customer clicks on the Purchase button, they are taken to the checkout page bypassing the shopping cart page. Express Checkout is best used for single product stores or stores where a customer would only buy a single product at a time. The Shopping Cart Style setting allows you to change the shopping cart to a light color scheme. If your website has a dark background, then the default dark color scheme may not show up well. Checking the Use Light Color Scheme ensures that it is visible against the darker background. Figure 4-9 shows this group of Checkout settings.

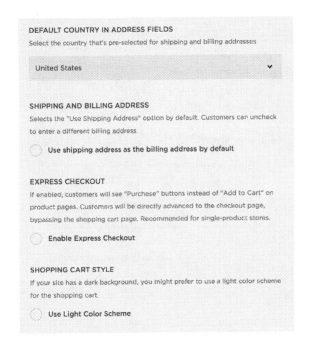

Figure 4-9. *Checkout settings group 2*

The Quantity Field for Service Products setting allows you to show or hide the Quantity field for all Service Products. This cannot be selected on a per-product basis. Hiding the Quantity field for some Service Products but not others takes custom coding. The Next Order Number field allows you to set the starting number for your next order. If you are switching from an existing web store you will want the Next Order Number to begin sequentially after your last order on the old system. For example, if your last order on the old system was number 1134, then you would put 1135 in the Next Order Number field. You could also start your new orders with a significantly different number, for example 2000, so it is obvious which orders are from the new system. The Quantity Field for Service Products, Next Order Number, Additional Fields, Checkout Page: Store Policies, and Invoices settings can all be seen on Figure 4-10.

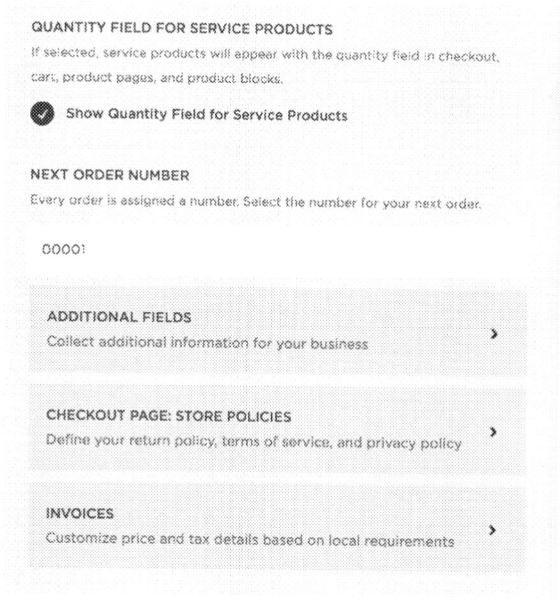

QUANTITY FIELD FOR SERVICE PRODUCTS

If selected, service products will appear with the quantity field in checkout, cart, product pages, and product blocks.

✓ Show Quantity Field for Service Products

NEXT ORDER NUMBER

Every order is assigned a number. Select the number for your next order.

00001

ADDITIONAL FIELDS
Collect additional information for your business ›

CHECKOUT PAGE: STORE POLICIES
Define your return policy, terms of service, and privacy policy ›

INVOICES
Customize price and tax details based on local requirements ›

Figure 4-10. *Checkout settings group 3*

Clicking the Additional Fields option brings up the Additional Fields menu, as seen in Figure 4-11. Squarespace recommends that you only collect this information if you need it for your business. The first option is phone numbers. You can select whether to collect a phone number with the shipping or billing address. There is also the option to make the phone number required. The Checkout Page: Custom Form section enables a Custom Checkout Form. This will allow you to collect additional information from the customer during the checkout process. One of my clients needed a tax-free version of their store. I set it up using Service Products since Service Products aren't taxed. However, at checkout, a shipping address isn't collected for Service Products. As a workaround, I used a custom form to collect the shipping address from the tax-exempt customers.

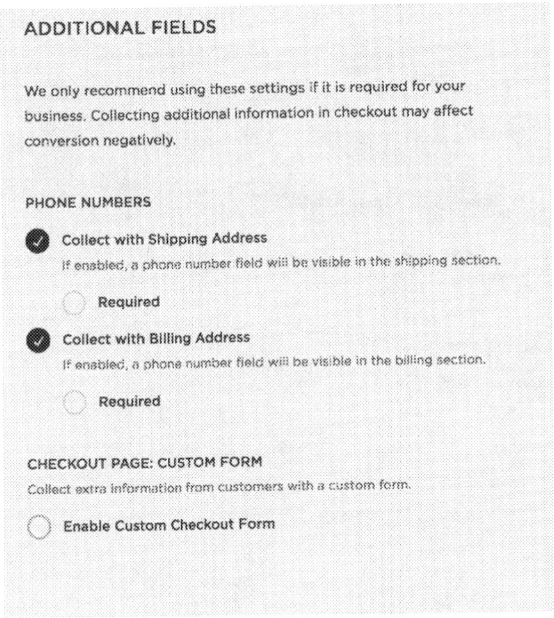

Figure 4-11. Additional Fields menu

The Checkout Page: Store Policies option allows you to add a Return Policy, Terms of Service, and Privacy Policy to your online store. Figure 4-12 shows the Checkout Page: Store Policies panel. The Return Policy, Terms of Service, and Privacy Policy each have their own entry field. The field is a text editor where you can enter content and include links. You cannot include images or other types of content in these fields. These policies are shows during the Review & Purchase portion of the checkout process.

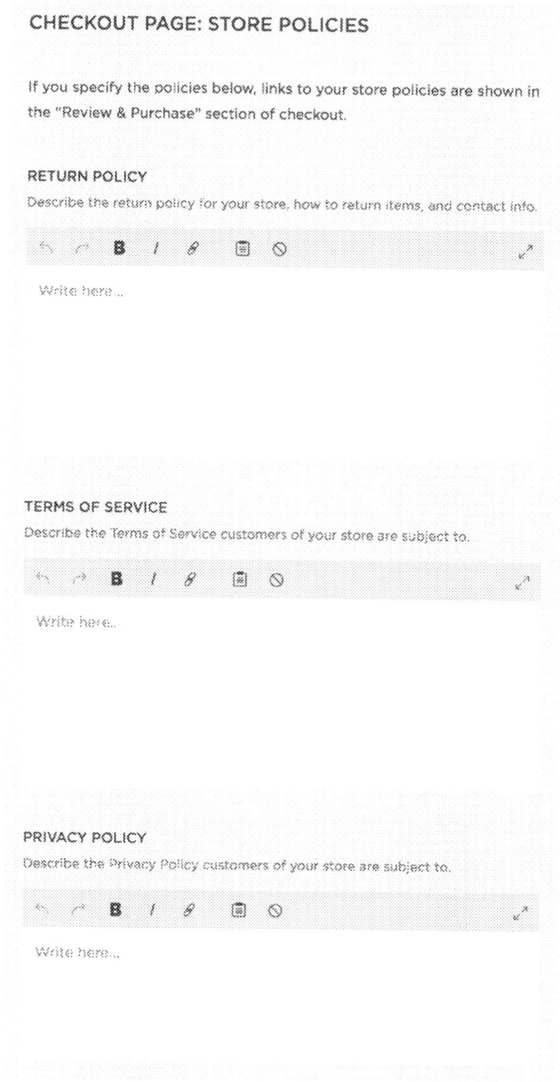

Figure 4-12. *Store Policies panel*

The Invoices option opens the Price and Tax Details menu. This section allows you to select which price and tax information will be displayed on your invoices. The Show Pre-Tax Price with Item Price option will allow both pre-tax and post-tax price to display for each item. The Show Tax for Each Item, when selected, will display the amount of tax charged for each item. The Show Pre-Tax Order Total, when selected, will display a net total in the order summary. The net total is the sum of the item cost plus shipping before tax was added. The Show a Tax Breakdown Table option will display a table summary of tax rates and amounts charged. It will appear below the order summary if an order includes tax. The business owner is responsible for choosing the correct tax and invoice options for their business. Figure 4-13 shows the Price and Tax Details options.

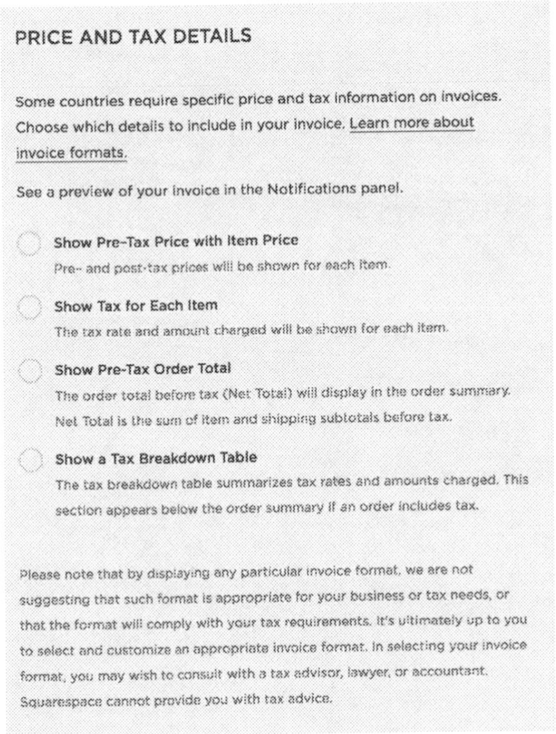

PRICE AND TAX DETAILS

Some countries require specific price and tax information on invoices. Choose which details to include in your invoice. Learn more about invoice formats.

See a preview of your invoice in the Notifications panel.

○ **Show Pre-Tax Price with Item Price**
Pre- and post-tax prices will be shown for each item.

○ **Show Tax for Each Item**
The tax rate and amount charged will be shown for each item.

○ **Show Pre-Tax Order Total**
The order total before tax (Net Total) will display in the order summary. Net Total is the sum of item and shipping subtotals before tax.

○ **Show a Tax Breakdown Table**
The tax breakdown table summarizes tax rates and amounts charged. This section appears below the order summary if an order includes tax.

Please note that by displaying any particular invoice format, we are not suggesting that such format is appropriate for your business or tax needs, or that the format will comply with your tax requirements. It's ultimately up to you to select and customize an appropriate invoice format. In selecting your invoice format, you may wish to consult with a tax advisor, lawyer, or accountant. Squarespace cannot provide you with tax advice.

Figure 4-13. Price and Tax Detail menu

Notifications

The Notifications panel has the settings for all of the email notifications the commerce system sends. Figure 4-14 shows all of these Notifications settings. The Customer Support Email: Reply-To setting allows you to specify where you receive emails that are sent by the customer, if they reply to a system-generated email. The Customer Support Email: From setting lets you set the address that system emails appear to be sent from. This is only recommended if you own the domain you are using. Using a third-party email service like Gmail or Hotmail could result in the message being marked as spam. The Automatic Stock Level Alert Email is sent to you when the stock level of a product drops below the set level. For example, if I set the level to 5, then I would receive an email when there were only 4 of those products left in stock. The Customize Emails settings allow you to control the content of system-generated emails.

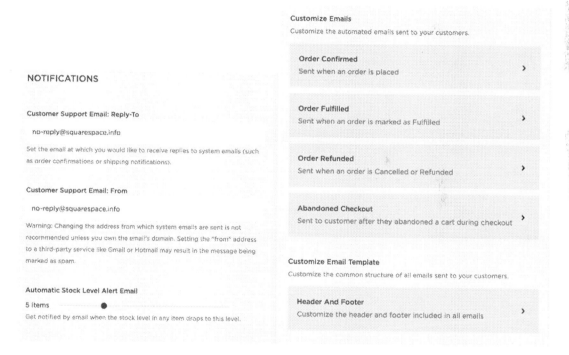

Figure 4-14. Notifications panel options

The Customize Emails options consist of the Order Confirmed, Order Fulfilled, Order Refunded, and Abandoned Checkout notifications. All four of these options provide the same editor that can be seen in Figure 4-15. The fields that can be customized for these notifications include the Subject Line, Title, and message. There is also a button to send a test email and restore the default values. The fields take a number of special characters and content injection. The %s seen in the Subject Line field inserts the site title in that location. The %o value inserts the order number. The header and footer of the email can also be configured. Using HTML the company logo and some style elements can be inserted into the email to allow the email branding to match the website branding.

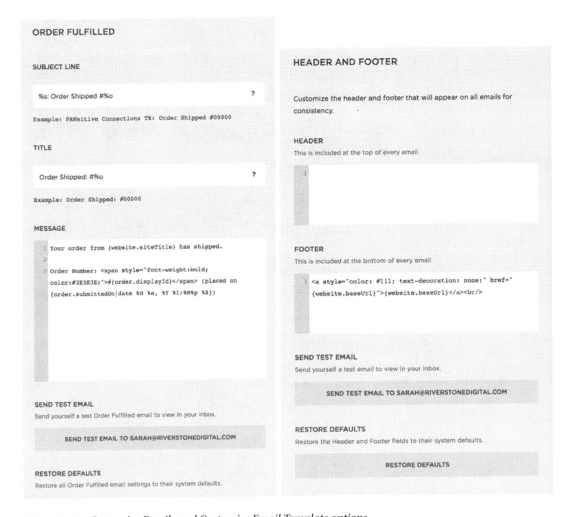

Figure 4-15. *Customize Emails and Customize Email Template options*

Shipping

The Shipping panel controls what shipping options are available to customers. Figure 4-16 shows the Shipping panel options and the Add Shipping Option menu. The two main forms of shipping options are Flat Rate and Depending on Weight. The shipping methods can be restricted to a particular country. The shipping options cannot be limited to a particular zip code. You can set up multiple shipping zones, but it would be up to the customer to self-select the correct shipping option. For example, if my business was in New York City, I might charge one flat rate to New York customers and a more expensive flat rate to other U.S. customers. The shipping portion of the checkout process would always show both shipping options. It would be up to the customer to select the correct one that applies to them. For Advanced Online Store plans it is also possible to add Carrier Calculated shipping rates. This does a real-time calculation of shipping cost based on weight, distance, and package size. Finally the Shipping panel also has the option to connect to ShipStation. ShipStation is an additional subscription service. It allows you to print shipping in a batch and send automatic notifications to customers with tracking numbers.

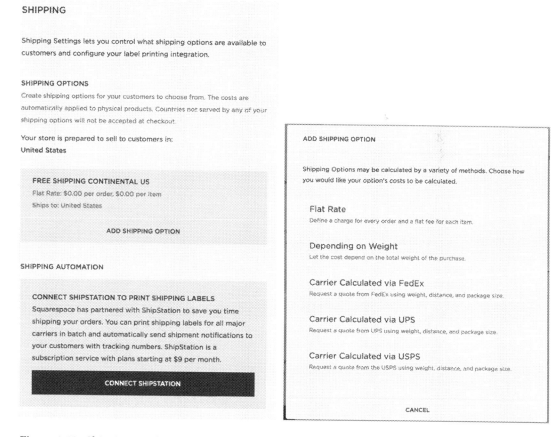

Figure 4-16. *Shipping panel and Add Shipping Option menu*

Taxes

The Taxes menu is where you can add tax rates. You can set the tax rate based on country and state or Province for the United States and Canada. For companies in the United States you can also add a local tax rule. The local tax rules can apply to a single zip code or a group of zip codes. Click Add Country to add a new tax rule. From the Create Country Tax Rate menu you can select whether shipping or services are taxed. Once you have a country rule set you can then add the state and local tax rules. Figure 4-17 shows the Taxes menu and Create Country Tax Rate menu.

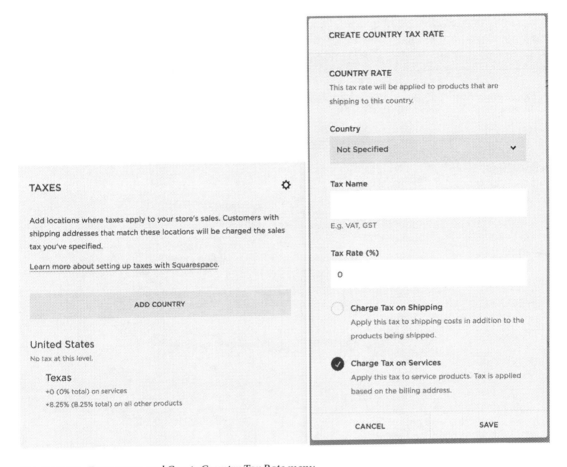

Figure 4-17. Taxes menu and Create Country Tax Rate menu

Accounting

The Accounting menu allows you to connect the Squarespace web store with Xero bookkeeping software. This allows you to automatically export your store data into Xero. Xero is a subscription plan and integration is only supported in the United States. Figure 4-18 shows the Accounting menu.

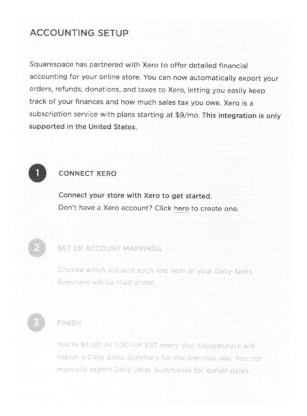

Figure 4-18. *Accounting menu*

Donations

The final section of the Commerce category is the Donations panel. Selecting Donations opens the Donation Confirmation settings. It is just like the email customizations options but specifically for transactions made through the Donation Block. The settings include Subject Line, Title, Message, Header, and Footer. It also allows you to send a text message or restore the defaults.

Analytics

Squarespace has built-in analytics tools. These are found in the Analytics menu. Squarespace provides information for Sales Overview, Traffic Overview, Traffic Sources, Popular Content, Purchase Funnel, Abandoned Cart, Site Search Queries, RSS Subscribers, Search Engine Queries, and Activity Log. Squarespace is actively improving its Analytics capabilities, so check the Squarespace website for current capabilities. Google Universal Analytics is the industry standard for tracking code. I include it in addition to the Squarespace analytics for most websites. We will talk more about Google Analytics later in the book.

Settings Menu, General Category

Next we will look at the settings within the General category of the Settings menu. We will cover most of the settings within this category. The settings we skip we will be looked at later in this chapter in the site launch section.

Business Information

The Business Information settings contain all of the basic business information. This information is displayed in some of the templates and populated to the commerce section. The Business Name and Business Address fields need the legal name and address of the business. These will appear on all invoices and emails sent to customers. The Tax Registration ID is optional but is required for some businesses. It will also appear on invoices and emails sent to customers. The Contact Phone Number and Contact Email are the primary contact information. This information will be made public and displays on the homepage of some templates.

The Physical Location allows you to enter a separate physical location for your business. For example, the Physical Location could be the retail store address while the Business Address is located somewhere else. Always include a physical location for the website. Search engines rank websites with a physical address higher than websites without one. Search engines assume businesses with a physical location are more trustworthy than ones without. The physical location should be consistent across all business listings. The Business Hours fields allow you to add specific business hours to the website. The business hours will be visible on the Mobile Info Bar if it is enabled. Figure 4-19 shows the Business Information fields.

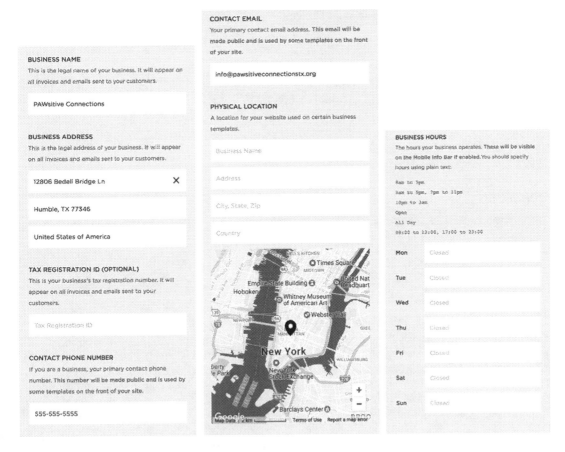

Figure 4-19. *Business Information settings*

Regional

The Regional settings allow you to set a number of location-based values. In Figure 4-20 you will see that the Time Zone is set for Central Daylight Time. Chicago is listed as the Nearest City based on what was available in the drop-down selection. The Language is set to English (United States). United States and Texas are selected in the Geography fields' Country and State / Providence options. The final Regional setting is the Measurement Standard. The Measurement Standard is used for defining the size and weight of physical products. The options are Imperial or Metric.

Figure 4-20. *Regional Settings*

Permissions

The Permissions menu is where you can add other users to the site. There are options to Invite Contributors and Add Basic Authors. Figure 4-21 shows the Permissions menu. The Allow Non-Admins to Purchase Assets check box allows other users to purchase Getty images and other licensed assets. The ownership of the site can be transferred to another admin user. I will often start out the website as the owner and when the site is ready to launch, I transfer the ownership to the business owner via the Transfer Ownership button. Only admins and owners can add users or Basic Authors to the site.

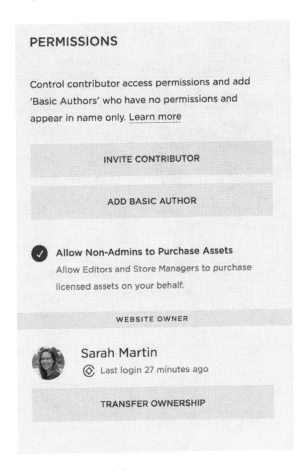

Figure 4-21. *Permissions menu*

A Basic Author is any name that can be attributed to content but does not have a login. Basic Authors appear in a drop-down menu where they can be selected. The author drop-down option appears on Gallery Images, Blog Posts, Events, and Tracks. This is a great way to highlight a guest author or another business. Basic Authors also appear in Archive and Summary Blocks. Figure 4-22 shows the Basic Author menu. The Basic Author information includes an image, name, google+ profile URL, website URL, bio, and location fields.

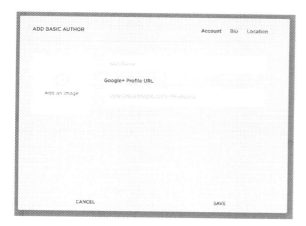

Figure 4-22. *Add Basic Author menu*

The Invite Contributor button opens the Invite Contributor menu. When inviting a contributor, you add a name, email address, and select their permission level. Figure 4-23 shows the Invite Contributor menu. There are a number of different permission levels. An Administrator has full permission and access to the site. The Content Editor is the basic user setting. The Content Editor can edit content but cannot change settings. Billing permissions let the user update the credit card on file for the site. Reporting permission gives access to the Analytics panel. A Comment Moderator can edit comments and comment on the site. The Trusted Commenter can bypass the comment moderation step. The Store Manager can receive store notifications, manage customer orders, and edit content on the site. The Content Editor and Store Manager are the most popular user permission levels.

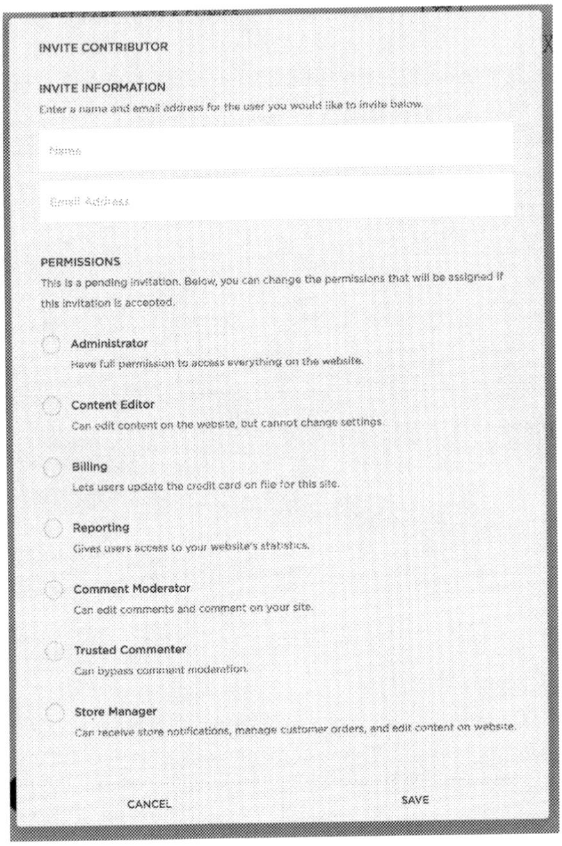

Figure 4-23. *Invite Contributor menu*

Billing & Account

The Billing & Account menu has settings for Billing, Invoices, Login History, and for trial sites, Delete Site. We will discuss the Billing section when we walk through launching a site. The Invoices section contains the invoices that Squarespace has issued to you. Login History provides a list of who has accessed the site. It shows the Browser, Operating System, and the IP address of the user. The Delete Site option is available on trial websites. To delete an active website you would need to contact Squarespace customer care.

Settings Menu, Website Category

There are a number of options in the Settings menu, Website category. We will cover Connected Accounts, Marketing, and Blogging now. The other settings we will go over later in this chapter.

Connected Accounts

The Connected Accounts menu allows you to connect your Squarespace website to a large number of other services. The options include social media, images services, video, music, location, and code accounts. More integrations are being added all the time, so check Squarespace's website for the latest integrations.

Marketing

The Marketing menu option has settings for Share Buttons, Pin it Buttons, Facebook page, and Google AdWords Credit. The Share Buttons option allows you to set which sharing options to include as part of the site. The Pin it Buttons option sets where the Pinterest Pin it buttons appear on the site. The options are Disabled, Enable for Blogs, and Enable for Blogs, Pages, and Products. The final marketing option is the Google Adwords credit. Squarespace is offering a promotion of a $100 Google AdWords credit with a Business or Commerce subscription. Figure 4-24 shows the Marketing menu and Share Buttons menu.

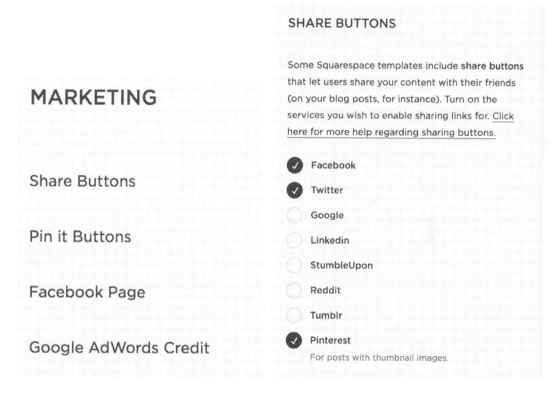

Figure 4-24. *Marketing menu and Share Buttons menu*

Blogging

The Blogging menu option contains the advanced settings for the Blog. Figure 4-25 shows the Blogging menu. The Post URL Format allows you to set the default post URL format. The default value is %y/%m/%d/%t. This stands for year/month/day/post title. If you only want the title in the URL then you could set it to be %t. The Comments Settings menu has the sorting, moderation, and other comments options. The Disqus Shortname field allows you to enter your Disqus shortname, which then replaces Squarespace's commenting system with Disqus throughout the site. Disqus is another popular commenting program you can sign up for. Simple Liking allows users to like posts without having to log in. The Accelerated Mobile Pages option, when enabled, creates optimized blog posts for viewing on mobile devices.

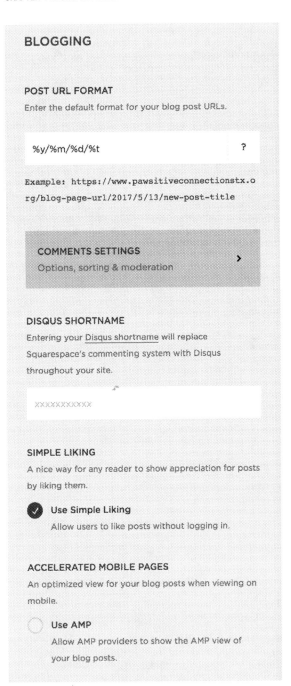

Figure 4-25. *Blogging menu*

Advanced

The Advanced menu contains a number of advanced options for the site. Figure 4-26 shows the Advanced menu. We will cover Developer Mode and Code Injection later in this book. As always you can refer to Squarespace's website for detailed information on any of these features.

Figure 4-26. *Advanced menu*

404 Error Page

If a website visitor tries to go to a page that doesn't exist, they are presented with the 404 Error Page. It is called a 404 error after HTTP code that is sent by a server if it can't find the requested resource. Squarespace includes a default 404 Error page. If you would like to have a custom 404 Error page, then create your preferred 404 error page in the not linked section of your site. Then in the 404 Error / Page Not Found menu you can select your new 404 Error page from the drop-down menu. Figure 4-27 shows this menu.

Figure 4-27. *404 Error / Page Not Found menu*

Default Text Editor

The Default Text Editor allows you to choose between a Rich Text Editor and a Markdown Editor as the default text block in your posts and pages. Text Blocks and Markdown Blocks can always be added to any page. The Rich Text Editor is similar to a traditional word processor and is the simplest to use. The Markdown block allows more control and requires an understanding of the Markdown language. Figure 4-28 shows the Default Text Editor menu.

Figure 4-28. *Default Text Editor*

Escape Key

The Escape Key setting is enabled by default in Squarespace. If you are logged into the site it will shrink or expand the site's preview panel. If you are not logged in it takes you to the login screen. Figure 4-29 shows the Escape Key menu. You can disable the Escape Key functionality by unchecking it. For websites that reach out to domestic abuse victims, the Escape Key is usually programmed to redirect the browser to a "safe" page like the weather. Squarespace's Escape Key setting needs to be disabled in order to enable a different use for the Escape Key.

Figure 4-29. *Escape Key menu*

Import / Export

The Import / Export menu gives you the option to move content between websites. Squarespace can import content from WordPress, Tumblr, Blogger, Etsy, Shopify, Big Cartel, and Products via .csv file. Squarespace content can be exported to Wordpress. You may have noticed, but there is currently no option to export Squarespace content from one Squarespace website to another Squarespace website. This is something to keep in mind as you work. If you have an existing Squarespace customer that wants to update their site, you have a couple options. You could temporarily replace the site with a lock screen so you can make the updates on the current website. The other option is starting a new Squarespace website and re-entering all of the content yourself.

External Services

The External Services menu gives you the option to add an Amazon Associates ID or classic Google Analytics account to your site. Figure 4-30 shows the External Services menu. Learn more about Amazon Associates IDs on the Amazon website. I highly discourage using the built-in Google Analytics integration. It uses the classic Google Analytics and is inferior to the Google Universal Analytics. Squarespace will not update the Google Analytics integration until Google retires the Classic analytics. We will cover how to add the Google Universal Analytics later in this book.

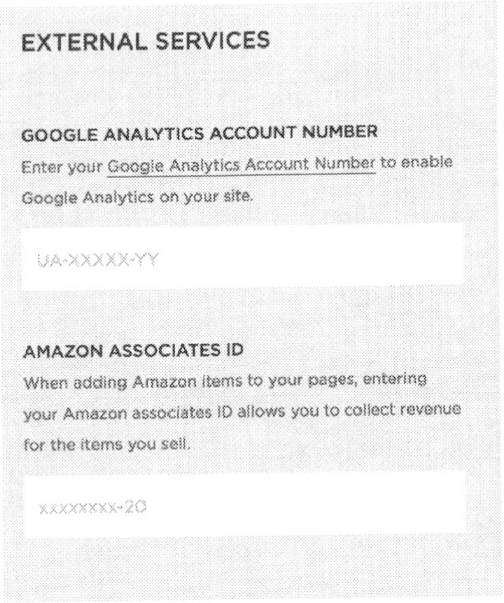

EXTERNAL SERVICES

GOOGLE ANALYTICS ACCOUNT NUMBER

Enter your Google Analytics Account Number to enable
Google Analytics on your site.

UA-XXXXX-YY

AMAZON ASSOCIATES ID

When adding Amazon items to your pages, entering
your Amazon associates ID allows you to collect revenue
for the items you sell.

XXXXXXXX-20

Figure 4-30. *External Services menu*

URL Mappings

URL mapping is the process of assigning a new URL to an existing URL. This is useful when a website is updated to a new one. On the old website the URL for the blog might have been /journal/ but on the new site it is /blog/. URL mappings allow you to convert all /journal/ URLs to /blog/ URLs. This change is all done in the URL Mappings menu shown in Figure 4-31. The URL Mappings take the original URL, new URL, and redirect type. You can see the formatting in Figure 4-31. Each mapping should be on its own line. The redirect type options are 301 and 302 redirects. 301 redirects tell search engines that the page has permanently moved. This allows the old page's Page Rank to be assigned to the new page. 302 redirects are temporary. The Page Rank is not reassigned to the new page.

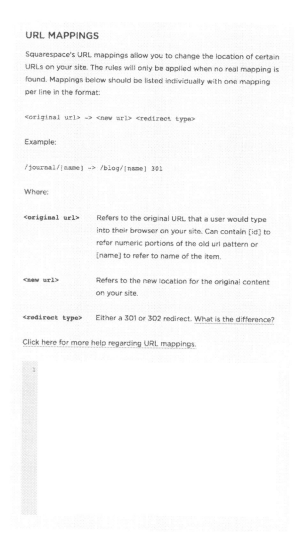

URL MAPPINGS

Squarespace's URL mappings allow you to change the location of certain URLs on your site. The rules will only be applied when no real mapping is found. Mappings below should be listed individually with one mapping per line in the format:

```
<original url> -> <new url> <redirect type>
```

Example:

```
/journal/[name] -> /blog/[name] 301
```

Where:

`<original url>`   Refers to the original URL that a user would type into their browser on your site. Can contain [id] to refer numeric portions of the old url pattern or [name] to refer to name of the item.

`<new url>`   Refers to the new location for the original content on your site.

`<redirect type>`   Either a 301 or 302 redirect. What is the difference?

Click here for more help regarding URL mappings.

Figure 4-31.   *URL Mapping menu*

Image Metadata Importing

Many photos are created with metadata embedded in them. The Image Metadata Importing menu allows you to enable importing this metadata. When the Enabled Image Metadata Importing option is checked, uploading an image into a gallery will import the metadata. The metadata will auto-populate the title, description, tags, and location of the image.

Home Menu

As we discussed in Chapter 1, there are two versions of the Home menu. One version is the default version for non-commerce websites and the other is the commerce-focused menu. The Home Menu settings allow you to switch between these two menu views. Figure 4-32 shows the Home Menu settings. You can select whichever Home Menu gives you the best access to your frequently used features.

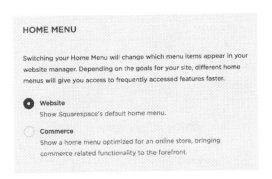

Figure 4-32. *Home Menu settings*

EU Cookie Banner

Current European Union laws require websites to inform their visitors of cookies placed by their website and to get the visitor's consent. Squarespace's website has step-by-step instructions for creating a cookie banner. The EU Cookie Banner menu links to these instructions. The check box option in the EU Cookie Banner menu enables the Restrict Squarespace Analytics feature. Enabling this feature prevents Squarespace from sending Analytics cookies to visitors who haven't dismissed the cookie banner. This enforces the implied consent part of the law. Figure 4-33 shows the EU Cookie Banner menu.

Figure 4-33. *EU Cookie Banner menu*

SEO Best Practices

Search engines, like Google, try to keep track of all public websites in an index. That way when a person types in search terms the search engine can provide good results. Search engines use a robot, which is a computer programmed to look at websites, to populate the index. Search Engine Optimization, or SEO, is the process of optimizing a website's content so that the robot correctly indexes the website. There are a couple components of SEO. One component is on-site SEO and is the optimization done to the website itself. The other component is the online reputation management. Online reputation management, also known as domain authority, consists of ensuring the business information is listed uniformly across the Internet and getting backlinks. A backlink is when another website links back to your site. On-site SEO and reputation management both try to get organic search traffic. Organic search traffic is free search traffic. There is also paid search traffic. Search Engine Marketing, or SEM, is the process of paying for small ads that appear at the top of a Search Engine's listing.

This next section of the book will cover on-site SEO using Squarespace. Before any SEO work can be done a keyword list needs to be created. Keywords are the search terms that a person would type into a search engine to find a website. A good keyword analysis will determine the best keywords to use for the website. These keywords should be used when the website's content is written. Keywords will also be used when writing on-site SEO descriptions.

Site Content

The first part of SEO is ensuring the content of the site is set up well. Text should be structured with headings. Headings allow the robots to prioritize content. When using a text block you can select Heading 1, Heading 2, or Heading 3 as the font size. When using a markdown or code block it is <h1></h1>, <h2></h2>, and <h3></h3> tags. The Heading 1 content has the highest priority with Heading 2 and Heading 3 being subheadings.

Every Page has a Page Title and Navigation Title that can be edited in the Page Settings. Figure 4-34 shows the Navigation Title and Page Title fields. By default the Page Title and Navigation Title are the same when a Page is created. Navigation Titles generally need to be shorter in order to appear in navigation menus. Page Titles do not have the same constraint. Page Titles appear at the top of the browser window or tab. Page Titles also appear in search engine results. Search engines give a lot of priority to a Page Title. Therefore Page Titles should reflect the content of the page and when possible include keywords.

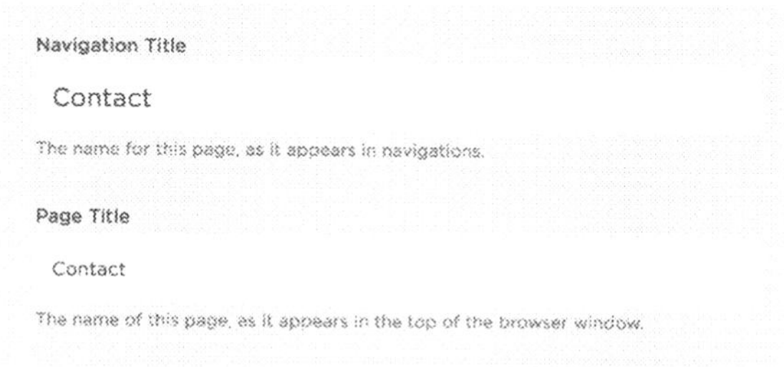

Navigation Title

Contact

The name for this page, as it appears in navigations.

Page Title

Contact

The name of this page, as it appears in the top of the browser window.

Figure 4-34. Navigation Title and Page Title fields in Page Settings menu

The Page Settings menu also contains the Description field. The page Description is indexed by search engines and appears as the content after the Page Title in the search engine results. Site Description and Site Type settings are found in the Settings menu, Website category, under Basic Information. Figure 4-35 shows the page Description field and the Basic Information menu. The Site Description should give a description of the site and include keywords. The Site Description is not displayed in search engine results but is surfaced in some templates.

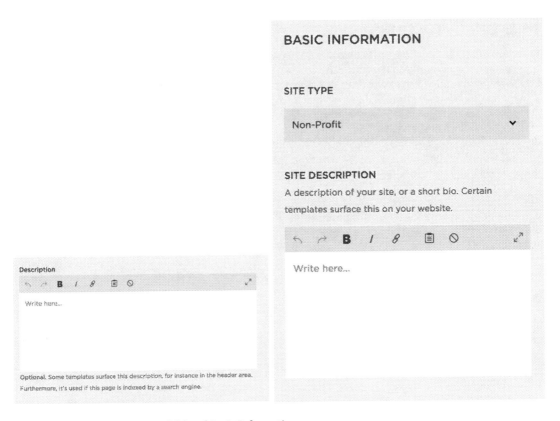

Figure 4-35. *Page Description field and Basic Information menu*

Tags and categories are another way of helping organize content. Tags and categories are always visible to robots, even when they are hidden in the Style Editor or Block settings. Therefore, the words used for tags and categories should overlap with the keyword list

Settings Menu, Website Category, SEO Menu

Squarespace has a SEO menu section. It is found in the Settings menu, under the Website Category. The Search Engine Description is a couple of short sentences that describe the website. This description is displayed after the page title in search results. If a page has a page Description set, then the page Description will display, rather than the Search Engine Description, in the search results. Figure 4-36 shows the Search Engine Description option in the SEO menu.

Figure 4-36. *Search Engine Description*

The SEO menu also contains fields to format the various titles of the site. Figure 4-37 shows the title format options. The title format options determine how the page title appears in the browser window or tab and in search engine results. The system default value is %s, which will display the Site Title. If you want a different title to display you can type it into the field. The Collection Title Format determines how the page title of collections, like blogs or galleries, is listed. It can take two values %c, which is the collection name, and %s for the site title. You can also add any spacing character that you want. I often use | since it takes up less space. For example, I might enter %s | %c into the Collection Title Format field. The final format is the Item Title Format. This takes the same values %s, %c values as well as %i for item title. Items are the things inside of a collection, like a blog post or product item.

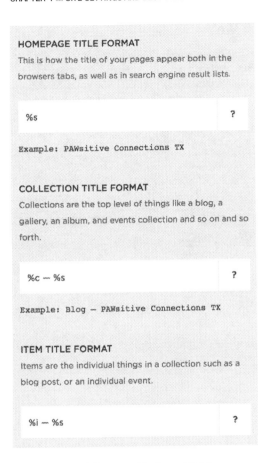

HOMEPAGE TITLE FORMAT

This is how the title of your pages appear both in the browsers tabs, as well as in search engine result lists.

%s   ?

Example: PAWsitive Connections TX

COLLECTION TITLE FORMAT

Collections are the top level of things like a blog, a gallery, an album, and events collection and so on and so forth.

%c — %s   ?

Example: Blog — PAWsitive Connections TX

ITEM TITLE FORMAT

Items are the individual things in a collection such as a blog post, or an individual event.

%i — %s   ?

Figure 4-37. *SEO menu title format fields*

Image Block

Every image has a field attached to it called an alt tag. Alt tags appear in the code of the webpage but are not visible to site visitors. Alt tags are read by search engine robots and by screen readers. Since robots and screen readers can't determine the content of an image file, it is important to provide meaningful alt tags for your images. Alt tags are added as the caption in the Inline layout of an Image. Every image should have an alt tag. If you do not want the caption to be visible with an Inline layout Image Block, then under the Design menu select Do Not Display Caption. This hides the caption from the website visitor but allows the robots to read it. For the other Image Block layouts, add the alt tag by temporarily switching to the Inline layout and adding the desired alt tag to the Inline layout caption. Then switch back to your desired layout. Figure 4-38 shows the Image Block caption area and the Image Block settings menu.

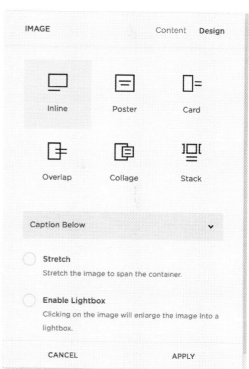

Figure 4-38. *Image Block Caption area and Image Block settings*

117

Gallery Block and Gallery Page

For Gallery Blocks and Gallery Pages alt tags are added to each individual image. Inside the Gallery Page or Gallery Block, click on the image settings gear icon to enter the image editor. Figure 4-39 shows the image editor. Enter the desired alt text into the Title field and save.

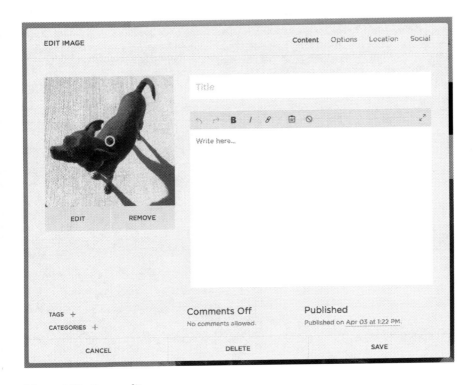

Figure 4-39. *Image editor*

Product Image

To add alt tags to Product images, first enter the Product editor for the selected Product Item. Then click on the gear icon for the desired image. An Edit Image Metadata menu will appear with a single field to enter the image title. Squarespace populates the alt tag with the image title. Figure 4-40 shows the Edit Image Metadata menu.

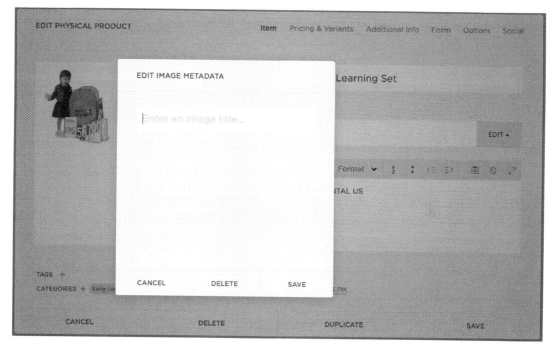

Figure 4-40. *Edit Image Metadata menu*

Cover Page and Thumbnail Images

To add alt tags to Cover Page images, navigate to the Media menu of the Cover Page. Then click on the gear icon for the image and enter a page title. For Thumbnail Images the file name populates as the alt text, except when the thumbnail appears in a blog post banner. Then the blog post title populates the alt text. Therefore, keep the keywords in mind when you create the file name for thumbnail images.

Settings Menu, Website Category, Security & SSL

This next section we will discuss security settings for the site. In the Settings menu, Website Category under Security & SSL there are a number of security-related settings. The first section is the status of the SSL Certificate. An SSL certificate establishes an encrypted link between the browser and webserver. This allows for private information to be passed securely. SSL encryption is required for all e-commerce transactions. Squarespace automatically supplies SSL certificates for all Squarespace websites. This includes domains registered via Squarespace and domains registered with a third party. It can take up to 72 hours for the SSL certificate to be created when a new domain is added to a Squarespace website. The Certificate Status section will tell you the status of the SSL certificate. Figure 4-41 shows the Certificate Status.

Figure 4-41. *SSL Certificate Status*

119

SSL

The Security Preference gives the option to require the use of the SSL certificate or allow the browser to communicate without it. Websites that use SSL certificates have https:// URLs. Websites that are insecure have plain http:// URLs. If the website is secure and uses https:// URLs then everything linked to the website also needs to use https:// URLs. For example if you are adding an iframe then the iframe URL needs to be https://. Figure 4-42 shows the Security Preference option. While a new SSL certificate is processing, before it becomes active, it is best to have the Security Preference option set to Insecure. If the Security Preference is set to Secure, without an active SSL certificate, a security warning will display in the browser. The security warning prevents the site visitor from accessing your website. Once the SSL Certificate has the status of active, you can set the Security Preference to Secure.

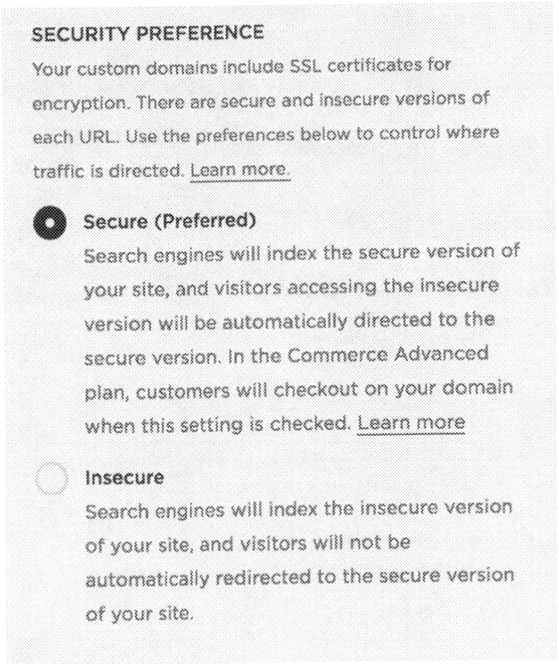

SECURITY PREFERENCE

Your custom domains include SSL certificates for encryption. There are secure and insecure versions of each URL. Use the preferences below to control where traffic is directed. Learn more.

● **Secure (Preferred)**
Search engines will index the secure version of your site, and visitors accessing the insecure version will be automatically directed to the secure version. In the Commerce Advanced plan, customers will checkout on your domain when this setting is checked. Learn more

○ **Insecure**
Search engines will index the insecure version of your site, and visitors will not be automatically redirected to the secure version of your site.

Figure 4-42. Security Preference

Password Protection

The final setting under the Security & SSL menu is the Site-Wide Password. The Site-Wide Password creates a private website. No one can view the website without the password. Search Engines no longer index a site after the password has been set. Squarespace password protection is incredibly secure. No one can access content without the password. Figure 4-43 shows the Site-Wide Password setting.

SITE-WIDE PASSWORD

Create a private website. Hide your website behind a
password so visitors can't view it. This is useful while
building your site. Customize the lock screen in the
Design Panel.

Enable Site-Wide Password   ∨

•••••••••••••••

Figure 4-43. *Site-Wide Password*

Launching the Site

Finally we will wrap this chapter up by going over the process of launching the website. Once the site is designed and all the content is entered, it is ready to be launched. First the website account needs to be switched to an active account from a trial account. This means that a subscription plan needs to be selected and paid for. The subscription and billing information can be found in the Settings menu, General category, Billing & Account menu, under Billing. Figure 4-44 shows the Billing menu. Since my example site is a trial site, the Upgrade Your Site menu is displayed. If this were an active site the information for the current subscription would be displayed. Clicking on the Upgrade option opens the Select a Plan menu. It shows all the available subscription plans and the features available with each plan. The Select a Plan menu is also seen in Figure 4-44.

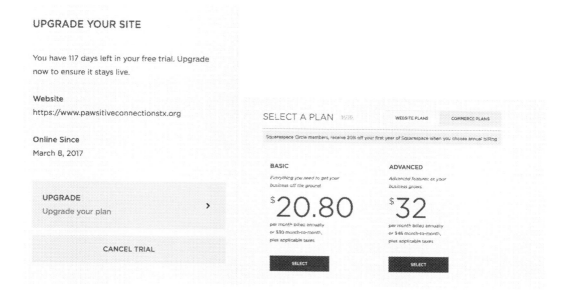

Figure 4-44. *Billing menu and Select a Plan menu*

The second step in the process is to update the website to the desired domain. All Squarespace websites come with a default Squarespace domain. It usually is a combination of the user name, letters, and numbers. The Settings menu, Website category, Domain menu allows you to control the domain of the site. I like to update the Built-In Squarespace domain when I start a new site. For the example website, I updated it to pawsitiveconnectionstx.squaresapce.com. It is meaningful and easy for me to remember. To change the Built-In Domain click on the Built-In Domain option and the Built-In Domain menu appears. The Domain menu and Built-In Domain menu are both shown in Figure 4-45. Selecting the Get a Domain or Use A Domain I Own options will take you through step by step adding a new domain. In the example website I have added www.pawsitiveconnectionstx.org domain.

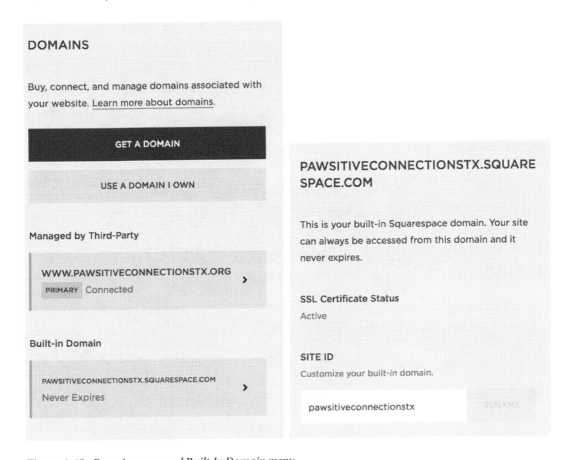

Figure 4-45. Domain menu and Built-In Domain menu

A final option that you can offer your clients is to set up their email. Squarespace partners with G Suite to provide businesses with branded email, along with the other G Suite services. This allows businesses to have email addresses like info@pawsitiveconnections.org. It also allows your client to manage all of their online accounts from a single location. Many small businesses appreciate the simplicity of the setup. The G Suite integration is found in the Settings menu, Website category, under Email. It will open a window with the different G Suite subscription options.

Wrap-Up

You should now feel familiar with all of Squarespace's built-in settings and tools. This solid understanding of the Squarespace platform is the foundation you will build your websites on. The rest of the chapters in this book will cover how to do advanced customizations using custom code.

CHAPTER 5

■ ■ ■

HTML, CSS, and JavaScript

This chapter begins the second portion of the book, custom code! A solid understanding of the Squarespace platform is vital to writing custom code. High-quality code works with the Squarespace platform rather than around it. Working with the platform means that you use the built-in Squarespace tools to get as close as possible before adding custom code. If there is a Style Editor Tweak or Block setting to adjust something, use it! Writing custom code when there is already a provided Tweak or setting only increases your workload. Squarespace has detailed documentation on all features and settings on their website. You can also refer back to earlier chapters of this book. In Chapter 9 we will take a deeper look at what it means to work with the Squarespace platform.

Web Languages

There are many programming languages that can be used to create websites. The foundational ones are HTML, CSS, and JavaScript. HTML, CSS, and JavaScript are browser-side languages, meaning they run in the web browser. Every webpage is made up of HTML, CSS, and JavaScript by the time it reaches the browser window. Squarespace provides code injectors to allow us to add HTML, CSS, and JavaScript to the website.

There are also server-side languages that run on a web server, and generate HTML to send to the browser. Squarespace does not allow us to use server-side programming languages. It is important to understand the difference, and be able to recognize, different programming languages in order to understand if a solution can be applied to a Squarespace website. PHP is a popular server-side programming language. WordPress and many other programs are built using PHP. I have seen many novice web professionals try to copy and paste a WordPress code solution into Squarespace, and then wonder why it doesn't work. By the end of this chapter, you will be able to be a discerning user when searching the Internet for code snippets.

HTML – The Structure

HTML stands for Hyper Text Markup Language. It is a markup language because the elements, or pieces of content, are wrapped in tags, also known as markup. These tags tell the browser what the element is and set the initial display qualities. Every piece of content is inside an element. The Squarespace platform provides the initial HTML for the site. When customizing a site we can manipulate the HTML elements. However, before manipulating the elements, it is important to understand the different elements. Listing 5-1 shows the most basic HTML markup for a page.

© Sarah Martin 2017
S. Martin, *The Definitive Guide to Squarespace*, https://doi.org/10.1007/978-1-4842-2937-8_5

Listing 5-1. Basic HTML structure

```
<!DOCTYPE html>
<html>
    <head>
        <title>Page Title</title>
    </head>
    <body>
        <h1>This is a Heading</h1>
        <p>This is a paragraph. <a href="http:www.weather.com">
            This is a link.</a></p>
    </body>
</html>
```

The first tag is the <!DOCTYPE> declaration. It tells the browser what type of document it is reading since there are many different markup languages. Every webpage has the <!DOCTYPE> declaration as the very first line. In this case it is an HTML document <!DOCTYPE html>. The rest of the elements are all wrapped in the <html></html> tags. The <html></html> tags tell the browser that everything within them is HTML content. For most elements there is an opening and a closing tag. Opening tags have an opening angle bracket <, the name of the element, and a closing angle bracket >. Closing tags have an opening angle bracket <, a slash /, the name of the element, and a closing angle bracket >. You can see how <html> is the opening tag and </html> is the closing tag.

If the opening and closing tags don't match up correctly then the browser will take a guess at where the missing tag should be. This usually results in a page that looks broken. Another common mistake is to forget the slash / for a closing tag. In this case the browser will think they are two opening tags that were never closed.

HTML elements are talked about in terms of their relationship to other elements. Elements that are directly nested inside a containing element are considered children of the containing element. For example in Listing 5-1 the <body></body> tag has two children, the <p></p> and <h1></h1> elements. The <a></a> tag is also a descendant of the <body></body> tag. However, the <a></a> element is not its child since it is within the <p></p> element. The <p></p> element is the parent of the <a></a> element. Elements that are both children of the same parent element are considered siblings. In Listing 5-1 <p></p> and <h1></h1> are sibling elements.

HTML tags can also have attributes associated with them. Attributes provide additional information that is not part of the content to display. Attributes appear inside the tag's angle brackets. They consist of the attribute name and value. The <a> tag in Listing 5-1 has the attribute of href="http://www.weather.com". The name of the attribute is href. The value of the link is "http://www.weather.com." The value of the attribute is always wrapped in quotes. The quotes can be single or double quotes. Like the tags the quotes need to be matched up. Forgetting to include a closing quote is another common source of errors. It is recommended to use double quotes around attribute values, unless the attribute value itself contains double quotes, in which case single quotes can be used.

The less than <, greater than >, slash /, double quotes ", and the ampersand & are all part of the HTML language. If we want to use these characters in our HTML content then we need to use special HTML codes for them. These codes go in place of the desired character. If my content said "Shop & Save" then the HTML version should say Shop & Save. The HTML codes start with an ampersand & and end with a semicolon ;. Listing 5-2 is a list of frequently used HTML codes.

Listing 5-2. HTML Codes

```
&lt;   Less Than
&gt;   Greater Than
&quot; Double Quotes
&amp;  Ampersand
&copy; Copyright Sign
```

Basic HTML Elements

Looking back at Listing 5-1, there are two elements that wrap the rest of the HTML content. The first element is the `<head></head>` tags. Content in the `<head></head>` tags is not part of the displayed webpage. The content inside the `<head></head>` tags instead is metadata only readable to the browser or search engines. In Listing 5-1 there is only one element inside the `<head></head>` tags, and it is the `<title></title>` element. The `<title></title>` tags define the page title. The page title displays at the top of the browser window and is indexed by search engines. We will explore additional meta tags later in this chapter.

The second element that goes immediately inside the `<html></html>` tags is the `<body></body>` element. The `<body></body>` tags wrap up the content that will display on the webpage. The webpage content is made of up three types of tags, heading 1`<h1></h1>`, paragraph `<p></p>`, and link `<a></a>`. Figure 5-1 shows the HTML from Listing 5-1 if you open the page with a web browser.

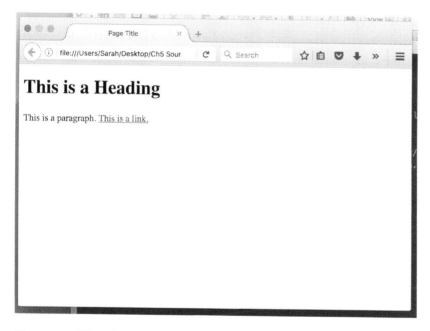

Figure 5-1. *HTML from Listing 5-1 opened in browser*

As you can see the `<title></title>` tag content appears in the browser tab. The elements inside the `<body></body>` tags all appear in the browser window. The webpage is displaying with the default browser styles since we haven't added any additional styling yet. The heading 1 style is larger than the paragraph or link style. The heading 1 style is the largest of the headings. They decrease in size and importance as the number increases. There are six heading elements available in HTML. The Squarespace text block provides styling for the first three `<h1></h1>`, `<h2></h2>`, and `<h3></h3>`. To use the other heading elements `<h4></h4>`, `<h5></h5>`, and `<h6></h6>` you need to use a code block or markdown block. For SEO purposes every page should have an `<h1></h1>` element since it is the highest priority heading.

Attributes

There are many different types of attributes and each element can have multiple attributes. Some attributes are available to use for CSS styling. Other attributes are data attributes that are used by the Squarespace platform. The ID attribute, `id="feature"`, defines the ID of the particular element. ID attribute values should be unique to the element. That means if you have a banner area with the id of `id="hero_banner"`, then you shouldn't use that id anywhere else on that page. You can use the same id across different webpages. You can have two separate pages in your site that each have one banner area with the id of `id="hero_banner"`. In Squarespace every single page has a unique id to identify it.

The class attribute can be used on multiple elements within the same page. It can be used by CSS to define the style for a whole class, or group, of elements. An example of this is if you want to style the `<h2></h2>` tags on the banner overlay sections of an index. A class can be added to the desired tags like this: `<h2 class="overlay_banner"></h2>` tags. Then in the CSS we can define the style of the class and the `<h2></h2>` elements will look different than the `<h2 class="overlay_banner"></h2>` elements.

The `href` and `src` attributes both take URLS for a value. The `href` attribute specifies the URL the browser should go to when clicked. The `src` attribute specifies a source file that should be imported into the document. For example an `<a></a>` tag takes the attribute of `href` since it links to a different location. The `src` attribute is used inside an image element to define the source of the image file. For `<a></a>` elements the attribute of `target="_blank"` tells the browser to open the link in a new tab or window.

The `style` attribute contains CSS style rules. Inline CSS is CSS that exists inline with the HTML in the style attribute. It is most commonly used in HTML emails. It is the least used method for styling webpages. Internal CSS styles sheets and external CSS style sheets are more efficient. We will discuss all three methods in depth later in this chapter.

Head Elements

As we discussed earlier there are a number of different metadata elements that can go inside the `<head> </head>` tags. These elements include `<link>`, `<script></script>`, `<meta>`, and `<style></style>`. Before we go any further into these you may have noticed that a couple of these tags look different. They are missing a closing tag. That is because the `<link>` and `<meta>` tags are self-closing. They are self-closing because all the information needed is included in the tag and it never takes any other content. Therefore there is never a reason to have a separate closing tag. Another example of a self-closing tag is the image `<img>` tag. The source attribute for the image tag provides all the information necessary `<img src="image.png">`.

The `<link>` tag takes two attributes, `href` and `rel`. The `rel` attribute tells the browser what type of information is in the link. In this case it is a stylesheet `rel="stylesheet"`. The `href` attribute tells the browser where the information is located and the name of the file `href="mystyle.css"`. Here is a complete link element `<link rel="stylesheet" href="mystyle.css">`.

The `<script></script>` element can either contain JavaScript within the tags, or it can call on an external JavaScript document. If the `<script></script>` tags are calling an external JavaScript file the source attribute is used `<script src="myscript.js"></script>`. With an external source the closing script tag `</script>` is still necessary. The `<script></script>` tag doesn't magically become self-closing if it has a source attribute. The other way to use the `<script></script>` tags is to include the JavaScript directly inside the tags. Listing 5-3 shows an example.

Listing 5-3. JavaScript inside a script element

```
<script>
  document.getElementById("demo").innerHTML = "Hello JavaScript!";
</script>
```

The `<style></style>` element can contain CSS. This is called an internal CSS style sheet. Multiple CSS style rules can be put in this element. This example includes a CSS style rule that changes the color of the body font to red `<style> body{color: red; }</style>`. The `<style></style>` tags can group multiple CSS style rules together. Each style rule should not have it own set of `<style></style>` tags.

The `<meta>` tag is another type of head element that specifically takes metadata for use by search engines or social media sites. The `<meta>` tag is another self-closing element. Meta elements have a `name` and a `content` attribute. The `name` attribute specifies the type of `<meta>` element. The `content` attribute specifies the value of the `<meta>` element. Search engines look for the meta description when they crawl a webpage. The meta description is found in a meta element that has the `name` attribute of description, for example, `<meta name="description" content="The Definitive Guide to Squarespace Chapter 5">`.

Body Elements

Elements inside the `<body></body>` tags have default layout properties. There are block elements, which create boxes of content. Then there are inline elements, which style text where it is inline with other text. We have already looked at heading `<h1></h1>` and paragraph `<p></p>` elements. These are both examples of block elements. The link element `<a></a>` is an inline element, which is why the link text is inline with the rest of the sentence.

A very common HTML element is the `<div></div>` element. The `<div></div>` element is a block element used to group sections of content together. You will see it used to create rows, columns, or group other content like social media icons together. Another block element is the `<img>` element, which we know adds an image to the page. The `<br>` tag stands for line break. It forces content within an element to wrap to the next line. It is often used to format text like addresses. It is also a self-closing tag. The `<hr>` element stands for horizontal rule. The `<hr>` element creates a horizontal line on the page and is another self-closing tag.

Links `<a></a>` are a common inline element. As mentioned they have a `href` attribute to specify the URL. The URL can be a relative or absolute URL. An absolute URL contains the entire link including the domain. For example, this link has an absolute URL, `<a href="http://www.weather.com">Local Weather</a>`. A relative links points to another page or file within the same site. The browser assumes that the rest of the domain is the same. For example, we were on the homepage of our example website `www.pawsitiveconnectionstx.org` and there is a link to the contact page. A relative link would be entered leaving off the domain `<a href="/contact">Contact Us</a>`. The absolute link would be created by including the domain name `<a href="http://www.pawsitiveconnectionstx.org/contact"> Contact Us </a>`. The default layout for a link `<a></a>` tag is inline but CSS can be used to make it behave like a block element. This is how many call-to-action buttons are created.

Other inline elements include `<span></span>`, italics `<i></i>`, and `<em></em>`, bold `<b></b>`, and `<strong></strong>`. The `<span></span>` element is the inline equivalent of the `<div></div>`, a generic container. It is typically used with a `class` attribute to change the visual properties of the text. The `<i></i>` and `<em></em>` tags both italicize content. The meaning of them is slightly different. The `<i></i>` tag would be used for content that should look different from the normal text. Examples of this are book titles, foreign words, and lyrics. The emphasis `<em></em>` tags convey the meaning of emphasizing the text. This is often used in dialog. For example *"Please* take out the trash!" would be written like this `<p><em>Please</em> take out the trash!</p>`. The tags `<b></b>` and `<strong></strong>` both bold text by default. However `<strong></strong>` tags stand for strong emphasis and can be styled to convey the extra emphasis another way. Instead of bolding the text, CSS can make the `<strong></strong>` tags change the text color or even switch the font, whereas bold `<b></b>` tags would typically only ever bold the text. The `<em></em>` and `<strong></strong>` elements were the first semantic elements, or elements that convey meaning to the developer as well as the browser.

Semantic Elements

The introduction of HTML5, the most recent HTML specification, introduced new semantic elements. Websites were being created using hundreds of <div></div> elements, which conveyed no additional meaning. Developers were using classes like "header," "footer," and "nav" to be able to convey the purpose of the <div></div>. HTML5 added semantic elements that convey meaning to both the browser and developer to replace <div></div> and <span></span> tags for specific purposes. The new semantic elements include <header></header>, <footer></footer>, <article></article>, <nav></nav>, <main></main>, <time></time>, and many more. You will see these semantic elements used in the Squarespace templates.

Form Input Elements

Form elements are another category of HTML elements. The <form></form> element defines the form for user input. The form is then populated with different types of input areas. The <input> element is a self-closing element that can take several different forms depending what type of input it is. The type of input is assigned by the type attribute. <input> elements also have name attributes so that they can be uniquely identified. Here is an example of a text input for a first name, <input type="text" name="first_name">. <input> elements can also be type="submit" that creates a submit button for the form. <input type="submit"> elements have an additional attribute of value. The value content will be the text displayed on the input button. Listing 5-4 shows the HTML for a simple contact form.

Listing 5-4. Simple form

```
<form>
  First name:<br>
  <input type="text" name="firstname"><br>
  Last name:<br>
  <input type="text" name="lastname">
  <input type="submit" value="Send">
</form>
```

Radio buttons and check boxes can be created using type="radio" and type="checkbox". Another common element of forms is a <select></select> element. The <select></select> element creates a drop-down list. Listing 5-5 shows the structure of a <select></select> element with the <option></option> elements that populate the drop-down. It is a drop-down to select a dog breed.

Listing 5-5. Select element for dog breed drop-down

```
<select name="breed">
  <option value="beagle">Beagle</option>
  <option value="dachshund">Dachshund</option>
  <option value="husky">Husky</option>
  <option value="lab">Labrador Retriever</option>
</select>
```

The <textarea></textarea> creates a box for typing text into. This is typically used for Message fields in contact forms. The field can be labeled for the site visitor using the <label></label> that has an attribute of for which connects the label with the input field. Listing 5-6 shows our sample page from Listing 5-1 with a form added to it. Figure 5-2 shows how the browser displays this example page. I rarely create HTML forms since they are usually integrated with other programs. However, it is important to understand form elements so you can style them.

Listing 5-6. Sample HTML Page with form

```
<!DOCTYPE html>
<html>
   <head>
      <title>Page Title</title>
   </head>
   <body>
      <h1>This is a Heading</h1>
      <p>This is a paragraph. <a href="http:www.weather.com">This is a link.</a></p>

      <h2>Dog Form</h2>
      <form>
        <label for="firstname">Dog's First Name</label><br>
        <input type="text" name="firstname"><br>

        <label for="lastname">Dog's Last name:</label><br>
        <input type="text" name="lastname"><br>

        <label for="breed">Breed:</label><br>
        <select name="breed">
          <option value="beagle">Beagle</option>
          <option value="dachshund">Dachshund</option>
          <option value="husky">Husky</option>
          <option value="lab">Labrador Retriever</option>
        </select><br>

        <label for="notes">Notes:</label><br>
        <textarea name="notes" rows="10" cols="30">
        </textarea><br>

        <input type="submit" value="Send">
      </form>
   </body>
</html>
```

Figure 5-2. Sample page as displayed by Firefox browser

CSS – The Style

CSS stands for Cascading Style Sheets. CSS tells the browser how to display the HTML elements. The webpage in Figure 5-2 is boring because it has no CSS styling. CSS is made up of style rules that are applied to specific elements. CSS can control the visibility, color, font, size, position, and layout of HTML elements. There are even CSS transitions that can create animation effects without using JavaScript. CSS is powerful but it can only style existing HTML elements; it cannot change them.

In CSS, if an item has multiple style rules that could apply to it, then the browser displays the rule with the highest priority. As we mentioned earlier, there are three different ways to add CSS style rules: an external style sheet, an internal style sheet, and inline within the element's style="" attribute. Inline styles have the highest priority. Internal style sheets have the second highest priority, followed by external style sheets. If there are multiple external style sheets, then the last one loaded has the higher priority. Web browsers load HTML by reading the file top to bottom and left to right, just like how we read. The first <link> in the <head></head> element would be added first, and the second <link> would have higher priority. The default browser style rules have the lowest priority.

Within a given style sheet, the rules later in the sheet have priority over the earlier rules. That is why style sheets are typically set up with the most general styling rules at the top of the CSS and the more specific style rules further down. When working with CSS it is common to see comments. Comments are text that is added to code for the developer to read. Browsers ignore comments and do not display the content. In CSS comments are wrapped in /* */ for example /* comment text here */. This is useful for adding reminders about what the CSS is doing.

CSS style rules are made of up selectors and declaration blocks. The selector defines the HTML elements that the rule will apply to. Declaration blocks contain individual declarations separated by semicolons. Each declaration is made up of a CSS property and a value. Listing 5-7 contains an example of a CSS rule that changes the background color of the <body></body> tag to light grey. The word body is the selector. The declaration block is wrapped in curly brackets {}. The declaration is background-color: lightgrey;. The CSS property is background-color and the value is lightgrey.

Listing 5-7. CSS style rule

```
body{
  background-color: lightgrey;
}
```

CSS Selectors

HTML elements can be selected by id, class, and element type. The CSS rule in Listing 5-7 uses the body element selector. Any HTML elements can be selected using the element name, for example, body, h1, a, and p. An element can be selected by id by placing a # in front of the id name. If we have a heading <h1 id="page-desc">Coming Soon!</h1> then we can select that element using #page-desc. Class names can be selected by using a period in front of the class name. For example, if we have <h1 class="heading-main">Heading</h1> then we could select all headings with that class name using .heading-main.

Just like style sheets have a priority, so do the selectors. Ids are the highest priority followed by classes and finally element names. Multiple selectors can also be grouped together using combinators. The most common combinator is the space. The space is the descendant selector. Given the selector div h1, then the CSS rule will apply to all <h1></h1> elements that are a descendant of a <div></div> element. There is also the child selector >. This selects only the elements that are a child of the parent element. For example, div > h1 selects all <h1> </h1> elements that are a child of a <div></div>. There are also sibling selectors. The + is the adjacent sibling selector. The ~ is the general sibling selector.

Let's consider Listing 5-8 to demonstrate the combinators. The selector div p will select all the <p></p> elements. The selector .top p will select all the <p></p> elements found inside the <div></div> that has the class of "top." The selector div #current will select only the <p></p> element that has the id of "current." The selector of #current ~ p will select all the siblings of the <p></p> element that has the id of "current." That would be the <p></p> tags that contain Red, Green, and Purple. The other <p></p> elements are in another <div></div> so they are not siblings of the #current element. The selector of #current + p will select only the siblings following the #current element. This means the <p></p> tags containing Green and Purple will be selected. The <p>Red</p> element will not be selected since it is before the #current element.

Listing 5-8. Combinator example

```
<div class="top">
 <p>Red</p>
 <p id="current">Blue</p>
 <p>Green</p>
 <p>Purple</p>
</div>
<div class="bottom">
```

```
    <p>Orange</p>
    <p>Yellow</p>
</div>
```

Selectors can be combined without spaces to select an element that has multiple classes associated with it. For example, the first `<div></div>` in Listing 5-8 could have two classes, `<div class="top left"></div>`. There could be another `<div></div>` with the classes of `<div class="top right"></div>`. Using the selector `.top` would select both of these `<div></div>`s. To select just the "top left" `<div></div>` we can use the `.top.left` selector. The class names are combined without any spaces. The element, id, and class selectors can all be combined without spaces, for example, `div.top p#current`. If you are combining the element selector, then the element type is listed first, followed by the id and class values.

Each declaration block can also have multiple CSS selectors. A comma separates the different CSS selectors. Still referring to Listing 5-8, the selector `#current, .bottom p {}` would select the `<p id="current">Blue</p>` from the top `<div></div>` using the first selector `#current`. The second selector `.bottom p` would select `<p>Orange</p>` and `<p>Yellow</p>` from the bottom `<div></div>`.

CSS has what is known as pseudo-classes. A pseudo-class defines a particular state of an element and acts like a class has been added. The `:hover` pseudo-class defines the element when it is being hovered over. This is commonly used to change the style of a link or button when the user is hovering over it. For example `a:hover{color: red;}`changes the color of a link to red when the user is hovering over it. There are also `:first-child` and `:last-child` pseudo-classes. These select the element only if it is the first child or last child respectively. The `:nth-child()` pseudo-class is used to select a particular child in numeric order. For example I can select the second child in a list using `:nth-child(2)`. The selector `:nth-child(1)` selects the same element as `:first-child`. There are many more pseudo-classes, but these are the ones you will frequently use.

In addition to pseudo-classes, there are pseudo-elements. In CSS3 pseudo-elements should be distinguished by using two colons `::`, but in reality you can use one or two colons. The older CSS specification CSS1 and CSS2 both used single colons for pseudo-elements and browsers accept both versions. The most common pseudo-elements are `::before` and `::after`. Pseudo-elements have a content property that accepts a little bit of text. This effectively creates additional elements on the page, which is why they are called pseudo-elements. We will explore the uses of pseudo-elements later in this book. They are useful for adding design elements and injecting little bits of content without using JavaScript.

CSS Properties

There are many CSS properties and they define everything from color and font to position and visibility. Every element has a `color` and `background-color` property. The `color` defines the text color and `background-color` defines the background color of the element. There are several different types of color codes that can be used as the color value. There are hex colors that take the form of a # followed by six characters. The six characters can be numbers zero through nine and letters a through f. For example the color white is `#ffffff`. There are RBG and RGBa colors. RGB stands for red, green, and blue, which is the composition of light colors. The RGBa includes an opacity value. The color white defined as an RGB value is `rgb(255,255,255)`. A transparent white can be defined with `RGBa(255,255,255,.5)`. The opacity value is a number between 0 and 1. 0 is completely transparent and 1 is completely opaque. There are also HSL and HSLa colors. HSL stands for Hue, Saturation, and Lightness. HSLa colors take the format of hsla(0, 100%, 100%, 1). My personal preference is to use rgba or hex colors. However you are welcome to use whatever you are most comfortable with. There are many color-picking tools that can help you get the right color codes. Most image editing tools will provide the color value in multiple formats.

There are several properties that control how fonts display. The `font-family` property specifies the font. The `font-family` property accepts a list of fonts with the first font listed, given the highest priority and the subsequent fonts being fallback fonts. For example, in the declaration `font-family: Arial, sans-serif;`, the main font is Arial. However, if Arial doesn't exist then the browser's default sans-serif font would be used. The `font-size` property specifies the size of the font. It accepts values in px, em, and percentages. I could set the font to be 40px using this declaration font-size: 40px;. Fonts also have weights associated with them. Bold fonts have a higher weight value than thin fonts. Many fonts have multiple weights including light, regular, and bold. They typically have numeric values from 100 to 900 in increments of 100. If I want all of my main headings to be bold, I could use this declaration h1{font-weight: 700;}. The font-style property can set the font to be italic or normal. The text-transform property tells the browser how to display the text in terms of uppercase and lowercase letters. The declaration text-transform: uppercase; displays all the letters as uppercase letters. The value of lowercase displays all the letters as lowercase. The value of capitalize transforms the first letter of each word to uppercase. To return a style to the browser default the declaration text-transform: none; can be used.

There are three different properties that control how an element displays. These are display, visibility, and opacity. The display property has a number of values. The most common are block, inline-block, inline, none, and flex. The value of block tells the element to behave like a block element. For example, the inline element of <a></a> can have the declaration display: block; and it will behave like a block element. The value of inline makes the element behave like an inline element. The value of inline-block makes a series of blocks line up. This is often used in horizontal navigation. The value of none hides the element. It no longer appears on the screen, and it no longer has a place in the flow of the page. The value of flex tells the browser to use the flexbox model for displaying the content. You can learn more about the flexbox model at https://css-tricks.com/snippets/css/a-guide-to-flexbox/. CSS-TRICKS is a great resource for learning more about different CSS techniques.

The visibility property is another way to show or hide text. The value of visible is the default value. The value of hidden makes the element invisible but it still takes up its space on the page. The opacity property is growing in popularity as a way to show and hide elements. The opacity property takes any value between 0 and 1, with 0 being transparent and 1 being opaque. A popular technique is to fade elements in or out, rather than having them suddenly change appearance. The display and visibility properties can't fade. The use of CSS transitions can be used with the opacity property to create the fade effect.

An element's position can be controlled using the position property. The default positioning is static. If we want to move an element outside of its default position, there are the options of relative and absolute positioning. Relative positioning means that the element moves relative to its default position. The properties top, bottom, left, and right can be used to define how far the element moves. The CSS property position:relative; can be used to change the position of the <h1></h1> element. Figure 5-3 shows an example of an <h1></h1> element inside a container <div></div> before and after the position has been changed. Listing 5-9 shows the CSS that generated the change.

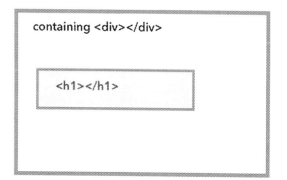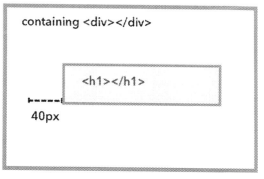

Figure 5-3. The heading position before and after position is changed

Listing 5-9. CSS applied to Figure 5-3

```
h1{
  position: relative;
  left: 40px;
}
```

The top, bottom, left, and right properties can take positive and negative numbers in px, em, or percentages. In Figure 5-3 if we wanted to move the heading up we could use position: relative; and top: -20px; to move the heading 20px up.

Absolute positioning gets a little trickier. The element is positioned absolutely relative to the nearest ancestor that has a position value of relative or absolute. If no ancestor has a position value set, then it is positioned relative to the browser window. Let's look at the same container and heading from Figure 5-3. If we apply absolute positioning to only the <h1></h1> element, then it will be positioned relative to the browser window and fall outside the container <div></div>. Figure 5-4 shows the image and Listing 5-10 shows the CSS.

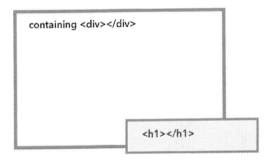

Figure 5-4. *Heading with absolute positioning*

Listing 5-10. CSS that positioned the heading

```
h1{
  position: absolute;
  bottom: 0;
  right: 0;
}
```

Let's assume that we didn't want the heading to flow outside of the container. Instead we want it to be in the bottom-right corner of the container. We can add the property of position:relative; to the container. Then the heading element will be positioned absolutely, relative to the container. Figure 5-5 shows the desired position of the heading and Listing 5-11 shows the CSS. You will notice that we only included position:relative; for the container and not left, right, top, or bottom properties. Adding the other positioning properties would have moved the container <div></div> and in this example we don't want to do that. We will explore positioning in greater detail later in the book.

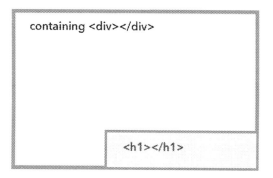

Figure 5-5. *Container with desired heading position*

Listing 5-11. CSS to correctly position the heading

```
div{
  position: relative;
}

h1{
  position: absolute;
  top: 0;
  bottom: 0;
}
```

The `!important` flag can be used to force the browser to use a property's value even if it doesn't have priority given the declaration's selectors. It is best practice to use the `!important` flag as sparingly as possible. It is much better to increase the priority of the CSS rule by adding selectors. However, there are times when it is necessary to add the `!important` flag. This will sometimes happen when we are trying to override a template's built-in CSS. The `!important` flag is put at the end of the property value before the semicolon. For example, `text-transform: uppercase !important`; will add extra priority to the `text-transform` declaration. If multiple CSS rules that apply to the same element have `!important` flags, then the rule with the highest selector priority and the `!important` flag will be used.

Media Queries

Media queries allow us to target our CSS rules to specific screen sizes. For example, we want to change the background color to white on mobile devices so it is easier to read. Listing 5-12 shows the CSS media query to do this. The media query starts with `@media`. This tells the browser that a media query rule is starting. The next part tells the browser what to apply the rule to. In our example we want the rule to apply to screens so we include the media type of `screen`. CSS rules are sometimes used for print styles in which case the media type `print` is used. The media query then specifies what media feature we want the rule to apply to. The most common values are `min-width` and `max-width`. These media features apply to the display area, typically the browser window. Since the browser window displays on a screen, it is measured in pixels. The media feature of `max-width: 480px` tells the browser that the rule applies to screens where the browser window is at most 480px wide. The media query includes and to let the browser know that both the media type and media feature value are to be considered. Then the media feature is included in parentheses with a colon separating the name and value (`max-width: 480px`). All of the CSS rules that we want in the media query, so they only apply to the specified screen size, are grouped in curly brackets. A single media query can have any number of CSS rules grouped in the curly brackets. A common error with media queries and CSS rules is to miss a closing curly bracket.

Listing 5-12. CSS media query

```
@media screen and (max-width: 480px){
  body{
    background-color: #ffffff;
  }
}
```

JavaScript – The Interaction

JavaScript is the programming language that provides the interactions for the site. Without JavaScript a webpage is static and doesn't change. Another way to think about it is that JavaScript is the electricity for a house. The HTML is the house structure, the CSS is how you decorated the house, and the JavaScript is the electricity that turns everything on. JavaScript is responsible for the power that submits a form when a user clicks a button. It allows us to add next and previous arrows to a slideshow, allowing the user to switch slides. JavaScript is also responsible for carousels that auto transition between slides. You can tell you are looking at JavaScript because it will be in a `<script></script>` tag or a .js file.

JavaScript is so powerful because it can control the HTML and CSS of a webpage. JavaScript code injection can be used to add HTML elements to a webpage or remove unwanted ones. It also can add classes to particular elements. It also powers many web applications. As you can imagine, JavaScript opens up a world of possibilities when it comes to styling Squarespace websites.

JavaScript is an object-oriented language. This means that objects are created and stored and the objects have properties and functions associated with them. The properties are the values assigned to the object. Functions are things that the object can do. Objects and values can be stored as variables. Variables are containers with names that can hold an object, number, string, or other value. For example, we can create the variable sedan and save a new car object to that variable, `var sedan = New Car();`. The word `var` is a keyword that says, "make a new variable named sedan." `New Car()` is a constructor that makes a new object of type car. Variables can also just contain data. For example, a variable can contain a number `var doors = 4;`, or a string `var color = "blue";`. Objects, like our Car, have properties. The Car can have a wheels property that says our sedan has four wheels `sedan.wheels = 4;`. The Object can also have functions that do something, just like a car can drive. We can tell our car to drive by calling the `drive()` function, `sedan.drive();`. JavaScript also allows us to write our own functions. We will be writing some functions later in this book.

The key thing to take away from this section is the ability to recognize if some code is JavaScript. Functions will have a name followed by a period and another name that ends in parentheses `sedan.drive()`. Variable names will be preceded by the keyword `var` and then used throughout the code. Properties will be a variable name followed by a period and another variable name with no break, `sedan.wheels`. We will go into the use of JavaScript in more detail later in this book.

JavaScript Libraries

In addition to basic JavaScript, often called vanilla JavaScript, there are JavaScript libraries. JavaScript libraries are external JavaScript files that add specific functionality to the site. There are many JavaScript libraries that can be set up to work. I used the GSAP (Green Sock Animation Platform) https://greensock.com/gsap to add an animation to the homepage of the Math Stackers website http://www.mathstackers.com. I used GASP to code the position and timing of the blocks and bubbles as they drop and bounce onto the page. Figure 5-6 shows the Math Stackers homepage hero section after the animation.

Figure 5-6. *Math Stackers animation*

There are two main JavaScript libraries that you will encounter when working with Squarespace: the YUI library and jQuery. They are both DOM (Document Object Model) libraries, which is a fancy way of saying they give us tools to make it easier to manipulate the HTML structure of the page. JQuery is a very popular DOM library. It is characterized by the dollar sign $ since the library saves the jQuery library object to a variable named $. JQuery is an external library so it has to be added to the site via a <script></script> element in order to use it. Since jQuery is so popular, Google hosts a version on its CDN (Content Delivery Network) for anyone to use. Listing 5-13 shows the <script></script> element that adds the jQuery library and then a little bit of JavaScript in a second <script></script> element that uses the jQuery library. You can see the dollar signs $ that indicate it uses jQuery.

Listing 5-13. jQuery library script

```
<script src="https://ajax.googleapis.com/ajax/libs/jquery/3.2.1/jquery.min.js"></script>
<script>
$(document).ready(function() {
    $(".Mobile-overlay-nav-item").click(function() {
        $("body").removeClass("is-mobile-overlay-active");
        });
});
</script>
```

The YUI library is a similar DOM library created by Yahoo. It didn't have as much use as jQuery and in 2014 Yahoo announced that they were no longer going to maintain the library. Now you may be asking, why are we talking about an old JavaScript library? That is a very good question. We are talking about it because the YUI library is deeply embedded into the Squarespace platform. There are components of the Squarespace platform, when initially created, that made YUI the best choice for the job. It is a huge undertaking to try and change the Squarespace platform to a different DOM library and it has no benefit to users. Therefore, Squarespace has decided to maintain their version of the YUI library. We are safe to use YUI scripts until a major upgrade occurs to the whole platform, comparable to the Squarespace 7 update from Squarespace 6.

You can tell that JavaScript code is using the YUI library because the library is stored in a variable named Y. So in the same way that jQuery uses $, the YUI library uses Y. Listing 5-14 shows the same script as in Listing 5-13 but is coded using the YUI library instead of jQuery. You will notice that there is only a single <script></script> element. This is because Squarespace has already added the YUI library so we don't need to add it again.

Listing 5-14. YUI library script

```
<script>
Y.on("domready", function(){
  Y.all("a.Mobile-overlay-nav-item").on("click", function() {
    Y.one("body").removeClass("is-mobile-overlay-active");
  });
});
</script>
```

How do you know which JavaScript library to use? Different web developers will give you different answers to that question. If I need to add a few lines of code, and the site doesn't already include jQuery, then I will usually use YUI. I do not want to add jQuery unless necessary because it is a large library and can impact the page load time, especially for mobile devices. Some third-party integrations and plug-ins require the use of jQuery. If jQuery has already been added to the site then I will write my code in jQuery. If I need to write a fair amount of code, jQuery is not present, and it can easily be done in YUI, then I will use YUI. I will add jQuery to a site if jQuery is superior for that task. One such case is if I need to do something when the user scrolls. For example, I want the site's fixed header to change background color once the user has scrolled past a particular part of the page. YUI does not have an easy way to calculate how far the user has scrolled while jQuery has some great scroll utilities.

Anatomy of a Squarespace Page

Now that we have covered the basic aspects of HTML, CSS, and JavaScript, let's look at how it all works together inside a Squarespace website. All browsers come with an inspector tool. You can right-click on the item that you want to inspect and the developer tools will open up with the details of that element. For my examples I will be using the Firefox browser. Let's start by looking at the Brine demo site `http://brine-demo.squarespace.com`. When I right-click on the Brine logo the developer tools opens up. Figure 5-7 shows the browser window, with the logo highlighted, and the developer tools window. The developer tools window shows me the HTML for the site on the left-hand side. The right-hand side is showing the CSS rules that are applied to the selected element. Since I right-clicked on the logo, the logo's `<img>` tag is highlighted in blue. The browser window and developer tools window both highlight the logo to show what element is being selected and how it appears on the page.

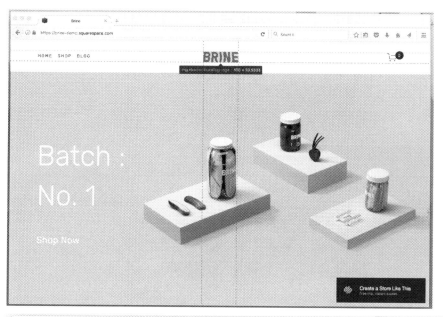

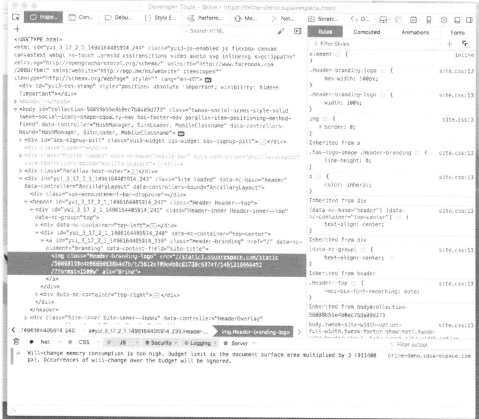

Figure 5-7. *Brine demo site with logo inspected and developer tools window*

We can edit the CSS in the developer tools window. This doesn't change the code that is saved in the site. It gives us a quick way to test out new CSS rules before we add them into the site. In Figure 5-7 we can see in the CSS rules section that the logo has a class of `.Header-branding-logo` and a property of `max-width: 100px;`. However we would like our logo to be bigger. If I change the max-width value to 300px then we can see in the browser that the logo is larger. Figure 5-8 shows the edited CSS rule and the enlarged logo.

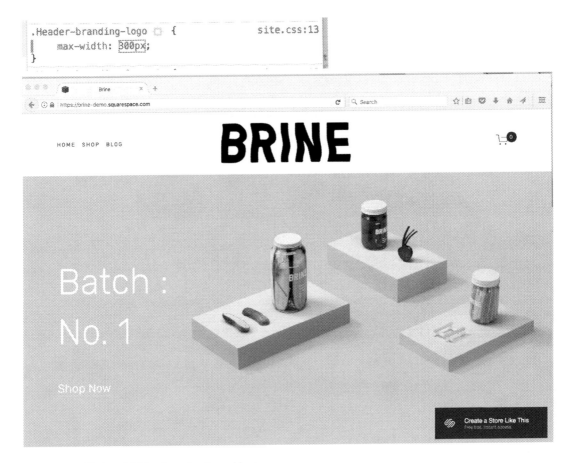

Figure 5-8. Updated CSS rule and enlarged logo

The inspector has little triangles that indicate whether a section has been collapsed and can be expanded. In the developer tools we can see that the `<head></head>` element is currently collapsed. By clicking on the arrow I can expand it and see the elements that are nested inside of the `<head></head>` element. Figure 5-9 also shows the expanded `<head></head>` element. In Figure 5-9 you can see `<meta>`, `<link>`, and `<script></script>` tags. There are many meta tags targeting social media sites. You can also see the style sheets and scripts that make up the Squarespace platform.

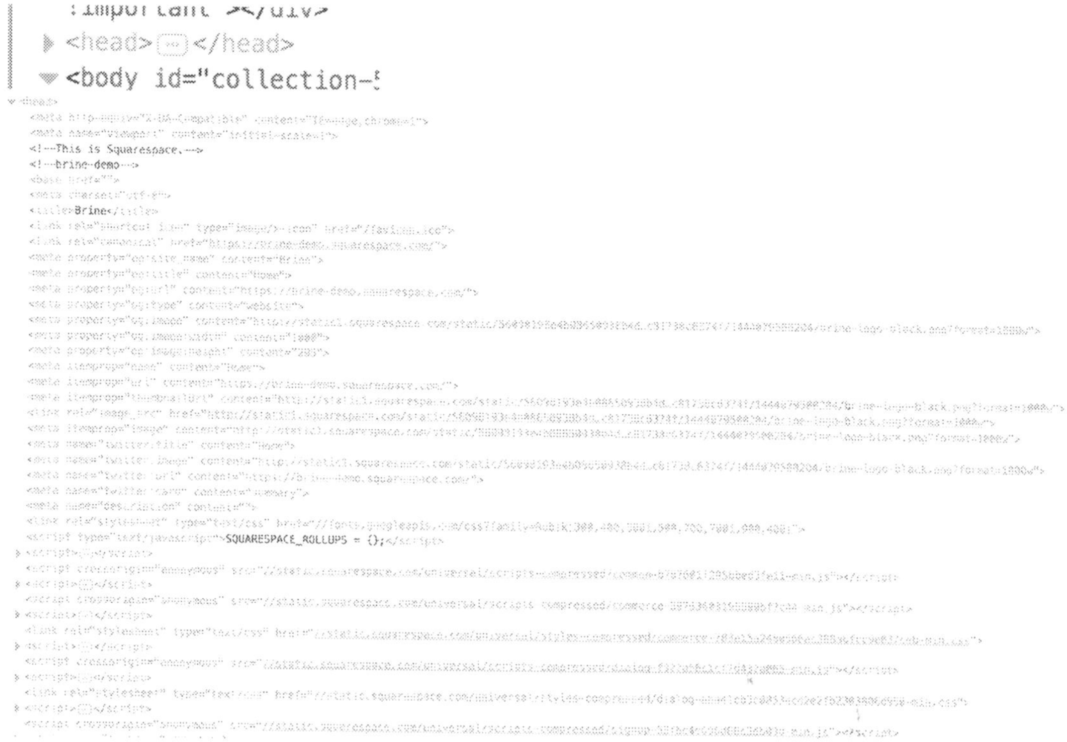

```
  !important ></div>
  ▶ <head> ... </head>
  ▼ <body id="collection-!
```

Figure 5-9. Brine Demo Site head element expanded

We can also look at the elements inside of the <body></body> tag. If you inspect the logo again you should see the elements shown in Figure 5-10. As you can see there are a number of different <div></div> tags as well as semantic elements like <header></header> and <footer></footer>. There are also additional <script></script> tags right before the closing </body> tag. It is common to put large JavaScript files at the bottom so that the content can be displayed and the visitor can begin to view it while the browser finishes running the scripts.

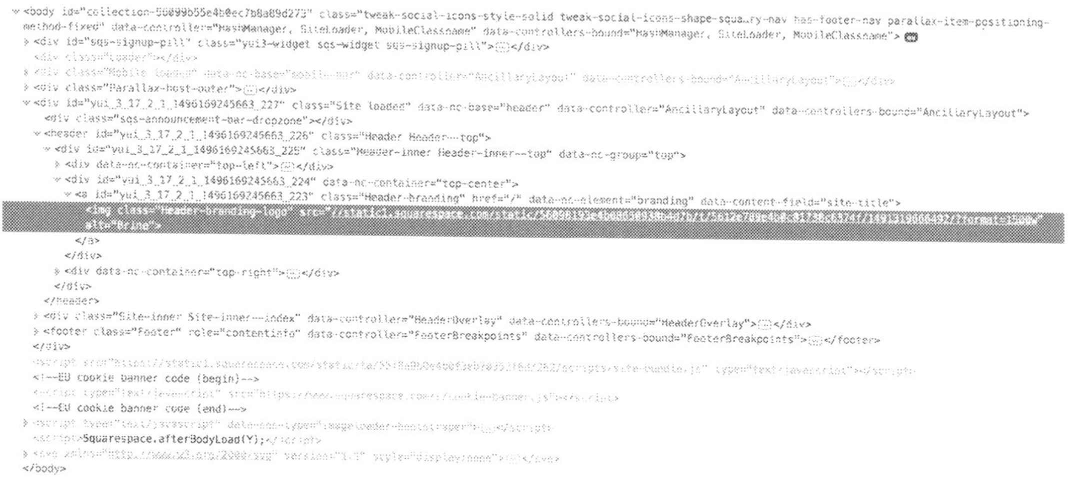

Figure 5-10. Inspecting the logo and viewing elements within the <body></body> tag

Finding the Right Selector

The challenge in using Custom CSS with Squarespace is ensuring that you have the right selector for the element and that the selector has the highest priority. Squarespace template families are all build differently and have different classes and ids. This means that CSS that works on one template will not necessarily work for another template. Let's work through how to find the correct selector. On the Brine homepage we want to change the words "Batch: No. 1" to black. The first step is to right-click on the element to inspect it. Figure 5-11 shows the <h1></h1> element and the CSS rules applied to it. We can see that the element does not have a class or id attribute. The styles are also fairly generic and apply to all the <h1></h1> elements on the page.

Figure 5-11. Heading element and CSS rules in development tools

In order to update the color I want to first find an id or class I can use to target the element. Each section of an Index Page is wrapped in a `<section></section>` element with an id. I move around the inspector to find the `<section></section>` tag for the first section of the page. Figure 5-12 shows the section, and it has an id of `welcome-brine`.

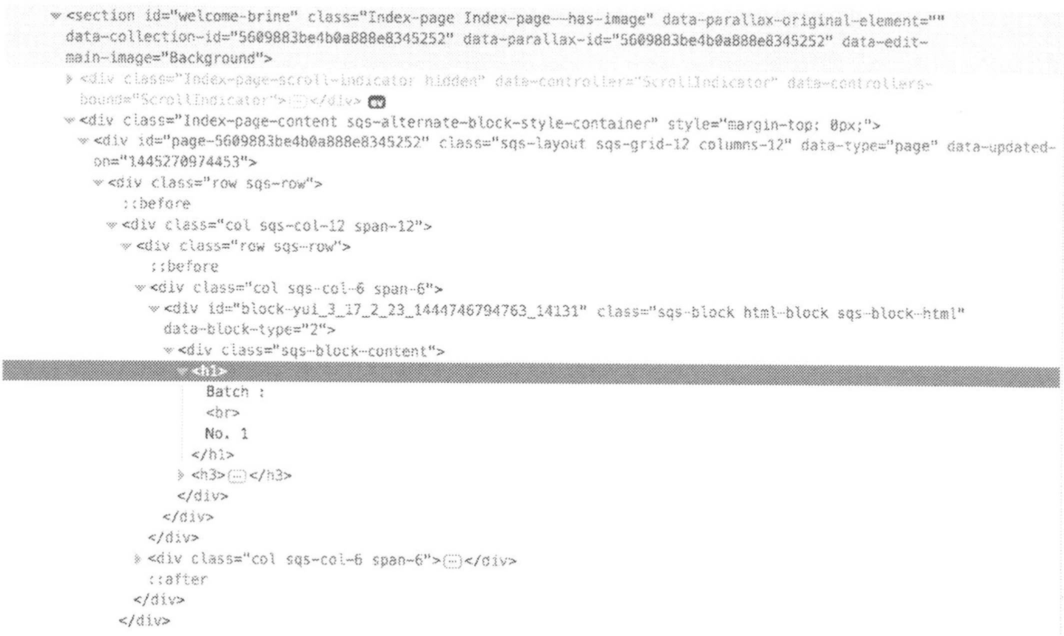

```
▼ <section id="welcome-brine" class="Index-page Index-page--has-image" data-parallax-original-element=""
   data-collection-id="5609883be4b0a888e8345252" data-parallax-id="5609883be4b0a888e8345252" data-edit-
   main-image="Background">
   ▶ <div class="Index-page-scroll-indicator hidden" data-controller="ScrollIndicator" data-controllers-
      bound="ScrollIndicator"> </div>  ○○
   ▼ <div class="Index-page-content sqs-alternate-block-style-container" style="margin-top: 0px;">
      ▼ <div id="page-5609883be4b0a888e8345252" class="sqs-layout sqs-grid-12 columns-12" data-type="page" data-updated-
         on="1445270974453">
         ▼ <div class="row sqs-row">
            ::before
            ▼ <div class="col sqs-col-12 span-12">
               ▼ <div class="row sqs-row">
                  ::before
                  ▼ <div class="col sqs-col-6 span-6">
                     ▼ <div id="block-yui_3_17_2_23_1444746794763_14131" class="sqs-block html-block sqs-block--html"
                        data-block-type="2">
                        ▼ <div class="sqs-block--content">
                           ▼ <h1>
                              Batch :
                              <br>
                              No. 1
                           </h1>
                           ▶ <h3> … </h3>
                        </div>
                     </div>
                  </div>
               </div>
               ▶ <div class="col sqs-col-6 span-6"> … </div>
               ::after
            </div>
         </div>
      </div>
```

Figure 5-12. *First section of the index page*

The `<h1></h1>` didn't have any ids associated with in when we inspected it in Figure 5-11. Therefore I will write my CSS using the id of the section followed by the h1 element selector, #welcome-brine h1. Listing 5-15 shows the entire CSS rule. Figure 5-13 shows how the first section looks after the CSS rule has been applied. You can see that the header text is now black.

Listing 5-15. CSS rule

```
#welcome-brine h1{
  color: #000000;
}
```

Figure 5-13. *First section of Brine homepage with the CSS from Figure 5-7 applied*

Wrap-Up

You should now be able to identify HTML, CSS, and JavaScript code and understand its role in a website. We will use these languages throughout the rest of the book. I will provide you with the coding basics to get started customizing Squarespace sites. However, there is a lot more to all of these languages. There are many great resources available to learn more. There are online classes with interactive lessons at codeschool.com and codeacademy.com, as well as great books and webinars available. Building websites is a constantly changing field, and I enjoy continually learning and growing my skills.

CHAPTER 6

▦ ▦ ▦

Code Injectors—Add Custom Code

The previous chapter explored the different programming languages used in Squarespace websites. You learned to recognize the difference between HTML, CSS, and JavaScript and the different roles these languages have within a website. This chapter will explore the tools for working with custom code and the Squarespace code injectors. There are many different places to inject, or add, custom code. However, before we can add custom code you need the right tools for writing the code.

Use a Code Editor

Code needs to be written in a code editor, also known as a text editor. What is a code editor, you ask? A code editor is a program designed for writing code. Before we discuss code editors further, I want to introduce an important rule: **do not use a word processor to write code**. A word processor program, like Microsoft Word, or Google Docs, is designed to create text documents. A word processor adds all kinds of extra formatting to enhance the readability of text. The primary example is straight quotes and smart quotes, also known as curly quotes. As we discussed in the previous chapter, quotes are a part of the coding languages. Straight quotes are used in code. However, word processors automatically change straight quotes to smart quotes. Word processors make the substitution because smart quotes are used in print documents since they enhance readability.

The automatic substitution is a problem in code because browsers read straight quotes and smart quotes as different characters. It is the equivalent of substituting the letter O with the number zero (0). They look very similar, but mean very different things. See Figure 6-1 for an enlarged example of straight and smart quotes. Straight quotes are the quote characters located next to the return key on your keyboard. Straight quotes are straight. They do not bend or curve and can be used as opening or closing quotes. Smart quotes curve or tilt and have an opening and closing version. When a browser is reading code and finds smart quotes it treats them like every other character. Smart quotes do not have the special meaning that straight quotes have. It is a good practice when copying code from the Internet or an email to check it for smart quotes. I have seen many people spend hours frustrated that their code isn't working, only to realize there was a set of smart quotes in the code.

© Sarah Martin 2017
S. Martin, *The Definitive Guide to Squarespace*, https://doi.org/10.1007/978-1-4842-2937-8_6

Straight and Smart Quotes

"	Straight Double Quote
'	Straight Single Quote
"	Smart Opening Double Quote
"	Smart Closing Double Quote
'	Smart Opening Sinlge Quote
'	Smart Closing Single Quote

Figure 6-1. *Straight Quotes and Smart Quotes*

Now that you understand why it is important to use a code editor, let's explore some code editor options! There are a number of great code editors out there. There are free and premium code editors. Premium editors usually come with advanced features and integrations designed for application programming. Even the free editors will have more features than you will probably ever use. What I look for in a good code editor is the ease of navigating around my project and good syntax highlighting. Syntax highlighting is where the editor displays different parts of the code in different colors. HTML tags may be one color while the content within the tag is another color. It helps make mistakes more obvious and makes the code easier to read. Figure 6-2 shows an example of syntax highlighting.

```
videoclose.html
1  <script>
2    Y.on('domready', function(){
3      Y.one('.sqs-slice-play-button').on('click', function(){
4        Y.one('.sqs-lightbox-close').on('click', function(e){
5          e.preventDefault();
6          e.stopPropagation();
7          window.location = "/home";
8        });
9      });
10   });
11 </script>
12
```

Figure 6-2. *Syntax highlighting example*

Some code editors will auto-close the code. Auto-close means that when you type in an opening character or tag, the editor will automatically add the corresponding closing one. For example, if you add a <div> HTML tag it will automatically add the </div>. Another example is when you add an opening curly bracket, the code editor will add the closing one. Some people find this really useful. Other people find it very annoying. It is all a matter of personal preference. There are also auto-complete features that make suggestions as you type in code. While auto features are helpful and can speed up productivity, they can also lead to bad habits. Relying on the code editor to close everything for you can lead to problems when you are working outside of the editor.

The code editor that I use is Atom by GitHub https://atom.io/. It is free and available for all major platforms. Atom is an open source code editor. This means that a number of extension packages have been created for it. I have added on a color picker package. The color picker enables me to easily update colors while I am working in the code editor. Figure 6-3 shows my current Atom setup. The project tree in the left column allows me to easily add and remove files and navigate within the project. I can also load multiple projects into the same window.

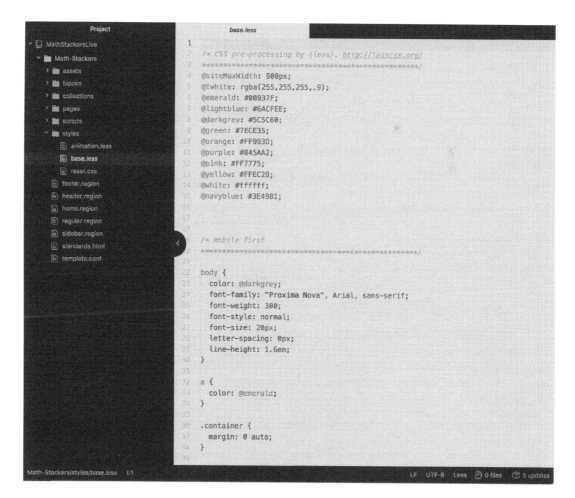

Figure 6-3. *Atom by GitHub*

Brackets, by Adobe `http://brackets.io/`, is another free code editor. It is designed especially for web designers and front-end developers. It is a minimalist code editor, which keeps it fast and easy to understand. Figure 6-4 shows a screen shot of the editor from the Brackets' website.

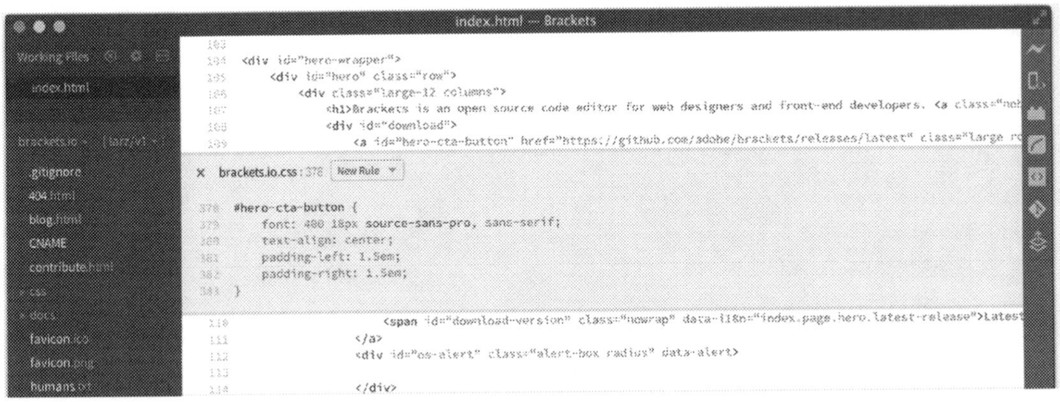

Figure 6-4. *Brackets by Adobe*

A very popular premium editor is Sublime Text `https://www.sublimetext.com/`. Sublime Text is a sophisticated and robust code editor. It is designed with the application developer in mind and has a lot of integrations. There are many more options out there as well. Find the code editor that fits your needs and is an enjoyable experience for you to work with.

It sometimes feels like duplicate work to update the custom code in the site and in a code editor. However, the code editor is what allows you to track history and undo changes. It is important to keep track of the history and versions of the code since the client may want a significant change and then not like it. A popular program for keeping track of code is GitHub. It is a cloud-based code storage system that allows you to keep all the different versions of your code together in a repository. The repository allows you to see what changed with the code and when it changed. At the very least you should store your custom code somewhere that keeps an automatic backup.

Web Developer Browser Tools

Another way to edit code is with the browser's developer tools. We already saw one type of developer tool, the inspector. There are also ways to test JavaScript and edit the HTML and CSS of the site within the browser. I will usually test new CSS rules with the developer tools before adding them to the Custom CSS Editor and code editor. The great thing about testing out the custom code in the browser is that it saves time. Changes made within the browser are visible immediately. You don't have to save the changes in Squarespace and refresh the site in order to see them.

Browsers will allow you to update the CSS right in the inspector window. In Figure 6-5 the cursor indicates where I can add new properties to the `.Index-page---has-image` `.Index-page-content` rule. Up at the top next to the Filter Styles search box there is a + icon that creates a new rule for the selected element.

Figure 6-5. Inspector CSS editing

Mozilla Firefox also has a few other tools I really like. The style editor tab lists the various style sheets in the left-hand column and displays the content of the style sheet in the right-hand column. The + icon allows a new style sheet to be added. You can also load a style sheet into the browser using the upload icon next to the + icon. Figure 6-6 shows the Mozilla Firefox style editor developer tool.

Figure 6-6. Mozilla Firefox style editor developer tool

The debugger developer tool will show you a list of all the JavaScript files loaded into the website. Figure 6-7 shows the debugger view of my River Stone Digital website. You can see where I have added additional fonts from Typekit and Google's Universal Analytics. If you want to know if a site is running jQuery, this is where you would look. If a site already had jQuery loaded, then it would appear in the list. If you have added additional JavaScript for a third-party integration, it would appear here as well.

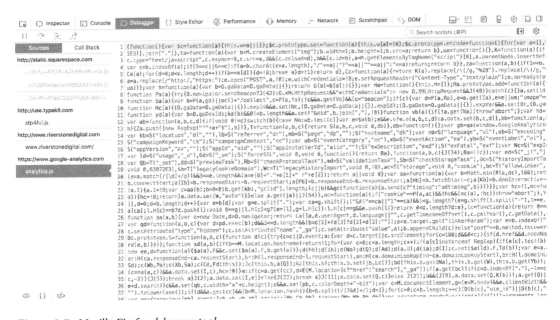

Figure 6-7. Mozilla Firefox debugger tool

All browsers have a console area that allows a user to type in and run JavaScript. The console consists of a single line where the code is entered. The code isn't saved and needs to be typed in each time it is to be run. In Mozilla Firefox there is the scratchpad tool. Scratchpad allows the user to enter an entire section of JavaScript and then click the Run button to run the script on the site. I can then edit the script and run it again. This allows me to quickly iterate and make changes to my code without having to type it out every time. Figure 6-8 shows Mozilla Firefox's console and scratchpad developer tool.

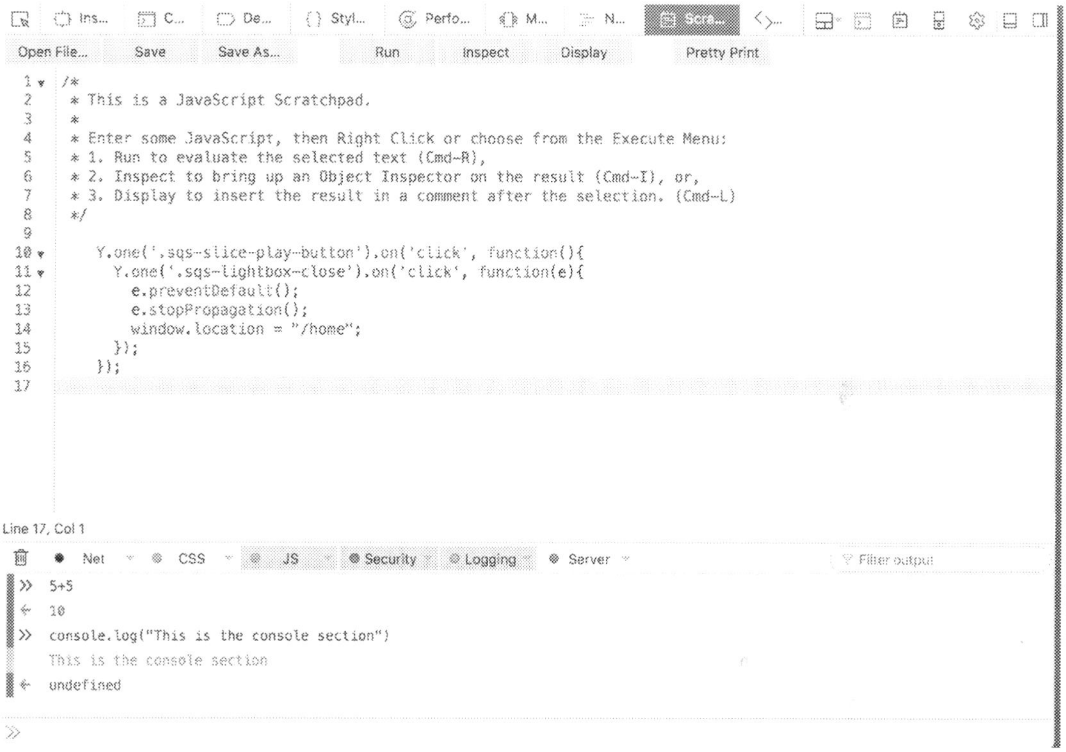

Figure 6-8. *Mozilla Firefox console and scratchpad tools*

Site-Wide Code Injection

The site-wide code injectors are found in the menu under Settings, Website, Advanced, Code Injection. The site-wide code injectors include the Header code injection and the Footer code injection. Any code entered into the Header code injection will be added into the <head></head> tag on every page of the site. Code entered into the Footer code injection is added into the template-defined footer of every page on the site. If code in the Footer code injection is not working correctly, try moving the code to the Header code injection. Any code added to the Header or Footer code injection has to be valid HTML. That means scripts need to be added using <script></script> tags and any CSS is added within <style></style> tags. Figure 6-9 shows the Google Universal Analytics script that I added to the Header code injection of my River Stone Digital site. Listing 6-1 is the HTML script. This is the same script is used for all Google Universal Analytics. The unique identifier is what changes for each website.

Listing 6-1. Google Universal Analytics Script

```
<script>
  (function(i,s,o,g,r,a,m){i['GoogleAnalyticsObject']=r;i[r]=i[r]||function(){
  (i[r].q=i[r].q||[]).push(arguments)},i[r].l=1*new Date();a=s.createElement(o),
  m=s.getElementsByTagName(o)[0];a.async=1;a.src=g;m.parentNode.insertBefore(a,m)
  })(window,document,'script','https://www.google-analytics.com/analytics.js','ga');

  ga('create', 'UA-XXXXXXXX', 'auto');
  ga('send', 'pageview');

</script>
```

CODE INJECTION

HEADER
Enter code that will be injected into the 'head' tag on every page of your site.

```
1  <script>
2    (function(i,s,o,g,r,a,m){i['GoogleAnalyticsObject']=r;i[r]=i[r]||function(){
3    (i[r].q=i[r].q||[]).push(arguments)},i[r].l=1*new Date();a=s.createElement(o),
4    m=s.getElementsByTagName(o)[0];a.async=1;a.src=g;m.parentNode.insertBefore(a,m)
5    })(window,document,'script','https://www.google-analytics.com/analytics.js','ga');
6
7    ga('create', 'UA-68105131-1', 'auto');
8    ga('send', 'pageview');
9
10 </script>
```

FOOTER
Enter code that will be injected into the template-defined footer on every page of your site.

```
1
```

***Figure 6-9.** Site-wide Header and Footer Code Injection with Google Universal Analytics script*

The site-wide Header and Footer code injectors are the most useful. This is where you will add code that you want on every page. However, the code within these can also be targeted to a specific page, or only a couple of pages.

Lock Page Code Injection

The next option in the Code Injection section is the Lock Page code injection. If the site has a site-wide lock page, then any code in the Lock Page code injection will replace the default Squarespace messages on that page. However, if you have styled the lock page using the Lock Screen Style Editor then the code is added to the page. Our example website for PAWsitive Connections TX is still under construction so it has a site-wide lock page on it. Figure 6-10 shows the PAWsitive Connections TX lock page before any code was injected. Figure 6-11 shows the Lock Page code injection where I added `<h1>This is the lock page code injection! </h1>`. Figure 6-11 also shows the lock screen after the Lock Page code injection was added. Like the Header and Footer code injections, the Lock Page code injection takes HTML code.

Figure 6-10. *Lock Screen before code injection*

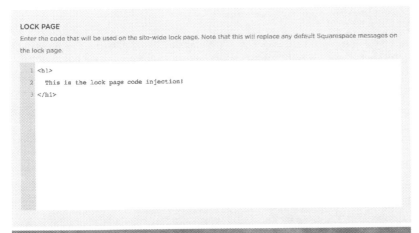

Figure 6-11. *Lock Page code injection and updated Lock Screen*

Order Confirmation Page Code Injection

The last site-wide code injector is the Order Confirmation Page code injection. Code that is added in this section will be injected into the footer of the Order Confirmation Page that displays after checkout. The Order Confirmation Page code injector takes HTML but it also will accept a few JSON-T tags. These tags allow us to capture order information to be used by a third-party service. The tags are {orderID}, {orderSubtotal}, {orderSubtotalCents}, {orderGrandTotal}, {orderGrandTotalCents}, and {customerEmailAddress}. Referral services sometimes have scripts that would be added here. To capture the email address we could add <div id="email" style="display: none;">{customerEmailAddress}</div> to the Order Confirmation Page code injection. Then we would add an additional script that collected that email address from the <div></div> and sent it to a third-party service like Zapier. From Zapier we could automatically add the email address to a number of different programs. Figure 6-12 shows the Order Confirmation Page code injection.

ORDER CONFIRMATION PAGE

Enter code that will be injected into the footer of the order confirmation page after checkout. If you'd like to pass the Order ID, subtotal, grand total, or customer email to a third party service, use the tags below in your code:

* {orderId}: The unique ID of the confirmed order
* {orderSubtotal}: The subtotal of the confirmed order
* {orderSubtotalCents}: The subtotal of the confirmed order, in cents
* {orderGrandTotal}: The grand total of the confirmed order
* {orderGrandTotalCents}: The grand total of the confirmed order, in cents
* {customerEmailAddress}: The customer's email address, as it was entered in the "Billing Info" section

```
1  <div id="email" style="display: none;">{customerEmailAddress}</div>
```

Figure 6-12. *Order Confirmation Page code injection with customer email tag*

Page Header Code Injection

The Page Header Code Injection is found in the page settings. Remember the page settings are opened using the gear icon to the right of the page's name in the Pages menu. The Page Header Code Injection is then under the Advanced tab. Figure 6-13 shows the Page Header Code Injection area. The Page Header Code Injection adds the code to that specific page. Code added here will not impact other pages of the site. If a single page needs the code, then this is a great choice. If you will be reusing the code on several pages, it is better to put it in the site-wide Header code injection. The Page Header Code Injection takes HTML just like the other code injectors that we have seen so far.

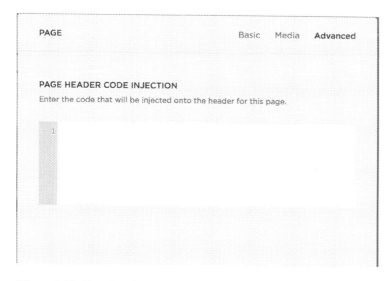

Figure 6-13. *Page Header Code Injection*

Post Blog Item Code Injection

The Blog Page has an extra code injector. Underneath the Page Header Code Injection area the Blog Page has the Post Blog Item Code Injection. Figure 6-14 shows the Post Blog Item Code Injection area. Any code entered here will be injected onto the Blog Page for each Blog Item. If the Blog Page is a stacked list, then the code is added after the item's content but before the item's footer. If the Blog Page is using a grid layout, the injection location varies depending on the template. The Post Blog Item Code Injection requires HTML but also accepts two JSON-T tags. The tags are {permalink} and {title}. These tags allow you to access the title and link for each blog post. It is important to note that the Post Blog Item Code Injection only injects the code onto the Blog Page, not into the individual blog post pages. If you want to add custom code to each individual blog post, you will need to add it to the Blog's Page Header Code Injection.

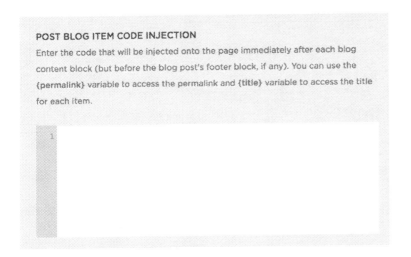

POST BLOG ITEM CODE INJECTION

Enter the code that will be injected onto the page immediately after each blog content block (but before the blog post's footer block, if any). You can use the {permalink} variable to access the permalink and {title} variable to access the title for each item.

Figure 6-14. *Post Blog Item Code Injection*

Custom CSS Editor

The Custom CSS editor is the main way to add CSS to the site. The Custom CSS editor is found in the Design menu. The Custom CSS editor accepts CSS and LESS. LESS is a CSS pre-processor language. This means that it extends the CSS language to add functionality that makes it faster to write the CSS for the site. LESS code is then run through a processor that outputs CSS. You can learn more about LESS here: http://lesscss.org/. The Custom CSS editor accepts LESS because Squarespace has a built-in LESS processor. Any CSS or LESS that is added to the Custom CSS editor is run through a LESS processor and added to the site.css file along with the template's included CSS. The Custom CSS is added at the very end of the site.css file. CSS added to the Custom CSS editor will be added every page except Cover Pages. Cover Pages do not use the site.css file and therefore are not changed by CSS in the Custom CSS editor.

The Custom CSS editor can also open in its own window. Figure 6-15 shows the Custom CSS editor as it appears as part of the left-hand menu and opened in its own window. Since code in this CSS editor is added to the site.css file, if you add broken CSS it could cause the whole site to look wrong. Squarespace customer support cannot help with websites that have Custom CSS added to them. Therefore there are warnings to use caution. The Custom CSS editor does check the code for major errors and won't let you save it if you are missing a closing bracket or semicolon. However it is can be very frustrating to suddenly have the whole site look wrong. This is why I like to test my CSS style rules in the browser developer tools before adding them to the Custom CSS editor.

Figure 6-15. *Custom CSS editor as part of the left panel and opened in a window*

The Custom CSS editor also allows files to be uploaded. The Manage Custom Files button appears under the CSS editor. The Manage Custom files section is for adding images or fonts used in the CSS. This is not the area to add any other type of files. PDFs, JavaScript files, external style sheets, and images not used in CSS should all be added to the regular file upload area. Figure 6-16 shows the Manage Custom Files upload section.

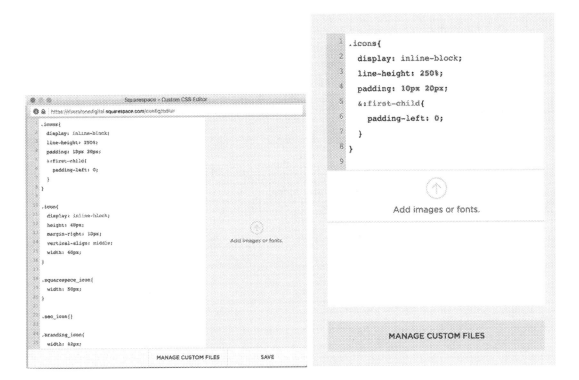

Figure 6-16. *Manage Custom Files upload section*

Code Blocks

The Code Block is another way to add custom code to the site. The Code Block is a Squarespace Block that can be added to a page just like the other Block types. The Code Block accepts HTML and therefore can include JavaScript and CSS inside `<script></script>` and `<style></style>` tags. Figure 6-17 shows the Code Block editor and the code displayed on the page. Code Blocks work best for HTML and CSS. I will include the CSS in the Code Block only if it applies to the HTML in the Code Block. If the CSS will change more than just the contents of the block, then it should be put in the Custom CSS editor. While JavaScript can be included in the Code Block, I avoid putting it there. For example, JavaScript in Code Blocks on Index Pages won't always run correctly. Therefore, I usually put the JavaScript portion of the custom code in the Page Header Code Injection or the site-wide Header Code Injection.

Figure 6-17. *Code Block editor and displayed code*

Form Block Post-Submit HTML

The final code injector is the Form Block's Post-Submit HTML injector. This is found in the Form Block's Advanced menu. Figure 6-18 shows the Post-Submit HTML injection area. The Post-Submit HTML is injected after the form's post-submit message. This is often used to redirect the user to another page after the form has been submitted or to add tracking code. It also allows you to add a more complex Post-Submit Message including social media links or images.

Figure 6-18. Form Block Post-Submit HTML code injection

Load Order

Now that you have been introduced to all of the different Code Injection areas, let's talk about the load order. Load order is the order in which the browser reads and executes the code. This has implications for how the code behaves. For example, JavaScript that adds a click hander to a button, like opening a lightbox, won't work if the JavaScript runs before the button exists. Custom CSS may not take effect if it is being loaded before other style rules that have the same specificity and are loaded later.

CSS Priority

As you learned in Chapter 5, CSS rules have a priority. The rule with the highest priority is the one that is rendered, or displayed. If rules have the same weight, or specificity, then the one that is loaded most recently will have priority. The Custom CSS editor adds the Custom CSS to the bottom of the site.css file. This means that the Custom CSS editor rules have priority over the template style rules if they are the same specificity. The site.css file is loaded before any other code injection is loaded. The site-wide Header Code Injection is loaded after the site.css file. This means that the Header Code Injection will have priority over the site.css style rules if they are the same specificity. The Page Header Code Injection is the next one to load. Therefore, the Page Header Code Injection CSS will have priority over the site-wide Header Code Injection rules if they are the same specificity. Finally, there are the Block level code injectors. The block level code injections run as the page content is loaded. The site-wide Footer Code Injection is the last to run. Generally you don't want to include CSS in the Footer Code Injection. This is because the page will first load for the site visitor and then the style rules will be applied. The site visitor will see the unstyled version of the page for a fraction of a second before it suddenly shifts to be styled.

JavaScript Load Order

Just like CSS, the load order for JavaScript is very important. Typically when we are adding JavaScript to a site, it is to manipulate part of the page. Therefore we need the HTML to be in place before the JavaScript runs. As we have discussed, the main places that JavaScript is added into a site are the Header and Footer Code Injections. However, if we add JavaScript to the Header Code Injection, we need the JavaScript to wait until the HTML has all loaded before running. The HTML is known as the DOM, or Document Object Model. Browsers will fire an event when the DOM has loaded and is safe to manipulate. There is also a Window Load event. The Window encompasses everything that the browser window currently contains. If a browser has multiple tabs open, then each tab is its own Window. The Window Load event fires when the DOM and all of the other files have fully loaded. This includes loading all the images and any other style or script files. Typically the DOM ready event is all we need to listen for. However, if your code is dependent on an image loading first, then the Window Load event should be used instead.

Listing 6-2 shows three different listeners. The first `<script></script>` tag is the `window.onload` event listener. This is the plain JavaScript option. The script is creating a function that will run when the `window.onload` event fires. The second `<script></script>` is the YUI DOM ready event handler. The YUI DOM ready script says, "When the DOM is ready, run the code in this function." The third `<script></script>` contains two versions of the jQuery DOM ready event handler. The jQuery DOM ready event handler and the YUI DOM ready event handler do the same thing using different JavaScript libraries. The first jQuery DOM ready handler is the full version and the second one is the shorthand version.

Listing 6-2. Plain JavaScript, YUI, and jQuery load and ready listeners

```
<script>
  window.onload = function(){
    // your code
  }
</script>

<script>
Y.on('domready', function(){
  // your code
});
</script>

<script>
$(document).ready(function(){
  // your code
});

//Shorthand version
$(function(){
  //your code
});
</script>
```

If the code that you are writing uses the jQuery library, or another JavaScript library, then that library needs to load before your script runs. Therefore you need to include the `<script></script>` tag to load jQuery before you add your `<script></script>` tag. However, you only need to add jQuery once. I often see sites that have jQuery added two or three times. The web designer has typically added a few third-party add-ons that require jQuery. The third party includes the jQuery script in the code they provide since their script relies on it. However, if you have several scripts that all use jQuery you only need to load the jQuery library once. The scripts may use different versions of jQuery. As long as you keep the latest version, the one with the highest version number, then you can delete the extra ones. Unnecessarily loading jQuery multiple times will slow down your website. It may not be noticeable from desktop devices, but it will definitely impact load time on mobile devices.

Wrap-Up

You should now have a solid understanding of the different code injectors within Squarespace. You should understand the purpose of each code injector and generally when it should be used. The next chapter builds on this understanding, adding another level of complexity with AJAX. The newest template families have AJAX page loading. The next chapter will explore what AJAX is and the implications for adding custom code.

CHAPTER 7

■ ■ ■

AJAX and AJAX Enabled Templates

In this chapter we will explore AJAX and how it is used in Squarespace templates. AJAX is a common source of confusion among novice web developers. The scenario usually goes like this: The web developer has added custom code to a particular page in the site. The customization looks great when the browser is refreshed. However, when navigating between pages the customization no longer works, or worse, the customization now runs on the wrong page altogether. What happened? The answer lies in understanding how AJAX is used in Squarespace templates.

What Is AJAX

First of all, let's define AJAX. AJAX stands for Asynchronous JavaScript And XML. It is pronounces as "A" (as in the letter A) and "jacks." AJAX is a way of using JavaScript and an XMLHttpRequest to request data from a web server and display, or use the data, on the web page. Figure 7-1 shows this interaction between the web browser and the web server.

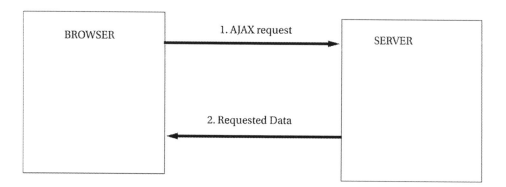

Figure 7-1. *AJAX request diagram*

AJAX can be used in many different ways in a website. A common use of AJAX is to create an Infinite Scroll blog. In an Infinite Scroll blog, an initial set of blog items is loaded onto the page. As a user approaches the bottom of the list, additional posts are loaded. This creates the feeling of being able to scroll forever; hence the technique is called Infinite Scroll. The benefit of using AJAX is that it keeps the page load time

© Sarah Martin 2017
S. Martin, *The Definitive Guide to Squarespace*, https://doi.org/10.1007/978-1-4842-2937-8_7

short. Without using AJAX, all of the blog posts would have to be loaded when the page first loads. For a blog that has 500 posts, this would mean a very slow page load time. When AJAX is used, the initial page load only has to load a small number of posts, for example, 30. Then the AJAX request asks for additional blog posts and loads them as the user scrolls down the page. This provides a much better user experience.

Another main use of AJAX is for faster page loads. When using AJAX for page loads, only the part of the page that changes is loaded rather than the entire page and all of the accompanying files. For example, the CSS style sheets, JavaScript libraries, and some images, like a logo, are consistent across the website. Every page uses the same base set of files. Therefore, using AJAX, when a page changes only the updated content needs to be loaded. The JavaScript, CSS style sheets, and images stay loaded from the previous page. This significantly reduces the page load time of complex pages and preserves the user experience.

Squarespace Template Families with AJAX

The new style Squarespace templates all have AJAX loading enabled. This includes the Brine, York, Farro, Skye, and Tremont template families. An important thing to note is that AJAX is disabled when you are logged into the Squarespace system. Therefore, if you are editing the site you will not see the AJAX happening. You need to view the site in a separate browser, where you are not logged in, to see the AJAX take effect.

All AJAX enabled Squarespace templates use AJAX requests to load page changes. In addition to the AJAX page change, some templates have additional AJAX features. The Brine and Farro template families include an optional Loading Bar that can appear at the top of the site. The York template uses AJAX to create page load animations.

Brine, York, and Tremont template families have a Style Editor Tweak to enable or disable AJAX loading. The Skye template family does not have the option to disable the AJAX loading. The Farro template family has a Style Editor Tweak to disable AJAX loading, but will only disable it for non-blog pages. The Farro template blog pages will still use AJAX loading no matter what.

When custom code doesn't work correctly with AJAX enabled, the answer you will see in a lot of forum responses is to disable AJAX. I disagree with this approach since it sacrifices the user experience. There has only been one time that I could not get a third-party tool to work with AJAX enabled. The developer of the third-party tool is now in the process of updating their program to work with AJAX enabled templates. AJAX page loading is the way of the future, and allows us to push the limits of our websites. As web professionals, it is up to us to continually improve our skills and deliver excellent user experiences.

Working Around AJAX

The first step to working around the AJAX is to understand the difference between a regular page load and an AJAX page load. First, we will review a standard page load. In a standard page load the entire page is retrieved from the web server and loaded. The load order includes the Global Header Code Injection, Page Header Code Injection, Page Content, and finally Global Footer Code Injection. Figure 7-2 shows a chart of the load order and an example webpage.

Standard Page Load

1. Global Squarespace Scripts and Files
2. Custom CSS Editor style rules
3. Global Header Code Injection
4. Page Header Code Injection
5. Page Content
6. Global Footer Code Injection

Figure 7-2. *Standard Page Load Order*

As discussed previously, only the page content is changed in an AJAX page change. The website sends an AJAX request to the web server asking for the new page's content. When the website receives the page content, it swaps out the original page content for the new page content. Figure 7-3 illustrates this process. The page content, which will be changed, includes the "Contact Us" header and contact form. Everything else will stay the same.

AJAX Page Change

1. Send AJAX Request to web server
2. Receive Page Content from server
3. Replace Page Content with new Page Content

Figure 7-3. *AJAX page change illustration*

The key to understanding why custom code doesn't work with AJAX page changes lies in understanding what doesn't happen during the AJAX page change. First of all, the Page Header Code Injection is not retrieved as part of the page change and therefore cannot be run. Therefore with AJAX page changes, any CSS or JavaScript in the Page Header Code Injection essentially doesn't exist. The previously loaded Page Header Code Injection, from the original page load, stays in place. If page specific CSS rules were in the Page Header Code Injection of the original page, those rules will still apply to the new page. The way to work around this in AJAX enabled templates is to ignore the Page Header Code Injection as well. All Custom CSS should be put in the Custom CSS Editor. You may need to add collection ids or other selectors to ensure the code only applies to correct pages. However any CSS that was in a Page Header Code Injection can be updated and put in the Custom CSS Editor.

As you learned in the previous chapter, most JavaScript is structured so that it runs after the onload or DOM ready events are triggered. The browser window triggers these events once it has finished loading for the first time. With an AJAX page change, these events are not triggered. Since the events are not triggered, all the JavaScript that depends on those triggers doesn't run. This accounts for why the custom code will work with a browser refresh, which is a standard page load, and not on page change, which is an AJAX page change. The solution to this problem lies in being able to trigger the JavaScript after the AJAX page change.

Mutation Observer

The answer to our AJAX page change problem is a Mutation Observer. A Mutation Observer is a JavaScript function created to watch for AJAX page changes. It actually watches for any insertion, removal, or updating of DOM elements. It is not limited to AJAX page changes. Listing 7-1 shows my version of a Mutation Observer. There is a more standard implementation of a Mutation Observer, where the Mutation Observer triggers a page change event rather than running a function. My version minimizes the chances of the Mutation Observer conflicting with the Mutation Observer included in a third-party plug-in. It is successfully running on numerous Squarespace websites and works with many different customizations.

Listing 7-1. Mutation Observer Script

```
<script>
//RSD Mutation Observer wrapper
function RSD_init(){
    //functions to call when mutation observer recognizes page change
}

window.onload = RSD_watch;

//RSD_watch function to look for page changes using Mutation Observer
function RSD_watch() {
    MutationObserver = window.MutationObserver || window.WebKitMutationObserver;

    var mo = new MutationObserver(function(mo) {
        var moCount = 0;
        for (var b = 0; b < mo.length; b++) {
            var c =mo[b];

            if ("attributes" === c.type  && moCount === 0) {
                RSD_init();
                moCount++;
            }
        }
    });

    var options = { attributes : true, attributeFilter : ['id']};

    mo.observe(document.body, options);
}
</script>
```

The first part of the Mutation Observer is the `RSD_init()` function. This function is a wrapper for any JavaScript we want to run after an AJAX page change. Typically anything included in an `onload` or DOM ready function should be repeated in the `RSD_init()` function. This ensures that all JavaScript that relies on those events is run after an AJAX page change. The other part of this script is the Mutation Observer itself. The Mutation Observer is contained in a function named `RSD_watch()`. The `window.onload = RSD_watch;` line of code assigns the `RSD_watch()` function to run at page load. Therefore the `RSD_watch()` function is created during the standard page load and stays active through all AJAX page changes.

The Mutation Observer itself is included inside the `RSD_watch()` function. The first line in the function, `MutationObserver = window.MutationObserver || window.WebKitMutationObserver;`, sets up the Mutation Observer based on which browser is being used. Browsers have different names for the MutationObserver, with some browsers using the WebKit prefix. Then the `RSD_watch()` function creates a variable `mo`, and saves the configured Mutation Observer to the variable. During an AJAX page change the MutationObserver will get an array, or list, of all the changes that occurred. The Mutation Observer will then look through the list to see if there were any ID attribute changes. The ID attribute changes signal an AJAX page change. Then if there was an ID attribute change the `RSD_init()` function is run. In order to simplify things I have ensured that the `RSD_init()` function is only called once with an AJAX page change. Many of the custom code snippets you will find in forums or online are designed to only be run once. By only forcing the `RSD_init()` function to only run once the custom code should need minimal updating. The `var options = { attributes : true, attributeFilter : ['id']};` line of code is where we tell the Mutation Observer to look for ID attribute changes. The last line of the `RSD_watch()` function, `mo.observe(document.body, options);`, is where we tell the Mutation Observer to watch everything inside the `<body></body>` tag of the page.

Google Analytics Example

Let's take a look at how to implement Google Analytics for an AJAX enabled template. Listing 7-2 shows the same Google Analytics implementation script from earlier. To implement it yourself, you will need to change the UA-XXXXXX to the number provided for your specific Google Analytics account.

Listing 7-2. Regular Google Analytics Script

```
<script>
  (function(i,s,o,g,r,a,m){i['GoogleAnalyticsObject']=r;i[r]=i[r]||function(){
  (i[r].q=i[r].q||[]).push(arguments)},i[r].l=1*new Date();a=s.createElement(o),
  m=s.getElementsByTagName(o)[0];a.async=1;a.src=g;m.parentNode.insertBefore(a,m)
  })(window,document,'script','https://www.google-analytics.com/analytics.js','ga');

  ga('create', 'UA-XXXXXXX', 'auto');
  ga('send', 'pageview');
</script>
```

Looking at the script there isn't a DOM ready or `onload` function. The Google Analytics script doesn't need to wait until the page is loaded to run. It runs immediately when it is loaded as part of the Global Header Code Injection. The problem with this is that it won't run again when AJAX page changes happen since the Header Code Injection isn't loaded again. Figure 7-4 shows the Real-Time view in Google Analytics. I have the test site running in 2wo browsers. I can change pages but the Real-Time view doesn't recognize these changes since the Google Analytics script didn't run again.

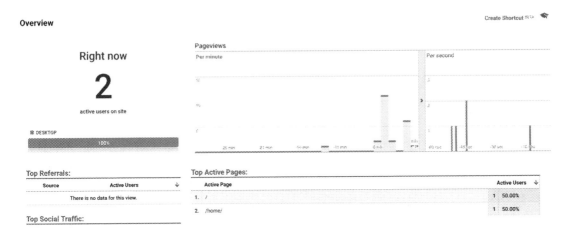

Figure 7-4. *Google Analytics Real-Time view*

Looking at the Google Analytics developer documents, `https://developers.google.com/analytics/devguides/collection/analyticsjs/pages`, it tells us that we can send a pageview hit to Google Analytics with the following code, `ga('send', 'pageview', window.location.pathname);`. If we look at our original Google Analytics script we see that this solution is a variation of the last line of the original script, `ga('send', 'pageview');`. The main difference between the two is that we are including the URL of the page in the second version. Listing 7-3 shows the implementation of our original Google Analytics script and the additional Mutation Observer code. When an AJAX page change happens we need to run this line of script `ga('send', 'pageview', window.location.pathname);`. The RSD_init() function is run when our Mutation Observer sees an AJAX page change. Therefore we add the `ga('send', 'pageview', window.location.pathname);` inside the RSD_init() function. Putting it all together, in Listing 7-3, we have the original Google Analytics Script, our additional line of Google Analytics code inside the RSD_init() function, and our Mutation Observer script.

Listing 7-3. Google Analytics with Mutation Observer

```
<script>
(function(i,s,o,g,r,a,m){i['GoogleAnalyticsObject']=r;i[r]=i[r]||function(){
(i[r].q=i[r].q||[]).push(arguments)},i[r].l=1*new Date();a=s.createElement(o),
m=s.getElementsByTagName(o)[0];a.async=1;a.src=g;m.parentNode.insertBefore(a,m)
})(window,document,'script','https://www.google-analytics.com/analytics.js','ga');

ga('create', 'UA-XXXXXXX', 'auto');
ga('send', 'pageview');

//RSD Mutation Observer wrapper
function RSD_init(){
  ga('send', 'pageview', window.location.pathname);
}

// add RSD_watch function to window.onload
window.onload = RSD_watch;

//RSD_watch function to look for page changes using Mutation Observer
function RSD_watch() {
  MutationObserver = window.MutationObserver || window.WebKitMutationObserver;
```

```
var mo = new MutationObserver(function(mo) {
  var moCount = 0;
  for (var b = 0; b < mo.length; b++) {
    var c =mo[b];

    if ("attributes" === c.type  && moCount === 0) {
      RSD_init();
      moCount++;
    }
  }
});

var options = { attributes : true, attributeFilter : ['id']};

mo.observe(document.body, options);
}
</script>
```

Having added the updated script from Listing 7-3 to the Global Header Code Injection of the test site, I can return to the Google Analytics Real-Time view. Now when I look at the Real-Time view I see page changes updated in real time. I can change pages in both of my browser windows and see those changes within seconds. Figure 7-5 shows the Google Analytics Real-Time view reflecting a page change to the portfolio page.

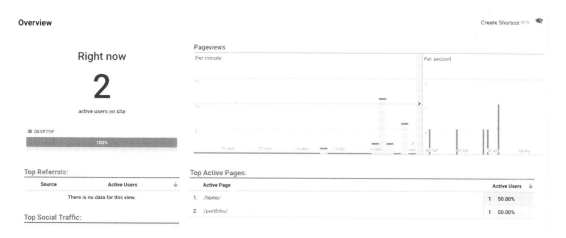

Figure 7-5. *Google Analytics Real-Time view with Mutation Observer page changes shown*

HTML Comment Box Example

Squarespace recommends a few resources for collecting customer reviews to add to the site. One of those resources is HTML Comment Box http://www.htmlcommentbox.com/. HTML Comment Box is a minimal comment or review collection tool to add to any page that doesn't have built-in comments. There are a number of configuration options available on the HTML Comment Box website when generating the initial script. Figure 7-6 shows the HTML Comment Box added to a webpage. Listing 7-4 shows the standard HTML Comment Box script that can be added to a Code Block.

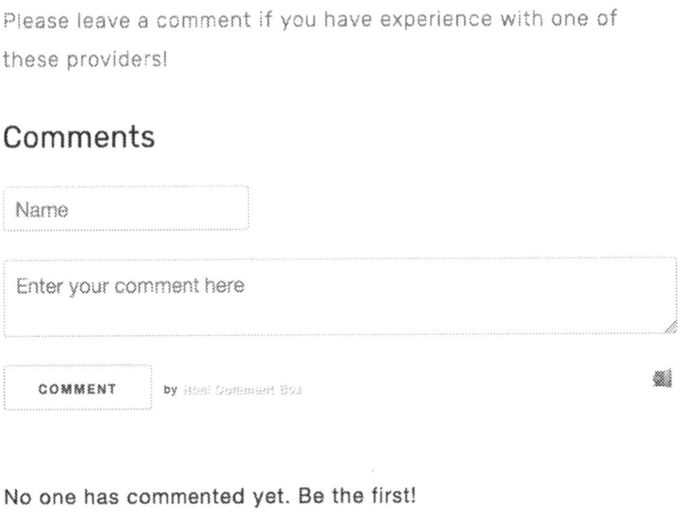

Please leave a comment if you have experience with one of
these providers!

Comments

Name

Enter your comment here

COMMENT   by Html Comment Box

No one has commented yet. Be the first!

Figure 7-6. *HTML Comment Box display on page*

Listing 7-4. *HTML Comment Box standard script*

```
<!-- begin www.htmlcommentbox.com -->
<div id="HCB_comment_box"><a href="http://www.htmlcommentbox.com">HTML Comment Box</a> is
loading comments...</div>
<link rel="stylesheet" type="text/css" href="//www.htmlcommentbox.com/static/skins/
skeleton/skin.css" />
<script type="text/javascript" id="hcb">
if(!window.hcb_user){hcb_user={};} (function(){var s=document.createElement("script"), l=hcb_
    user.PAGE || (""+window.location).replace(/'/g,"%27"), h="//www.htmlcommentbox.com";
s.setAttribute("type","text/javascript");s.setAttribute("src", h+"/jread?page="+encodeURI
Component(l).replace("+","%2B")+"&mod=%241%24wq1rdBcg%24.vdBkbSL28H.jpJLbYPw8."+"&opts=278&
num=10&ts=1499202414624");
if (typeof s!="undefined") document.getElementsByTagName("head")[0].appendChild(s);})();
</script>
<!-- end www.htmlcommentbox.com -->
```

For sites that don't have AJAX enabled, adding the HTML Comment Box script into a Code Block works well. However, as seen in Figure 7-7, it doesn't load on AJAX page change. If we take a closer look at the script in Listing 7-4 we see that it contains a <div> with a link in it, a link to a style sheet, and JavaScript. Since we know the JavaScript won't run inside the Code Block with AJAX page changes we know we need to move that code. We also know that it is best practice to move the link script out of the Code Block into the Global Header Code Injection.

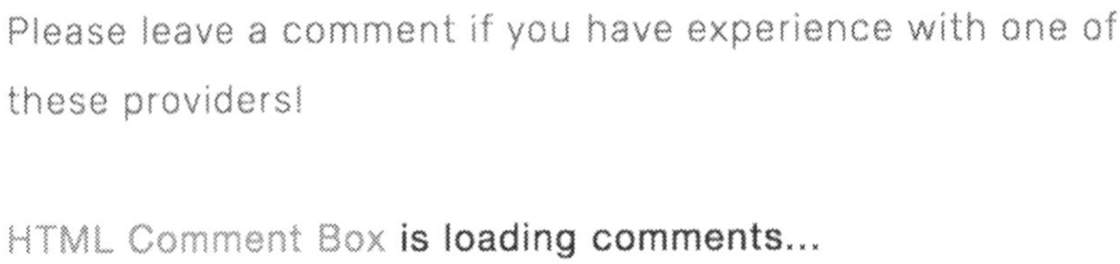

Please leave a comment if you have experience with one of

these providers!

HTML Comment Box is loading comments...

Figure 7-7. *HTML Comment Box not loading on page change*

Given what we know, the solution to making the HTML Comment Box work with AJAX loading is two-fold. The `<div>` from the HTML Comment Box script will stay where it is in the Code Block. The link to the style sheet and JavaScript will be moved to the Global Header Code Injection and we need to add the Mutation Observer. Listing 7-5 has the updated script that includes the Mutation Observer. There are comments `<!-- -->` in the code notating where the code goes. Any code inside `<!-- -->` is an HTML Comment. Comments aren't active code; they are just notes for the developer. In Listing 7-5 we see the `<div>` that we leave in the Code Block. Then comes the link and original JavaScript added to the Header Code Injection. Then a new `<script></script>` tag includes our Mutation Observer. The contents of the original `<script></script>` tag is what we want to repeat inside our RSD_init() function. You can see the original HTML Comment Box code and the repeat of it inside the RSD_init() function are both bolded. In this case it isn't important to understand every bit of the HTML Comment Box script. We just needed to know that it was the script that needed to run again.

Listing 7-5. HTML Comment Block script with Mutation Observer

```
<!-- Code for Code Block -->
<div id="HCB_comment_box"><a href="http://www.htmlcommentbox.com">HTML Comment Box</a> is
loading comments...</div>


<!-- Code for global Header Code Injection -->
<link rel="stylesheet" type="text/css" href="//www.htmlcommentbox.com/static/skins/
skeleton/skin.css" />
<script type="text/javascript" id="hcb">
if(!window.hcb_user){hcb_user={};}
(function(){var s=document.createElement("script"), l=hcb_user.PAGE || (""+window.
location).replace(/'/g,"%27"), h="//www.htmlcommentbox.com";
s.setAttribute("type","text/javascript");s.setAttribute("src", h+"/jread?page="+encodeURI
Component(l).replace("+","%2B")+"&mod=%241%24wq1rdBcg%24.vdBkbSL28H.jpJLbYPw8."+"&opts=278&
num=10&ts=1499202414624");
if (typeof s!="undefined") document.getElementsByTagName("head")[0].appendChild(s);})();
</script>


<script>
//RSD Mutation Observer wrapper
function RSD_init(){
  if(!window.hcb_user){hcb_user={};}
  (function(){var s=document.createElement("script"), l=hcb_user.PAGE || (""+window.
  location).replace(/'/g,"%27"), h="//www.htmlcommentbox.com";
  s.setAttribute("type","text/javascript");s.setAttribute("src", h+"/jread?page="+encodeURI
  Component(l).replace("+","%2B")+"&mod=%241%24wq1rdBcg%24.vdBkbSL28H.jpJLbYPw8."+"&opts=27
  8&num=10&ts=1499202414624");
  if (typeof s!="undefined") document.getElementsByTagName("head")[0].appendChild(s);})();
}

// add RSD_watch function to window.onload
window.onload = RSD_watch;

//RSD_watch function to look for page changes using Mutation Observer
function RSD_watch() {
  MutationObserver = window.MutationObserver || window.WebKitMutationObserver;
```

```
    var mo = new MutationObserver(function(mo) {
      var moCount = 0;
      for (var b = 0; b < mo.length; b++) {
        var c =mo[b];

        if ("attributes" === c.type  && moCount === 0) {
          RSD_init();
          moCount++;
        }
      }
  });

    var options = { attributes : true, attributeFilter : ['id']};
    mo.observe(document.body, options);
  }
</script>
```

FAQ Accordion Examples

Another popular customization is to add accordions to the page content. Accordions expand to reveal content and then shrink when another section is opened. These are often used in FAQ pages and other pages with multiple content sections. Figure 7-8 shows an accordion, as it should display on the page. There are three parts to an accordion. The first is the HTML content structure. The second is the CSS styling, and the third is the JavaScript interactions.

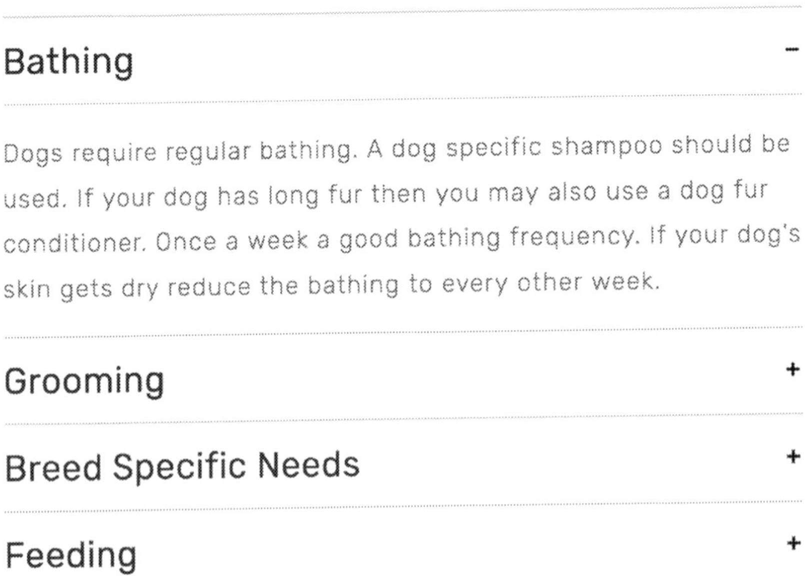

Bathing   --

Dogs require regular bathing. A dog specific shampoo should be used. If your dog has long fur then you may also use a dog fur conditioner. Once a week a good bathing frequency. If your dog's skin gets dry reduce the bathing to every other week.

Grooming   +

Breed Specific Needs   +

Feeding   +

Figure 7-8. *Accordion as displayed in the browser*

Listing 7-6 shows the code for the accordion if we put it all in a single Code Block. First is the heading and paragraph tags, `<h3></h3>` and `<p></p>`. Classes have been added to the heading and paragraph tags so that they can be selected for CSS styling and JavaScript interaction. The `<h3></h3>` tags have a class of info_head and the `<p></p>` tags have a class of info_text. Since this is a Code Block that takes HTML the styles are included in a `<style></style>` tag following the heading and paragraph tags. Finally there are a couple `<script></script>` tags that add jQuery and the accordion functionality.

Listing 7-6. Accordion regular example – all code in code block

```
<h3 class="info_head">Bathing</h3>
<p class="info_text">Dogs require regular bathing. A dog specific shampoo should be used.
If your dog has long fur then you may also use a dog fur conditioner. Once a week a good
bathing frequency. If your dog's skin gets dry reduce the bathing to every other week.</p>

<h3 class="info_head">Grooming</h3>
<p class="info_text">Your dog's nails may need regular trimming. If your dog walks a lot
on concrete then their nails may not need to be trimmed. If the nails click on the ground
then you should trim them.You can use dog nail scissors or a grinder. Be careful dogs have
a quick in the middle of their nail. If you take off too much it will bleed.If your dog has
long fur then they will also need regular brushing to prevent mats and regular trips to the
groomer.</p>

<h3 class="info_head">Breed Specific Needs</h3>
<p class="info_text">Different breeds of dogs require special care. Dachshunds are prone
to back problems and shouldn't be allowed to go up or down stairs, jump on furniture, or
play roughly with larger dogs. Smaller toy breeds like, Yorkies and Maltese, are prone to
allergies. Larger breeds are often prone to knee and hip problems.</p>

<h3 class="info_head">Feeding</h3>
<p class="info_text">Feed your pet a high quality food. Good ingredients ensures that your
pet's skin and coat remain healthy. It is also easier to train a well-fed dog.</p>

<style>
.info_head:after {
    content: '\02795';
    font-size: 13px;
    color: #777;
    float: right;
    margin-left: 5px;
}

.info_head.active:after {
    content: "\2796";
}

.info_head{
  border-top: 1px solid #ccc;
  padding: 15px 0;
  margin: 0;
}
```

```
.info_head.active{
    border-bottom: 1px solid #ccc;
}

.info_head.last{
  border-bottom: 1px solid #ccc;
}

</style>

<script src="https://ajax.googleapis.com/ajax/libs/jquery/3.2.1/jquery.min.js"></script>
<script>
$(document).ready(function() {
  $('.info_text:not(:nth-child(2))').slideUp();
  $('.info_head:nth-child(1)').addClass('active');

    $('.info_head').click(function(){
      $('.info_head').removeClass('active');
      $('.info_text').slideUp();
      $(this).addClass('active');
      $(this).next().slideDown();
    });
});
</script>
```

It is important to note that the jQuery won't run while logged into the site. Squarespace blocks it from running. Therefore when you are editing the page, all of the content sections will remain expanded. Figure 7-9 shows how the accordion script appears when logged into the website. You can see the Code Block indicator and the message that scripts have been disabled.

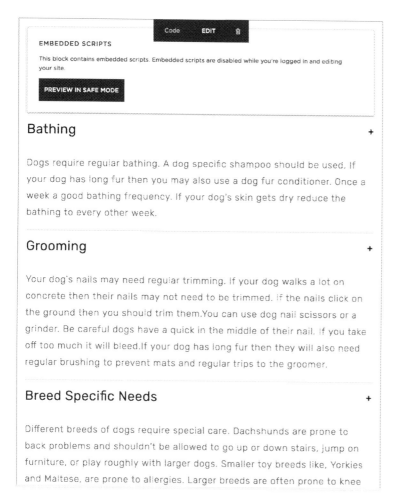

Figure 7-9. *Accordion code block as viewed in the Content Editor*

As we have seen with the previous examples. the script will work correctly on browser refresh. However when there is an AJAX page change the script won't run, and therefore it looks the same as when we are logged into the site. Figure 7-10 shows how the accordion looks in the browser with an AJAX page change and no Mutation Observer script.

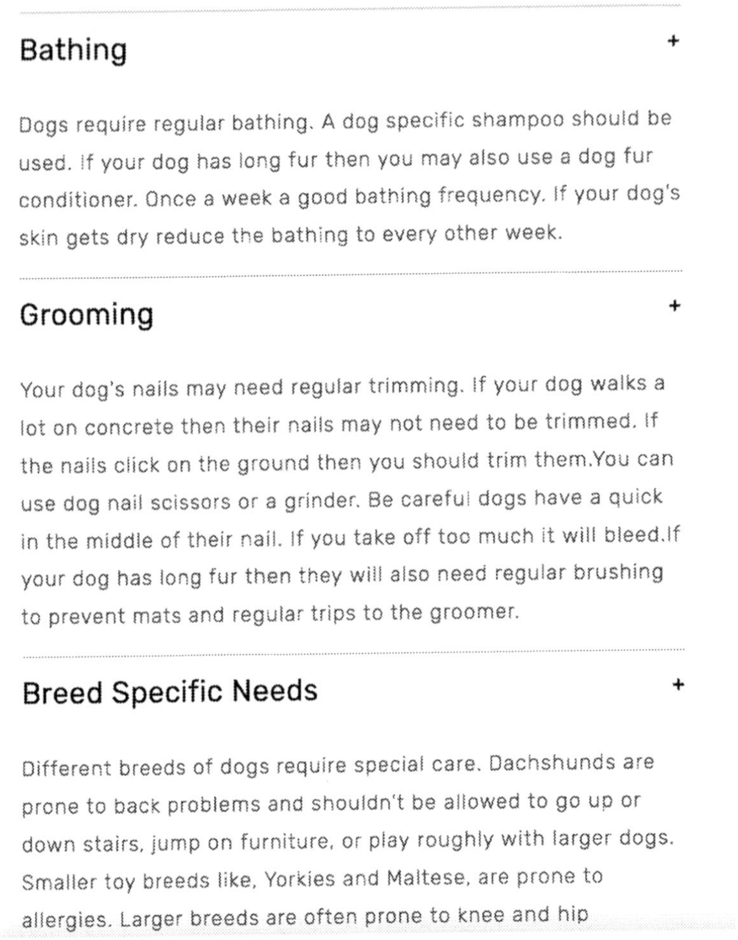

Bathing   +

Dogs require regular bathing. A dog specific shampoo should be used. If your dog has long fur then you may also use a dog fur conditioner. Once a week a good bathing frequency. If your dog's skin gets dry reduce the bathing to every other week.

Grooming   +

Your dog's nails may need regular trimming. If your dog walks a lot on concrete then their nails may not need to be trimmed. If the nails click on the ground then you should trim them.You can use dog nail scissors or a grinder. Be careful dogs have a quick in the middle of their nail. If you take off too much it will bleed.If your dog has long fur then they will also need regular brushing to prevent mats and regular trips to the groomer.

Breed Specific Needs   +

Different breeds of dogs require special care. Dachshunds are prone to back problems and shouldn't be allowed to go up or down stairs, jump on furniture, or play roughly with larger dogs. Smaller toy breeds like, Yorkies and Maltese, are prone to allergies. Larger breeds are often prone to knee and hip

Figure 7-10. Accordion loading incorrectly on page change

The accordion code needs to be restructured to work with the Mutation Observer. First of all we can leave the <h3></h3> and <p></p> tags inside the Code Block. A Markdown Block could also be used for this purpose. Everything else will be moved out of the Code Block. Listing 7-7 shows the HTML that we will keep in the Code Block.

Listing 7-7. Code to keep in Code Block

```
<h3 class="info_head">Bathing</h3>
<p class="info_text">Dogs require regular bathing. A dog specific shampoo should be used.
If your dog has long fur then you may also use a dog fur conditioner. Once a week a good
bathing frequency. If your dog's skin gets dry reduce the bathing to every other week.</p>

<h3 class="info_head">Grooming</h3>
<p class="info_text">Your dog's nails may need regular trimming. If your dog walks a lot
on concrete then their nails may not need to be trimmed. If the nails click on the ground
then you should trim them.You can use dog nail scissors or a grinder. Be careful dogs have
a quick in the middle of their nail. If you take off too much it will bleed.If your dog has
long fur then they will also need regular brushing to prevent mats and regular trips to the
groomer.</p>

<h3 class="info_head">Breed Specific Needs</h3>
<p class="info_text">Different breeds of dogs require special care. Dachshunds are prone
to back problems and shouldn't be allowed to go up or down stairs, jump on furniture, or
play roughly with larger dogs. Smaller toy breeds like, Yorkies and Maltese, are prone to
allergies. Larger breeds are often prone to knee and hip problems.</p>

<h3 class="info_head">Feeding</h3>
<p class="info_text">Feed your pet a high quality food. Good ingredients ensures that your
pet's skin and coat remain healthy. It is also easier to train a well-fed dog.</p>
```

Next we will move the CSS into the Custom CSS Editor. We do not copy the `<style></style>` tags into the Custom CSS Editor since the Custom CSS Editor only takes CSS. Listing 7-8 shows the CSS that is added to the Custom CSS Editor. The CSS adds the plus and minus signs that appear to the right of the accordion headers. The CSS also adds the borders to the accordion headers and uses an `.active` class to style the expanded section differently from the collapsed sections.

Listing 7-8. CSS to move to Custom CSS Editor

```
.info_head:after {
  content: '\02795';
  font-size: 13px;
  color: #777;
  float: right;
  margin-left: 5px;
}

.info_head.active:after {
  content: "\2796";
}

.info_head{
  border-top: 1px solid #ccc;
  padding: 15px 0;
  margin: 0;
}
```

```
.info_head.active{
  border-bottom: 1px solid #ccc;
}

.info_head.last{
  border-bottom: 1px solid #ccc;
}
```

Finally we will move the JavaScript to the Global Header Code Injection and add our Mutation Observer. Looking at the original code in Listing 7-6 we see that there are eight lines of code inside the $(document).ready() function. Rather than including all those lines of code twice we are going to wrap them in a function. Then we will call the function from the RSD_init() function and the $(document).ready() function. Since we are creating our own function, we choose the name. In this example I named it accordionInit() since the function initializes the accordion functionality. Inside the accordionInit() function are the eight lines of code inside the DOM ready function from Listing 7-6. In Listing 7-9 we have our updated accordion script and Mutation Observer. First included in the script is the jQuery library. Next is the DOM ready function that calls the accordionInit() function. Next is our accordionInit() function. Then the accordionInit() function is called inside the RSD_init() function. The rest of our Mutation Observer follows.

Listing 7-9. Accordion Script with Mutation Observer

```
<!-- Global Header Code Injection -->
<script src="https://ajax.googleapis.com/ajax/libs/jquery/3.2.1/jquery.min.js"></script>
<script>
$(document).ready(function() {
  accordionInit();
});

function accordionInit(){
  $('.info_text:not(:nth-child(2))').slideUp();
  $('.info_head:nth-child(1)').addClass('active');

 $('.info_head').click(function(){
   $('.info_head').removeClass('active');
   $('.info_text').slideUp();
   $(this).addClass('active');
   $(this).next().slideDown();
 });
}

//RSD Mutation Observer wrapper
function RSD_init(){
  accordionInit();
}

// add RSD_watch function to window.onload
window.onload = RSD_watch;

//RSD_watch function to look for page changes using Mutation Observer
function RSD_watch() {
  MutationObserver = window.MutationObserver || window.WebKitMutationObserver;
```

```
  var mo = new MutationObserver(function(mo) {
    var moCount = 0;
    for (var b = 0; b < mo.length; b++) {
      var c =mo[b];

      if ("attributes" === c.type  && moCount === 0) {
        RSD_init();
        moCount++;

      }
    }
  });

  var options = { attributes : true, attributeFilter : ['id']};
  mo.observe(document.body, options);
}
```

```
</script>
```

Now the accordion appears correctly every time we change pages. The accordion is a great example of why we only want the Mutation Observer to call the RSD_init() function once. If the RSD_init() function were called for each change in the Mutation Observer's list, then the accordion would open and collapse several times before taking on its updated state. The JavaScript that controls the interaction would need to be updated to ensure this didn't happen. Instead we control it in the Mutation Observer and don't need to worry about making additional changes to the accordion's JavaScript.

Accordion and HTML Comment Box Example

Up to this point we have added a single script to a site and made it work with AJAX enabled. Now we will look at how we could implement two or more scripts using our Mutation Observer. For this example we will add the HTML Comment Box and the Accordion to our test site. The Code Blocks and Custom CSS Editor content will remain the same from the previous examples. The Global Header Code Injection is the only thing that will need to be updated. We cannot have duplicate functions and do not want to include multiple Mutation Observers. Listing 7-10 shows the correctly combined code. First the stylesheet link and jQuery library are included at the top of the code injection. Next comes the original HTML Comment Box script in its own <script></script> tag. Then we have the rest of the script in a separate <script></script> tag. Ideally we would minimize the number of <script></script> tags, but some third-party tools need to be separate so that they don't conflict. You can always try grouping the code into a single <script></script> tag and if something strange happens, separate the code again.

Listing 7-10. Accordion and HTML Comment Box Global Header Code Injection

```
<!-- HTML Comment Box Styles -->
<link rel="stylesheet" type="text/css" href="//www.htmlcommentbox.com/static/skins/skeleton/
skin.css" />
<!-- jQuery -->
<script src="https://ajax.googleapis.com/ajax/libs/jquery/3.2.1/jquery.min.js"></script>

<!-- HTML Comment box dom ready script -->
 <script type="text/javascript" id="hcb">
   if(!window.hcb_user){hcb_user={};}
```

```
  (function(){var s=document.createElement("script"), l=hcb_user.PAGE || (""+window.
  location).replace(/'/g,"%27"), h="//www.htmlcommentbox.com";
  s.setAttribute("type","text/javascript");s.setAttribute("src", h+"/jread?page="+encodeURI
  Component(l).replace("+","%2B")+"&mod=%241%24wq1rdBcg%24.vdBkbSL28H.jpJLbYPw8."+"&opts=27
  88&num=10&ts=1499202414624");
  if (typeof s!="undefined") document.getElementsByTagName("head")[0].appendChild(s);})();
</script>

<script>
//Create accordion function
function accordionInit(){
  $('.info_text:not(:nth-child(2))').slideUp();
  $('.info_head:nth-child(1)').addClass('active');

  $('.info_head').click(function(){
    $('.info_head').removeClass('active');
    $('.info_text').slideUp();
    $(this).addClass('active');
    $(this).next().slideDown();
  });
}

//use dom ready script for accordion function
$(document).ready(function() {
  accordionInit();
});

//Set up Mutation Observer wrapper
function RSD_init(){
  //call accordion function
  accordionInit();

  //call HTML comment box script
  if(!window.hcb_user){hcb_user={};}
  (function(){var s=document.createElement("script"), l=hcb_user.PAGE || (""+window.
  location).replace(/'/g,"%27"), h="//www.htmlcommentbox.com";
  s.setAttribute("type","text/javascript");s.setAttribute("src", h+"/jread?page="+encodeURI
  Component(l).replace("+","%2B")+"&mod=%241%24wq1rdBcg%24.vdBkbSL28H.jpJLbYPw8."+"&opts=278
  &num=10&ts=1499202414624");
  if (typeof s!="undefined") document.getElementsByTagName("head")[0].appendChild(s);})();
}

// add RSD_watch function to window.onload
window.onload = RSD_watch;

//RSD_watch function to look for page changes using Mutation Observer
function RSD_watch() {
    MutationObserver = window.MutationObserver || window.WebKitMutationObserver;

    var mo = new MutationObserver(function(mo) {
    var moCount = 0;
    for (var b = 0; b < mo.length; b++) {
```

```
    var c =mo[b];

    if ("attributes" === c.type  && moCount === 0) {
      RSD_init();
      moCount++;
    }
  }

 });

  var options = { attributes : true, attributeFilter : ['id']};
  mo.observe(document.body, options);
}
</script>
```

In our Mutation Observer `<script></script>` tag, I first include the `accordionInit()` function. Then I include the DOM ready function that contained the `accordionInit()` function from Listing 7-9. I do not need to include the HTML Comment Box in the DOM ready function since that was already added in its separate `<script></script>` tag. Then follows the `RSD_init()`function and it contains the `accordionInit()` function and the HTML Comment Box code. We do not want to have duplicate `RSD_init()` functions. Therefore we combine the contents of the two `RSD_init()` functions from the previous examples into a single `RSD_init()` function. The rest of the Mutation Observer code follows just like the rest of the previous examples.

Let's recap how we combined the multiple scripts. First we added the external resources in the Global Header Code Injection. Next we included the stand-alone third-party scripts. Then we added our custom function and DOM ready function. Finally we updated the `RSD_init()` function to include both customizations. Finally we added the rest of the Mutation Observer code.

Mercury – Squarespace's Solution

Squarespace generates the AJAX page loading using a code module called Mercury. Mercury is Squarespace's proprietary code and is included in the Brine, Skye, Tremont, and Farro AJAX based templates. Mercury isn't included in the York template family. Recently Squarespace started releasing code to the developer community https://developers.squarespace.com/tools. This code is used internally by the Squarespace developers and they chose to share it with us. Knowing that Squarespace Developers depend on these tools, I use Mercury instead of a Mutation Observer with the templates that include it. To use Mercury, we replace the `window.onload = RSD_watch();` with `window.addEventListener("mercury:load", RSD_init);`. The rest of the `RSD_watch()` function that contained the Mutation Observer is unnecessary with this approach. Listing 7-11 shows the full code for using Mercury. Listing 7-11 serves the same purpose as our original code in Listing 7-1.

Listing 7-11. Mercury AJAX page loading

```
  <script>
//RSD AJAX Wrapper
function RSD_init(){
  //functions to call on AJAX page change
}

 window.addEventListener("mercury:load", RSD_init);
</script>
```

The Mutation Observer and Mercury approaches both have pros and cons. Mercury would be the more elegant lightweight approach, but Mercury isn't included in the York template family. The main benefit of using Mercury is that we can include multiple Mercury calls without any negative impact on the site. With the Mutation Observer there is a significant impact to page load if we use multiple Mutation Observers. The Mutation Observer also won't work with any other custom code that also relies on saving a function to the window.onload object. The Mutation Observer is a more resource-heavy solution, but it gets the job done. I have jokingly called it the sledgehammer approach. As is often the case in the world of web development, we make judgment calls based on the particular website's needs.

Wrap-Up

I highly suggest reading through this chapter a few times and trying out all of the code. This is the most challenging topic we have covered so far. Having a solid understanding of AJAX and how to make your custom code work with AJAX is a critical step in leveling up your developer skills. For a deeper look into the Mutation Observer and its capabilities, visit the David Walsh Blog at `https://davidwalsh.name/mutationobserver-api`. I also suggest ignoring most forum posts about AJAX. Due to significant changes to the Squarespace implementation of AJAX, almost all post answers are now out of date. In the next chapter we will explore popular customizations and all the code used to implement them. You will also learn how to think about customization challenges so you can figure out the best way to implement them.

CHAPTER 8

Popular Customizations

This chapter will walk through a number of popular customizations using the Brine family template. These customizations will provide a solid framework for beginning to create your own custom code. Each customization will be approached using a Structure, Style, and Interactions analysis. Structure changes indicate we will be manipulating HTML. Style changes require CSS coding. Interaction changes need JavaScript work.

Style Editor and Block Settings

The first step to creating custom code is to understand that the Style Editor settings can change the HTML structure of the website. The Style Editor settings also can change the CSS Style rules applied to the site. Therefore, if you are working on a customization, and you change the Style Editor setting, you may need to update your custom code. The Brine family template has two header areas: the top header and the bottom header. The position of the menu, logo, cart, and search icon inside these header areas is determined in the Style Editor. Figure 8-1 shows the header placement options in the Style Editor.

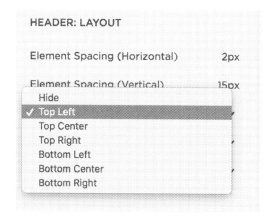

Figure 8-1. Brine template family's header placement Style Editor selections

S. Martin, *The Definitive Guide to Squarespace*, https://doi.org/10.1007/978-1-4842-2937-8_8

The two header areas exist as two separate <header> </header> tags in the HTML structure. The top header area has a class of Header--top. The bottom header area has a class of Header--bottom. An example we will work through later in this chapter is creating a fixed header. In our example the header elements are in the top header and we will code the CSS using .Header--top. Later, if we decide to move the header elements to the bottom header, we will need to update our CSS in order to keep the fixed header. Figure 8-2 shows the <header></header> tags for the top and bottom header areas.

```
▼ <header class="Header Header--top">
  ▼ <div class="Header-inner Header-inner--top" data-nc-group="top">
    ▼ <div data-nc-container="top-left">
      ▼ <a class="Header-branding" href="/" data-nc-element="branding" data-content-field="site-title">
          <img class="Header-branding-logo" src="//static1.squarespace.com/static/5774710bcd0f6811f303388d
          /t/5774887a46c3c4f7b4a39902/1500777034944/?format=1500w" alt="River Stone Digital">
        </a>
      ▶ <nav class="Header-nav Header-nav--secondary" data-nc-element="secondary-nav" data-content-
        field="navigation">⋯</nav>
      </div>
    ▶ <div data-nc-container="top-center">⋯</div>
    ▶ <div data-nc-container="top-right">⋯</div>
    </div>
  </header>
  ▼ <header class="Header Header--bottom Header--overlay">
    ▶ <div class="Header-inner Header-inner--bottom" data-nc-group="bottom">⋯</div>
  </header>
```

Figure 8-2. *Brine template family header HTML*

Block settings also can change the HTML and CSS of the Block. The Summary Block is a prime example of this. The Summary Block has a number of layout options, including a carousel and a grid. If custom code is applied to the grid layout, and the Block is switched to a carousel layout, the custom code will also need to be updated. Figure 8-3 shows the grid layout and the accompanying classes applied to the Block. Figure 8-4 shows the carousel layout and the accompanying classes applied to the same Block. You can see that the grid layout has a class of sqs-gallery-design-autogrid. The carousel layout has a different class of sqs-gallery-design-carousel.

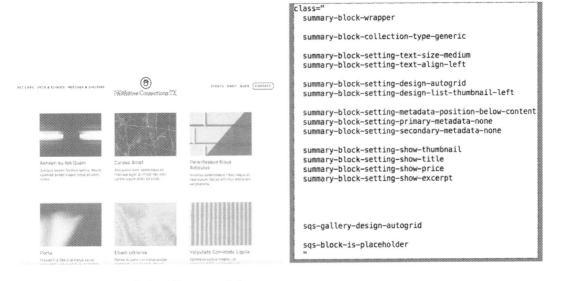

Figure 8-3. *Summary Block grid layout and classes*

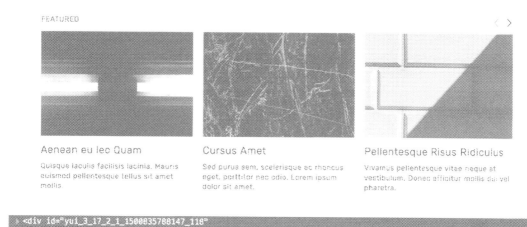

Figure 8-4. *Summary Block carousel layout and classes*

Even though Blocks might look similar, they usually have different structure and style. For example, both Gallery and Summary Blocks have a grid layout. CSS styling that works for the Gallery grid layout won't necessarily work for Summary grid layout and vice versa. It isn't uncommon for a web professional to be confused as to why the custom style isn't applying to a Block, only to realize it isn't the correct type of Block. If the client is adding their own content to the site, then they may not have used the correct Block, or given it the wrong settings. The first line of defense when trouble shooting Block specific custom code, is to ensure the Block's settings are correct.

Changing Styles on a Single Page

A lot of customizations start with the desire to change a style on a single page. For example, on my website, I have used an index page for the Home page, About page, and the My Work page. In my Style Editor settings I have the Index Navigation set to display as a Radio button on the right-hand side. Figure 8-5 shows the Index Navigation and the Style Editor setting.

INDEX: NAVIGATION

Style: Radio ⌄

Position: Right ⌄

Figure 8-5. *Index Navigation and Style Editor setting*

I love how the Index Navigation looks on the homepage; however it looks strange on my About page since there are only two sections in that Index. Figure 8-6 shows the Index Navigation as it originally appears on the About page. For this customization I want to hide the Index Navigation on just the About page. Time for the Structure, Style, and Interaction analysis. First the Structure: do we need to change the HTML structure? Well, removing the navigation from the HTML is certainly an option, but not the simplest solution. I know it is easier to hide the Index Navigation rather than removing it. Hiding the Index Navigation would be a Style change. This lets us know the solution will have custom CSS code. This customization doesn't have any Interaction changes involved, since our customization doesn't depend on the user to do something. Therefore we can conclude that our final custom code solution only needs CSS code.

Figure 8-6. *About page with Index Navigation*

The next step is determining the correct selectors for the CSS style rules. Fortunately for us, Squarespace assigns a unique Collection ID to every single page. When I inspect the About page I see that it has a Collection ID of `collection-596832b38419c27b439371fc`. Therefore my CSS selector will begin with `#collection-596832b38419c27b439371fc`. This ensures that the properties in the CSS style rule will only be applied to the About Page. When I inspect the Index Navigation directly I see that it has a class of `Index-nav`. Therefore, the second part of my selector will be `.Index-nav`. Remember, all class selectors begin with a `.` and all ID selectors begin with #. Figure 8-7 shows the Collection ID and `Index-nav` class as viewed in the browser developer tools.

```
▼ <body id="collection-596832b38419c27b439371fc" class="tweak-social-icons-style-solid tweak-social-icons-shape-
  squa...fects has-primary-nav parallax-item-positioning-method-fixed" data-controller="HashManager, SiteLoader,
  MobileClassname"> ⬚

  ▼ <nav class="Index-nav overlay">
    ▼ <div class="Index-nav-inner">
      ▼ <a class="Index-nav-item active" href="#header-2">
        ▶ <div class="Index-nav-indicator"> ⬚ </div>
        ▶ <div class="Index-nav-text"> ⬚ </div>
        </a>
      ▶ <a class="Index-nav-item" href="#about-2"> ⬚ </a>
      </div>
    </nav>
```

Figure 8-7. *Collection ID and Index-nav as seen in the browser developer tools*

Now that we have the correct selector we need to write the style rule. In this case, since I just want to hide the Index Navigation, I can use `display: none;`. This will hide the Index Navigation and remove it from the flow of the HTML document. Listing 8-1 shows the completed CSS rule exactly how it can be added to the Custom CSS Editor. Figure 8-8 shows the About page with the Index Navigation hidden.

Listing 8-1. Hiding Index Navigation on a single page style rule

```
#collection-596832b38419c27b439371fc .Index-nav{
  display: none;
}
```

Figure 8-8. *About page with Index Navigation hidden*

This example naturally leads to the question, what about Blogs and other collection types in Squarespace? If a website has two Blogs, can a style rule be applied to only one of them? More importantly, can it be applied without having to get the Collection ID of every single Blog Post? For collections like Blogs, Products, Events, and Galleries, the list page has a unique Collection ID, for example, `collection-1234`. Every child item of that collection has its own unique Collection ID, which identifies it as an individual item. However, it also has the Collection ID of the parent item as a *Class*. The individual blog post would have `id="collection-5678"` and `class="collection-1234"`, for example. Therefore every blog post within a particular blog can be targeted using `.collection-1234` as the CSS selector.

Styling a Single Navigation Item

Styling a single navigation item is another common customization. In our example we will style the Contact menu item to look like a button. It is very common for links to be styled to look like a button. The Brine template includes a style option for all the navigation items to look like buttons. However, we only want the Contact menu item to look like a button. On the example site, the right-side menu items are all styled the same. The original style is seen in Figure 8-9. Let's do the Structure, Style, and Interaction analysis. Structure – this customization requires no changes to the HTML. Style – this customization does require style changes. Our custom code will include CSS. Interaction – this customization isn't dependent on the user's actions. Therefore our solution will consist of CSS we put in the CSS Editor.

EVENTS   SHOP   BLOG   CONTACT

Figure 8-9. *Original right-side navigation items*

To start with, we will inspect the menu item we want to style. Figure 8-10 shows the Contact navigation item in the Inspector window. We can see that the Contact item has a class of Header-nav-item. The attribute selector property can be added to this class to select just the Contact item. The CSS selector would be .Header-nav-item[href="/contact/"]. The attribute is the href attribute and the value of that attribute is /contact/.

```
▼ <nav id="yui_3_17_2_1_1500836903408_411" class="Header-nav Header-nav--secondary" data-nc-
  element="secondary-nav" data-content-field="navigation">
  ▼ <div id="yui_3_17_2_1_1500836903408_410" class="Header-nav-inner">
      <a class="Header-nav-item" href="/events/" data-test="template-nav">Events</a>
      <a class="Header-nav-item" href="/shop/" data-test="template-nav">Shop</a>
      <a class="Header-nav-item" href="/blog/" data-test="template-nav">Blog</a>
      <a id="yui_3_17_2_1_1500836903408_409" class="Header-nav-item" href="/contact/" data-
      test="template-nav">Contact</a>
    </div>
  </nav>
```

Figure 8-10. *Inspector view of the Contact menu item*

Now that we have a starting selector for the style rule, let's work on the property changes. The button needs to have a border. The border CSS property takes a value that has three parts. It consists of the thickness of the border, the style of border, and the color. In this example the property border: 1px solid #000000; will create a 1px wide solid black border. To round out the corners of our border, so it is a rounded rectangle, we can use the border-radius property. The border-radius property can take a pixel or percentage value. Squares that have a border-radius value of 50% will appear as a circle. In this example we will use a border-radius of 10px. The property will be border-radius: 10px;. In order to have padding, or space between the border and the letters, we will need to have the link display like a block element. However, we also want it to stay inline with the rest of the navigation. Therefore we will give it the property of display: inline-block;. The padding properties will be defined as padding-left: 10px; and padding-right: 10px;. Listing 8-2 shows the completed CSS Rule and Figure 8-11 shows how the Contact menu item now looks.

Listing 8-2. Contact menu button CSS rule

```
.Header-nav-item[href="/contact/"]{
  border: 1px solid #000;
  display: inline-block;
  border-radius: 10px;
  padding-left: 10px;
  padding-right: 10px;
}
```

Figure 8-11. *Contact menu button with Listing 8-2 CSS style rule*

Wait! What happened? That isn't how the Contact menu button should look. We added padding to the right and left! When we go to the inspector we can see that our padding rule doesn't have enough specificity and a style rule in the template is taking priority. Figure 8-12 shows the Inspector view of how the rules are being applied. The style rule we made is the third one down. The padding-left and padding-right properties have a strike through them indicating that they are being ignored for a rule with higher priority. The rule with the highest specificity is the first one.

```
body:not(.tweak-header-          site.css:13
primary-nav-hover-style-
button) .Header-nav--primary .Header-
nav-item, body.tweak-header-secondary-
nav-inherit-styles:not(.tweak-header-
primary-nav-hover-style-button)
.Header-nav--secondary .Header-nav-
item ⚙ {
  ▶ margin: 0 .618em;
  ▶ padding: .618em 0;
}
.tweak-header-primary-nav-     site.css:13
hover-style-spotlight
.Header-nav .Header-nav-item ⚙ {
    color: ● #1d1d1d;
}
.Header-nav-                    site.css:15
item[href="/contact/"] ⚙
{
  ▶ border: 1px solid ● #000;
    display: inline-block;
  ▶ border-radius: 10px;
    padding-left: 10px; ▽
    padding-right: 10px; ▽
}
```

Figure 8-12. *Inspector view of the style rule in Listing 8-2*

We can make our style rule take priority in two ways. The first way would be to add the !important flag to our padding rules. This would give it the highest priority. The !important flag version of the CSS rule is the first style rule in Listing 8-3. A better way would be to add selectors to make our rule the highest priority. Looking at the inspector rule, we see that the one with highest priority has the additional selectors of body. tweak-header-secondary-nav-inherit-styles .Header-nav--secondary. We don't need to include the :not() part of the selector since we will be including the attribute selector instead. The second style rule in Listing 8-3 shows the updated CSS rule, including the additional selectors. Figure 8-13 shows how the Contact menu item looks in desktop view.

Listing 8-3. CSS rules for Contact Menu with !important flag and additional selectors

```
body.tweak-header-secondary-nav-inherit-styles .Header-nav--secondary .Header-nav-
item[href="/contact/"]{
  border: 1px solid #000;
  display: inline-block;
  border-radius: 10px;
  padding-left: 10px;
  padding-right: 10px;
}

.Header-nav-item[href="/contact/"]{
  border: 1px solid #000;
  display: inline-block;
  border-radius: 10px;
  padding-left: 10px !important;
  padding-right: 10px !important;
}
```

EVENTS   SHOP   BLOG   (CONTACT)

Figure 8-13. *Final Desktop view Contact menu button*

The desktop view contact button looks great! However, we are not done yet. Like many of the Squarespace templates the mobile navigation is a separate HTML structure from the desktop navigation. We need to use some additional CSS if we want the mobile navigation to have the same button appearance. Using the inspector we can determine which classes are different for the mobile menu. Figure 8-14 shows the Inspector view of the mobile menu contact item. For mobile navigation the .Header-nav-item class is .Mobile-overlay-nav-item. The <nav></nav> element also has a class of .Mobile-overlay-nav--secondary instead of .Header-nav--secondary. Therefore we will start by using our original style rule and adjusting the CSS selectors. I will also increase the padding a little since the font is bigger. Listing 8-4 has the updated CSS rule.

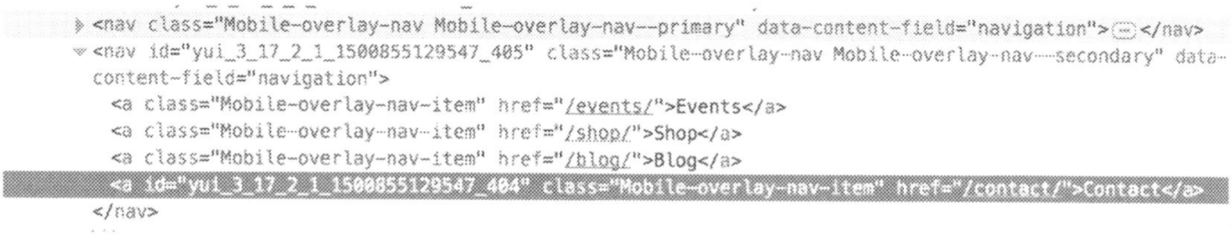

```
▶ <nav class="Mobile-overlay-nav Mobile-overlay-nav--primary" data-content-field="navigation">☺</nav>
▼ <nav id="yui_3_17_2_1_1500855129547_405" class="Mobile-overlay-nav Mobile-overlay-nav--secondary" data-
  content-field="navigation">
    <a class="Mobile-overlay-nav-item" href="/events/">Events</a>
    <a class="Mobile-overlay-nav-item" href="/shop/">Shop</a>
    <a class="Mobile-overlay-nav-item" href="/blog/">Blog</a>
    <a id="yui_3_17_2_1_1500855129547_404" class="Mobile-overlay-nav-item" href="/contact/">Contact</a>
  </nav>
```

Figure 8-14. *Inspector view mobile navigation Contact menu item*

Listing 8-4. Updated Contact menu item CSS rule

```css
body .Mobile-overlay-nav--secondary .Mobile-overlay-nav-item[href="/contact/"]{
  border: 1px solid #000;
  display: inline-block;
  border-radius: 10px;
  padding-left: 15px;
  padding-right: 15px;
}
```

We can see the updated mobile Contact menu button style applied in Figure 8-15. It is still not quite right. I need to add some padding at the top between Contact and the top border. It is also too wide. We left the display: inline-block value, so it should have fit the content. Using the inspector we can see that there is a .Mobile-overlay-nav-item class that has a property of width: 100%;. This is what is causing the button to be too wide. We want the style rule to revert to the default behavior. In this case we will add width: auto; to our CSS rule. Listing 8-5 has the updated CSS rule with the additional properties.

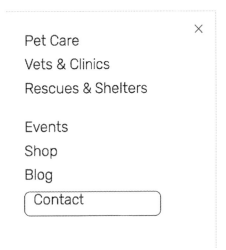

Figure 8-15. *Mobile menu Contact button with CSS form Listing 8-4*

Listing 8-5. Mobile menu Contact button updated CSS rule

```css
body .Mobile-overlay-nav--secondary .Mobile-overlay-nav-item[href="/contact/"]{
  border: 1px solid #000;
  border-radius: 10px;
  padding-left: 15px;
  padding-right: 15px;
  padding-top: 15px;
  width: auto;
}
```

Our mobile menu Contact button now looks correct. Figure 8-16 shows the final button. It is very easy when coding to focus on the desktop view and forget to check the mobile view. It is important to always check how your customization looks on the mobile view of the site. CSS rules can sometimes have unintended consequences, particularly if the mobile styles are significantly different from the desktop styles.

Pet Care   ×

Vets & Clinics

Rescues & Shelters

Events

Shop

Blog

Contact

Figure 8-16. *Final Mobile menu Contact button style*

Replace Logo with Mobile Logo

A popular customization is to use a different logo for mobile view. The smaller screens can sometimes benefit from a different version of the logo or an icon version. In the case of the example website, we will switch out the main logo for a stacked version. Figure 8-17 shows the original logo in the mobile header. The text is really hard to read at this small size.

Figure 8-17. *Original logo mobile header*

Let's start with a Structure, Style, Interactions analysis. Structure – we need to change the HTML structure of the site to use a different image source. This structure change cannot be completed using the Squarespace tools so we need to use JavaScript to update the HTML. Style – there is a good amount of style control over the mobile logo in the Style Editor. If we just update the src attribute of the <img> tag we can still use the Style Editor to control the sizing. However, we also know that the JavaScript will run after the page loads. The original logo will appear and then be replaced by the mobile logo after the JavaScript runs. Therefore we will use some CSS to hide the logo before the JavaScript runs and have it appear after the mobile logo has been added. Interactions – this change doesn't depend on user actions. We can conclude that this customization can be completed with CSS and JavaScript.

The first step is to upload the mobile logo version to the Manage Custom Files section of the Custom CSS Editor. Putting the cursor into the Custom CSS Editor and then clicking on the image file will insert the URL of the image file into the Custom CSS Editor. From there we can copy and paste it into our JavaScript. Figure 8-18 shows the mobile logo uploaded into the Manage Custom Files section and the URL in the Custom CSS Editor. Once I have copied the URL, I delete it from the Custom CSS Editor. The URL on its own is causing an error in the Custom CSS Editor, so I remove it.

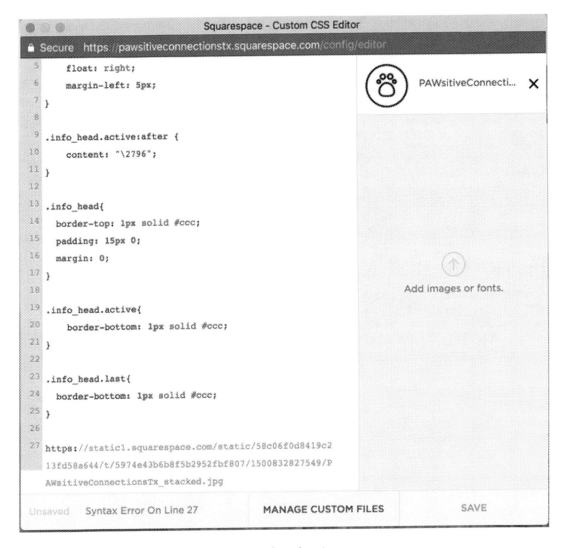

Figure 8-18. Manage Custom Files area with URL of new logo image

The next step is figuring out the correct selector for the current mobile logo. In the Inspector we see that the current logo has a class of Mobile-bar-branding-logo. This is the image we want to update the src attribute for. Figure 8-19 shows the Inspector view of the original mobile logo.

```
<img class="Mobile-bar-branding-logo" src="https://static1.squarespace.com
/static/58c06f0d8419c213fd58a…b2952fbf807/1500832827549
/PAWsitiveConnectionsTx_stacked.jpg" alt="PAWsitive Connections TX"
style="opacity: 1;">
```

Figure 8-19. Inspector view of Mobile Logo

We want to hide the original logo. There are a few ways to hide things with CSS. In the Index Navigation example we used the property `display: none;`. This removed the selected item from the flow of the HTML structure. In this case we don't want to do that. We want the space to remain there and just be updated with the new mobile logo. We could use the `visibility: hidden;` property to hide the logo. This would keep the space in the HTML structure. However, as we talked about in an earlier chapter, the visibility property cannot be animated. The new logo would flash in suddenly when we set the visibility property to `visible`. Our third option is to use the opacity property. Setting the opacity value to zero will hide the original logo. The opacity property can be animated so we can have the mobile logo quickly fade in once it has loaded. This will create a smoother user experience. The `transition` property can be used to create the fade in of the logo. The transition property takes four values: the property to be transitioned, the duration of the transition, the type of transition, and optionally a time delay prior to the transition. In this example we want to transition the opacity property. It should be a quick transition so we will set it to `.1s`. The transition can be `linear`, a consistent transition speed. Finally I will add a delay of `.4s` to ensure that the logo has time to load before being displayed. Listing 8-6 has the completed CSS style rule.

Listing 8-6. Custom CSS style rule

```
.Mobile-bar-branding-logo{
  opacity: 0;
  transition: opacity .1s linear .4s;
}
```

Next we will look at the JavaScript. The mobile header is a separate HTML structure from the desktop header as we discussed earlier in this chapter. Therefore it always exists in the HTML and we don't need to check for it. If the template had a single header for desktop and mobile, we would need to add an "if" statement that checked to see if the screen size was below a certain size. We know the Brine template is an AJAX template. However, the header area is not changed during an AJAX page change, so we do not need to use a mutation observer. We only need to switch out the logo on the original page load. In this example I am using the YUI library. Inside the `<script></script>` tags we will have the YUI DOM ready wrapper function. Inside of the DOM ready wrapper will be our code to switch the image. We first select the mobile logo using `Y.one('.Mobile-bar-branding-logo')`. Then we want to set the `src` attribute to the URL of the mobile logo. We can do this using the `.setAttribute()` function. In jQuery the function would be `.attr()`. The `.setAttribute()` function takes two parameters, the attribute and the value. In our case the attribute is the `src` and the value is the URL of the mobile logo. Finally after we have added the new logo URL, we want to set the `opacity` value back to 1. In YUI this is the `.setStyle()` function. In jQuery it is the `.css()` function. The function takes the CSS property name and value. Listing 8-7 has the completed JavaScript.

Listing 8-7. JavaScript for Mobile logo

```
<script>
Y.on('domready', function(){
  Y.one('.Mobile-bar-branding-logo').setAttribute('src', 'https://static1.squarespace.
      com/static/58c06f0d8419c213fd58a644/t/5974e43b6b8f5b2952fbf807/1500832827549/
      PAWsitiveConnectionsTx_stacked.jpg').setStyle('opacity', '1');
});
</script>
```

When the page first loads, the logo is hidden. Then the logo has a quick subtle fade in once the mobile logo is ready. It is a subtle transition and ensures that the logo is readable on mobile screens. Figure 8-20 shows the final view of the mobile header.

Figure 8-20. *Mobile header with second logo version*

This technique could also be used to add an extra call to action or second logo in the header. Instead of targeting the original `<img>` tag the JavaScript could create an additional `<img>` tag and append it to the header. You could use this technique to create almost any HTML structure you need to add to the header area. Figure 8-20 shows an example of the JavaScript to add an additional logo. The .append() function adds an element as the last child of the selected element. The `.prepend()` function would add it as the first child of the selected element. These functions have the same name in YUI and jQuery. Listing 8-8 shows an example of creating a new `<img>` element and adding it to the header. You would also need CSS to correctly style and position your new element. In the example code in Listing 8-8, I have added id=`"second_logo"` to the new image so I can easily target it with CSS.

Listing 8-8. Additional Logo JavaScript code injection

```
<script>
  Y.on('domready', function(){
    Y.one('.Header--top').append('<img id="second_logo" src="https://static1.squarespace.
        com/static/58c06f0d8419c213fd58a644/t/5974e43b6b8f5b2952fbf807/1500832827549/
        PAWsitiveConnectionsTx_stacked.jpg" alt="logo">');
  })
</script>
```

Changing Mobile Menu Icon

The mobile menu icon, also known as the hamburger icon, has become a user interface standard in recent years. However, some users are still unfamiliar with it. This is particularly true of websites that use the mobile navigation structure on desktop size screens. If a desktop user doesn't have a smart phone, then they are probably not familiar with the mobile menu icon. A common request is to replace the mobile menu icon with the word "Menu" or add the word "Menu" as a label. In this example we will add the word "Menu" to the mobile menu icon as a label. Figure 8-21 shows the original mobile header for my website.

Figure 8-21. *Original mobile menu icon*

Let's do the Structure, Style, Interactions analysis. Structure – we want to add the label; however it doesn't have to be a full HTML element. We can use the `:before` pseudo element to add the label. That way we can add the label using CSS rather than JavaScript. Style – we will need to style the new label, so we will certainly be using CSS. Interactions – there are no changes dependent on user actions in this example. First we need to identify the correct selector to use. Figure 8-22 shows the inspector view of the Mobile Menu icon. The <button> tag has a class of `.Mobile-bar-menu`. We will use this and add our label as the `:before` pseudo element of the `.Mobile-bar-menu` element.

```
<button class="Mobile-bar-menu" data-nc-element="menu-icon" data-controller-
overlay="menu" data-controller="MobileOverlayToggle" data-controllers-
bound="MobileOverlayToggle"> ev
  ▶ <svg class="Icon Icon--hamburger" viewBox="0 0 24 18">⬚</svg>
  ▶ <svg class="Icon Icon--hotdog" viewBox="0 0 24 14">⬚</svg>
  ▶ <svg class="Icon Icon--plus" viewBox="0 0 20 20">⬚</svg>
  ▶ <svg class="Icon Icon--dots-horizontal" viewBox="0 0 25 7">⬚</svg>
  ▶ <svg class="Icon Icon--dots-vertical" viewBox="0 0 7 25">⬚</svg>
  ▶ <svg class="Icon Icon--squares-horizontal" viewBox="0 0 25 7">⬚</svg>
  ▶ <svg class="Icon Icon--squares-vertical" viewBox="0 0 7 25">⬚</svg>
</button>
```

Figure 8-22. *Inspector view of mobile menu icon*

The word "Menu" will be added to our CSS rule using the `content` property of the pseudo element. The `position: relative;` property will allow us to position the label. I want to move it above the mobile menu so I use the property of `top: -6px;` that moves it up above the icon. Finally I want to make sure the font is a small size to span the width of the label. Listing 8-9 shows the complete CSS style rule. Figure 8-23 shows the final appearance of the mobile menu icon with its label in Firefox and Chrome. I have included screenshots from both browsers to illustrate the browser inconsistency. The placement of "menu" is the exact same for each browser in relation to the `.Mobile-bar-menu` element. However, it looks different because the menu icon is an .svg image inside the `.Mobile-bar-menu` element. The icon renders slightly differently in the two browsers. There is nothing that can be done to make the icons match. The browser inconsistency will come up a lot in web development. In this case a design compromise will need to be made. The word "menu" will either be too close in Chrome or too far in Firefox. Which way you choose depends on your client and your preferences.

Listing 8-9. CSS style for Mobile Menu label

```
.Mobile-bar-menu:before{
  content: "Menu";
  position: relative;
  font-size: 9px;
  top: -6px;
}
```

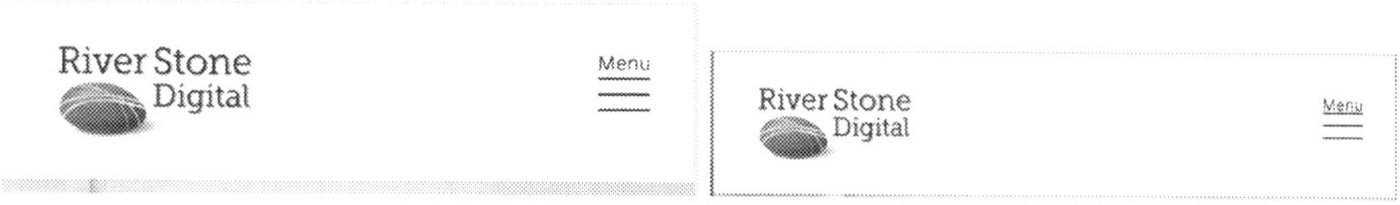

Figure 8-23. *Updated Mobile Menu Icon with Menu label in Firefox and Chrome*

Gallery Block Image Title Effect

Another popular request is to have gallery blocks that appear as tiles with a hover effect. During hover, the image title appears on a color overlay. Let's start with the Structure, Style, Interaction analysis. Structure – the title needs to be in the HTML structure in order for us to give it a hover effect. This is a Gallery Block setting. Therefore the only changes to the HTML can be done inside the Squarespace Block settings. Style – this effect will definitely require several CSS rules to create. Interactions – the effect is triggered by the hover user action. However, the hover action has been added to CSS as a pseudo class of :hover. If a CSS pseudo class did not support the user action, then we would need JavaScript.

First we set the Gallery Block to have the right HTML structure. In this case we select the option for the title to appear. Figure 8-24 shows the Gallery Block with its initial appearance. The image titles initially appear underneath the images.

 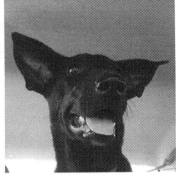 

Willy Puppy   Casper   Itty Bitty & Lil Girl

Figure 8-24. *Gallery Block with initial appearance*

If we want all of our grid gallery blocks to have this style then we could use the .sqs-gallery-block-grid class selector to target all of them. In this example, I will target just this particular Gallery Block. So the first thing I do is use the Inspector to find the block-yui id. The block-yui id is the id assigned to the outermost <div></div> of the Gallery Block. Sometimes the id will start with block-yui and occasionally it will simply be block. Using the inspector I find that the id for this Gallery Block is block-yui_3_17_2_3_1500835633766_27678. Using the LESS CSS precompiler language I will wrap the rest of the CSS style rules inside #block-yui_3_17_2_3_1500835633766_27678{   }. This ensures all the rules will only apply to this Gallery Block.

The next step is to position and style the image titles. I typically will do all the styling of position, font, and color first. Then I will add the hover styles. I inspect the Gallery Block until I find the structure that contains a single image and title. Figure 8-25 shows the Inspector view of a single image of the Gallery Block. I see that the outermost element, which contains a single image, has the class of slide. I also look at the next element in that has the class of margin-wrapper. The element with margin-wrapper has the image link and the image title as children. Therefore I know that I want to use the position: absolute; property on the image title element to position it relative to the margin-wrapper element. When I inspect the margin-wrapper element I see it does have the property of position: relative;. If it didn't already have that property, we would need to add it in order for the position: absolute; property of the image title to work properly. The inspection of the margin-wrapper element is also included in Figure 8-25.

```
▼ <div id="yui_3_17_2_1_1500908271473_126" class="slide sqs-
  gallery-design-grid-slide" data-type="image">
    ▼ <div class="margin-wrapper">
      ▼ <a class="image-slide-anchor content-fill" style="overflow:
        hidden;">
        ▶ <noscript>⬚</noscript>
          <img class="thumb-image loaded" data-
          src="https://static1.squarespace.com/static
          /58c06f0d8419c213fd58a…7330e35ff6/5974f15b37c581dd462fa00b
          /1500836254440/Casper.jpg" data-
          image="https://static1.squarespace.com/static
          /58c06f0d8419c213fd58a…7330e35ff6/5974f15b37c581dd462fa00b
          /1500836254440/Casper.jpg" data-image-dimensions="665x665"
          data-image-focal-
          point="0.5578231292517006,0.5374149659863946" data-
          load="false" data-image-id="5974f15b37c581dd462fa00b" data-
          type="image" style="opacity: 1; left: 0px; top: 0px; width:
          386px; height: 386px; position: relative;" data-position-
          mode="standard" data-parent-ratio="1.0" alt="Casper" data-
          version="module" src="https://static1.squarespace.com/static
          /58c06f0d8419c213fd58a…74f15b37c581dd462fa00b/1500836254440
          /Casper.jpg?format=1000w" data-image-resolution="1000w"> ⬚
      </a>
      <div class="image-slide-title">Casper</div>
    </div>
  </div>
```

```
.slide .margin-wrapper ⬚
{
✓   position: relative;
}
```

Figure 8-25. *Inspector view of Gallery Block image and position style rule*

To position the image title we will use the selector `.slide .image-slide-title`. The first property will be `position: absolute;`. We want to use absolute positioning since we want to remove the title from its original position and move it on top of the image without leaving the original space in the HTML flow. Then we will use a combination of positioning and the `transform` property to responsively center the title over the image. We start by using the properties `top: 50%;` and `left: 50%;`. These rules position the top-left corner of the title element in the center of the `margin-wrapper` element. Then we can use the `transform` property to move the title element to the left and up to center the title element. The transform property has the value of `translate(-50%, -50%);`. If we only needed to translate the X or Y axis then we could use `translateX` or `translateY`. The translate percentage is in relation to the width of the item itself. Figure 8-26 has an illustration of these properties in action. Listing 8-10 has the completed CSS rule. The transform property is a newer CSS property. As such it still needs to be prefixed for some browsers. The prefixed version is the same rule with `-webkit-transform` as the property name. I also changed the text color to white and made the font larger. Figure 8-27 shows the Gallery Block with the CSS rule from Listing 8-10 applied.

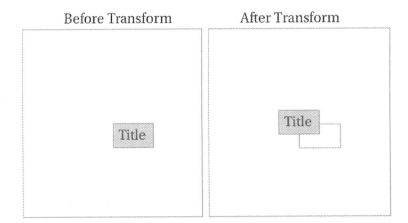

Figure 8-26. Before and after transform property

Listing 8-10. Image title positioning CSS rule

```
#block-yui_3_17_2_3_1500835633766_27678{
  .slide .image-slide-title{
    position: absolute;
    top: 50%;
    left: 50%;
    font-size: 30px;
    color: #ffffff;
    transform: translate(-50%, -50%);
    -webkit-transform: translate(-50%, -50%);
  }
}
```

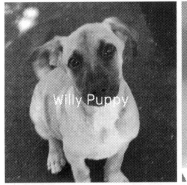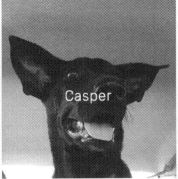

Figure 8-27. Image Title positioning without hover effect

Next we will add the hover effect. There are two parts to the hover effect. The first part is hiding the image title and having it appear on hover. The second part of the hover effect is changing the picture from color to black and white and darkening it. The first part can be accomplished by adding opacity: 0; and transition: opacity .2s ease; to the .slide .image-slide-title style rule. Next we add a hover rule where we set the opacity to be 1. The trick to this is where we add the :hover pseudo class. We want the title to appear when the image is hovered over, rather than when the title is hovered over. In order to accomplish this we will add the :hover pseudo class to the .slide selector. The final CSS selector for this part of the hover effect will be .slide:hover .image-slide-title.

The second part of the hover effect is selecting the image wrapper and applying a hover style. If we look at the inspector view in Figure 8-25 we see that the image is inside a <a></a> tag and has a class of image-slide-anchor. Therefore we can use .slide .image-slide-anchor as the selector to target the image wrapper. We don't need to make any changes to the default style. However, we do want the hover effect to have a fade transition. Therefore we do need to add the transition property to the default style. We should use the same transition property as the image title to ensure both parts transition at the same rate.

For the hover effect I will apply a filter. There are many different filter options but I will use the grayscale filter, which makes the image grayscale, and the brightness filter that allows us to darken the image. The filter property is another property that still needs to be prefixed. Listing 8-11 has the final CSS rules for this hover effect. Figure 8-28 also shows how the completed hover effect looks.

Listing 8-11. Final CSS for hover effect

```
#block-yui_3_17_2_3_1500835633766_27678{
  .slide .image-slide-anchor{
    transition: filter .2s ease;
  }
.slide:hover .image-slide-anchor{
   filter: grayscale(100%) brightness(70%);
   -webkit-filter: grayscale(100%) brightness(70%);
}

.slide .image-slide-title{
  position: absolute;
  top: 50%;
  left: 50%;
  font-size: 30px;
  color: #ffffff;
  transform: translate(-50%, -50%);
  -webkit-transform: translate(-50%, -50%);
  opacity: 0;
  transition: opacity .2s ease;
}

  .slide:hover .image-slide-title{
    opacity: 1;
  }
}
```

This same process can be used to achieve a color overlay rather than using filters. To create the appearance of a color overlay, a background-color needs to be added to the .image-slide-anchor element. Then on hover, the opacity of the <img> element would be reduced, allowing the color background to show through. This creates the illusion of a color overlay.

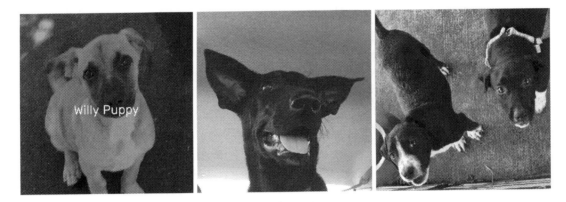

Figure 8-28. *Final Gallery Block hover effect*

Fixed Header with Scroll Styles

This next customization combines a couple of different elements. The first is turning the header of the Brine template into a fixed header. A fixed header stays visible at the top of the browser window as the user scrolls down. The second part of this is going to be providing a scroll style to the header so that the logo shrinks on scroll. This allows the header to reduce in size and take up less screen space. Figure 8-29 shows the original header and the header with the scroll styling applied.

Figure 8-29. *Original Header and Header with Scroll styling applied*

Let's begin by doing our Structure, Style, and Interaction analysis. Structure – the mobile header can be set as a fixed header in the Style Editor. Therefore this customization only impacts the desktop header area. No HTML structure changes are needed for this customization. Style – this will definitely need style changes. There will be the styles that make the header a fixed header. Then there will be styles used to reduce the size of the logo on scroll. Interactions – this customization has interactions! We want the header logo size to change when the user scrolls. Since this change involves scroll positioning, I will use jQuery as my JavaScript library. YUI doesn't have comparable scroll functions. Therefore we know this customization will involve CSS and JavaScript.

First we will add the styles to make the header a fixed header. Using the Inspector we see that the header of my website is in the `.Header--top` portion of the Brine template. To ensure that our rule has the specificity it needs, we will use `.Header.Header--top` as our selector. The property and value `position:fixed;` will make the header fixed to the top. That is only part of the work. As you can see in Figure 8-30 the header is fixed to the top. However, it is no longer full width and the website content is scrolling over the header. To ensure that it stays full width, we will add the property `width: 100%;` to our style rule. Adding the `z-index` property will ensure that the header stays on top of other content. The `z-index` is the order that the layers stack out from the screen. We can use the property `z-index: 10000;` to ensure the header is always on top of the other layers. Listing 8-12 shows the updated header CSS rule. Figure 8-31 shows the header with the CSS from Listing 8-12 applied.

Figure 8-30. *Fixed header with only* `position:fixed;` *property applied*

Listing 8-12. Completed CSS rule with width and z-index

```
.Header.Header--top{
  position: fixed;
  width: 100%;
  z-index: 10000;
}
```

Figure 8-31. *Fixed header with Listing 8-12 css rule applied*

We are making progress on our fixed header. However, now we have a different problem. Since elements with position:fixed; are pulled out of the HTML flow, the first part of our page content is actually hidden behind the header. Using the Inspector we find that all our main content is included in an element with the class Content-outer. If we add padding to the top of the .Content-outer element then the fixed header will no longer overlap the top of the content. We only want this change to apply to the desktop version. Checking the Style Editor settings tells us that the Mobile Breakpoint is set to 640px wide. Figure 8-32 shows this Style Editor selection. We need to use a media query with our CSS rule to ensure that only screens that are at least 640px wide are changed by our style rule. Listing 8-13 shows the updated CSS rule. Now the site looks the same as when we started, except that the header is fixed to the top of the browser window.

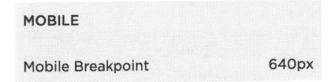

Figure 8-32. *Mobile Breakpoint Style Editor setting*

Listing 8-13. updated CSS rule with media query

```
.Header.Header--top{
  position: fixed;
  width: 100%;
  z-index: 10000;
}

@media screen and (min-width: 640px){
  .Content-outer{
    padding-top: 115px;
  }
}
```

The next part of this customization is the interaction part. When the user scrolls we want the logo to shrink in size. The logo can be selected with the selector .Header-branding-logo. I will add a transition property to the .Header-branding-logo selector so that the logo will shrink and grow gradually. The transition property will be transition: all .3s linear;. We will use jQuery to add and remove a class depending on how far the user has scrolled. We will call the class scrollNav. In the scrollNav style rule we will set a max-width of 110px on the logo. Listing 8-14 has the completed CSS.

Listing 8-14. Completed CSS for this customization

```
.Header.Header--top{
  position: fixed;
  width: 100%;
  z-index: 10000;
}

@media screen and (min-width: 640px){
  .Content-outer{
    padding-top: 115px;
  }
}
```

```
.Header-branding-logo{
  transition: all .3s linear;
}

.Header-branding-logo.scrollNav{
  max-width: 110px;
}
```

The next portion of this customization is the JavaScript. The first part of the JavaScript will add the jQuery library to the website. Then the rest of the code will include our `<script></script>` tag and a jQuery scroll event handler. The scroll event handler is triggered when the user scrolls. We can make our CSS changes inside the event handler. We will call the jQuery scroll handler on the entire browser window, `$(window).scroll(function(){});`. Inside the event handlers brackets we will use `$(window).scrollTop();` to find out how far down the page the user has scrolled. We will save the scroll value to a variable named `scroll`. Then we will use an if statement to see if the user has scrolled farther than 50px. If the user has scrolled farther than 50px we will add our `scrollNav` class to the logo. If the user has scrolled less than 50px then we will remove the class. If statements start with the word `if` and are followed by parentheses and brackets. The value you are testing goes inside the parentheses. In our case the if statement says `if(scroll > 50){}`. We then follow that with an else statement `else {}`. If the if statement is true the code inside the if's brackets will be run. If the if statement is false, the code inside the else brackets will run. Listing 8-15 has the completed JavaScript. The completed JavaScript would go in the Site-Wide Header Code Injection.

Listing 8-15. Completed JavaScript for Scroll Nav effect

```
<script src="https://ajax.googleapis.com/ajax/libs/jquery/3.2.1/jquery.min.js"></script>
<script>
$(window).scroll(function(){

  var scroll = $(window).scrollTop();
  if(scroll > 50){
    $('.Header-branding-logo').addClass('scrollNav');
  }
  else{
    $('.Header-branding-logo').removeClass('scrollNav');
  }

})</script>
```

You can view the complete effect at `www.riverstonedigital.com`. You can also add different properties or rules to the CSS to change other aspects on scroll. The background color, font color, and logo filter could all be changed using this structure.

Anchor Link Fixes

The last of the popular customizations we will discuss in this chapter is anchor link fixes. Index pages with anchor links to the various sections of the index are a very common website setup. Unfortunately with some of the Squarespace templates, the anchor links do not work correctly on mobile. For example, with the Brine family template clicking an anchor link doesn't close the menu and scroll to the correct section. An inspection of the template reveals that a class of `is-mobile-overlay-active` is added to the body element when the overlay navigation is visible. The mobile navigation anchor links can work by adding a click event handler that removes the `is-mobile-overlay-active` class from the body element. Listing 8-16 has this first version of the anchor link fix. For single page websites this is all that needs to be fixed. This same fix will work with other templates; you just have to update all of the class selectors.

Listing 8-16. Anchor Link Fix for Single Page Website

```
<script>
Y.all("a.Mobile-overlay-nav-item").on('click', function() {
  Y.one('body').removeClass('is-mobile-overlay-active');
});
Y.all("a.Mobile-overlay-folder-item").on('click', function() {
  Y.one('body').removeClass('is-mobile-overlay-active');
});
</script>
```

If the website consists of multiple pages, then a few more adjustments need to be made. The anchor link in the navigation needs to include the page URL and the anchor. For example, the navigation link would be /home#contact, rather than #contact. This ensures that the links will change page and then go to the section of the index. The other change is that the code needs to be added to a mutation observer. Listing 8-17 has the anchor link script, including the mutation observer.

Listing 8-17. Anchor Link Fix for Multi-Page Site

```
<script>
//Anchor link fix
 function anchorLinks(){
   Y.all("a.Mobile-overlay-nav-item").on('click', function() {
     Y.one('body').removeClass('is-mobile-overlay-active');
   });
   Y.all("a.Mobile-overlay-folder-item").on('click', function() {
     Y.one('body').removeClass('is-mobile-overlay-active');
   });
}

 // DOM Ready
 Y.on('domready', function(){
   anchorLinks()
 });

//RSD Mutation Observer wrapper
function RSD_init(){
 anchorLinks();
}

// add watch function to window.onload
window.onload = RSD_watch;

//watch function to look for page changes using Mutation Observer
function RSD_watch() {
   MutationObserver = window.MutationObserver || window.WebKitMutationObserver;

   var mo = new MutationObserver(function(mo) {
       var moCount = 0;
       for (var b = 0; b < mo.length; b++) {
           var c =mo[b];
```

```
        if ("attributes" === c.type  && moCount === 0) {
          RSD_init();

        }
      }

  });

var options = { attributes : true, attributeFilter : ['id']};

mo.observe(document.body, options);
}
</script>
```

The final anchor link fix includes navigation anchor links to anchors on non-index pages with AJAX enabled. When you add anchors to a non-index page you can add them in a code block. Any element with an id attribute can be used as an anchor. Like the previous example, the anchor links in the navigation would need to use the page URL followed by the anchor link, /home#contact. The problem with AJAX loading is that the content of the page changes but the window does not scroll to the anchor link. This can be fixed by adding another function. This new function will wait until after the page change has happened. Then it will check the URL for an anchor link. Then if there is an anchor link it will scroll down to it. Since this will include scroll-based positioning, the code will again require jQuery. If you have already included jQuery for another customization, remember you do not need to add it again!

We can name our new function scrollToURLAnchor. We will call this function only when the mutation observer sees a page change. We do not need to call it on page load because the anchor links behave correctly for a regular page load. ,Inside the scrollToURLAnchor function we will add a timeout, which tells the code to wait for a specific amount of time before continuing. We want the code to wait until the page has had a chance to fully load. , Then inside the timeout we will check to see if the window has an anchor in the URL using an if statement. Then, if it does, we will use a combination of the jQuery animate function and the distance the anchor is from the top of the page to scroll down to the anchor. , We do not need to include an else statement since the else statement would be empty. If there is no anchor in the URL we don't need to do anything. Listing 8-18 shows the new function by itself. Listing 8-19 is the function included with our other anchor link fix and Mutation Observer.

Listing 8-18. scrollToURLAnchor function

```
function scrollToURLAnchor(){
  setTimeout(function(){
    if(window.location.hash){

      $('html, body').animate({
          scrollTop: $(window.location.hash).offset().top
      }, 500,  function () {

      });
    }
  }, 500);
}
```

Listing 8-19. scrollToURLAnchor function combined with other anchor link fixes

```
<script src="https://ajax.googleapis.com/ajax/libs/jquery/3.2.1/jquery.min.js"></script>
<script>
//Anchor link fix
 function anchorLinks(){
  Y.all("a.Mobile-overlay-nav-item").on('click', function() {
    Y.one('body').removeClass('is-mobile-overlay-active');
  });
  Y.all("a.Mobile-overlay-folder-item").on('click', function() {
   Y.one('body').removeClass('is-mobile-overlay-active');
  });
}

function scrollToURLAnchor(){
 setTimeout(function(){
   if(window.location.hash){

     $('html, body').animate({
         scrollTop: $(window.location.hash).offset().top
     }, 500,  function () {

     });
   }
   }, 500);
}

 // DOM Ready
 Y.on('domready', function(){
   anchorLinks()
 });

//RSD Mutation Observer wrapper
function RSD_init(){
 anchorLinks();
}

// add watch function to window.onload
window.onload = RSD_watch;

//watch function to look for page changes using Mutation Observer
function RSD_watch() {
   MutationObserver = window.MutationObserver || window.WebKitMutationObserver;

   var mo = new MutationObserver(function(mo) {
       var moCount = 0;
       for (var b = 0; b < mo.length; b++) {
           var c =mo[b];

           if ("attributes" === c.type  && moCount === 0) {
             RSD_init();
```

```
        }
      }

  });

var options = { attributes : true, attributeFilter : ['id']};

mo.observe(document.body, options);
}
</script>
```

Wrap-Up

You should now have a good framework for approaching website customizations. You should feel confident in being able to conduct a Structure, Style, and Interaction analysis to determine the type of code that you will need for the customization. You should be able to use the Inspector to find the correct classes to target. It will take time to become familiar with the many CSS properties available, but over time you will get faster at doing these customizations. In the next chapter we will take a break from heavy coding. We will focus on identifying project scope and working within the limits of Squarespace.

CHAPTER 9

▦ ▦ ▦

Respecting the Limits

In this chapter we take a slight break from code to discuss respecting the limits of the Squarespace system. Every web platform was designed with specific users, and specific use cases, in mind. That means there will be cases where Squarespace isn't the best platform to use. It is very easy to determine whether or not something is possible with Squarespace and custom code. The harder question to answer is, is it a good idea? The rest of this chapter will discuss how I determine if a customization is a good idea to suggest to a client. We will also cover some of the hard limits within Squarespace, where I recommend doing the project on a different platform.

Preserve User Experience

First and foremost, all customizations should preserve the user experience. As web professionals we have to keep in mind that there are two types of users. There is our client, who will be using the back end of the website; and the web visitor, who will be using the front end of the site. It is easy to forget about the back-end user and only focus on the website visitor. The best websites optimize the experience of both users.

For the back-end user I think about what it will be like to update and maintain the site on a regular basis. Part of what makes Squarespace so popular is the easy-to-use page editor. I want to preserve that ease of use. I do not recommend solutions that require my client to add the same set of blocks on every page for consistency. An example of repeatedly adding the same blocks is to add a "fake" sidebar to blog templates that don't have one. The client would add the same set of blocks to every blog post. Figure 9-1 shows the layout of a "fake" sidebar. The user would put the regular blog post content in the 8 left-hand columns of the 12-column grid. Then the user would add the sidebar, noted by the dotted line, into the 4 right-hand columns of the grid. This solution leaves a lot of room for error and inconsistency, which would make the blog look sloppy and the site unprofessional.

© Sarah Martin 2017
S. Martin, *The Definitive Guide to Squarespace*, https://doi.org/10.1007/978-1-4842-2937-8_9

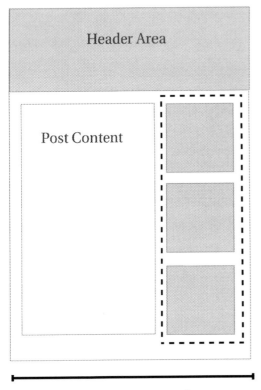

Figure 9-1. *"Fake" blog sidebar using repeated blocks*

The second solution is to add the sidebar by creating a separate sidebar page and loading the page content via AJAX into the blog post sidebar area. This approach essentially combines two pages into one. By adding the same sidebar page to every Blog post the client doesn't have to repeatedly add the same blocks. The client also has the ability to easily update the sidebar in one place, the sidebar page, and have it update across all blog posts. Both the Sidebar and the Blog Post have their own 12-column grid and are populated using regular Squarespace Blocks. Figure 9-2 shows how this layout works.

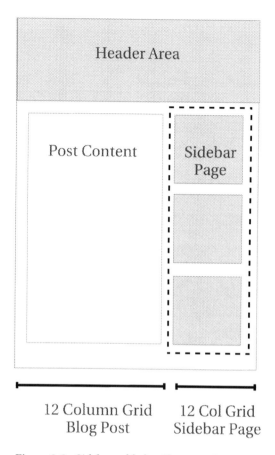

Figure 9-2. *Sidebar added to Blog post via AJAX*

The third approach to this solution is to use Developer Mode. In Developer Mode a sidebar area can be added as an additional content area. It would work the same as the footer area where it would be editable from all pages it appears on. If a site has other edits that require Developer Mode to be turned on, then I would suggest adding the sidebar using Developer Mode. If the site does not require Developer Mode for anything, then I would suggest the AJAX sidebar to my client.

To preserve the user experience, I don't want my client to ever have to edit the HTML or CSS themselves. This includes enabling or disabling scripts or CSS animation to allow for content update. To prevent my client from having to touch the code, I want to ensure that all content is accessible via the page editor. An example of this is adding a second page-specific popup to the site. In this case my client was already using the built-in Promotional Popup on most pages of their site. However, on a specific page they wanted a different popup. To accomplish this, for structure, I added the content for the custom popup at the bottom of the content area for the page. The CSS styling hid the content before it popped up and after it was closed. JavaScript adds a CSS class to display the popup after a slight delay. JavaScript also removes the class to hide the popup when the close icon is clicked. Figure 9-3 shows the final popup as it appears on the page.

Figure 9-3. Second page-specific popup

The problem with this approach is that the content blocks for the promotional popup are hidden when the site first loads. This means that they are hidden by the CSS in the page editor as well. Figure 9-4 shows the content, as it should appear in the Page Editor. However, without extra CSS the user couldn't see the popup content blocks to edit them. Figure 9-5 shows the Page Editor before the extra CSS was added. This is where one of my favorite CSS rules comes in. The `body:not(.sqs-edit-mode)` rule tells the CSS rule to apply only when the page is NOT being edited. In this particular example I would add `body:not(.sqs-edit-mode)` to the CSS rules that are hiding the content of the custom popup. That way when the user edits the page, they can edit the content of the popup. I have also used this CSS rule when the CSS creates a slide in animation, ensuring the blocks are in the normal position for editing.

Figure 9-4. *Second popup as it should appear in the content editor*

Figure 9-5. *Content blocks not appearing in Page Editor given initial CSS rules*

The volume of content in the site is another factor in the user experience. Unlike other platforms Squarespace doesn't have options to filter or sort collection items. Therefore updating large collections can be tedious and time-consuming work. If large volumes of content will need to be updated frequently, I would suggest looking for a third-party tool to use or switching to a platform with built-in filter and sorting capabilities. However, I have used this technique to successfully create a listing of preschool teachers. The school has about 25 teachers and the directory only needs to be updated once a year. Therefore, for that project, using a blog collection to create the teacher listing worked really well.

Risks of Customization

All customizations come with some level of risk. There is the risk that the user will change something that breaks the custom code. Code that relies on `block-yui` ids is the most fragile. If the user deletes the block, and then adds the exact same block type back in, the `block-yui` id still changes. Therefore the CSS will need to be updated. I avoid using the `block-yui` ids in my CSS and JavaScript as much as possible. If using `block-yui` ids is unavoidable, then make sure your client knows not to delete that block.

Another selector that would be easy for the client to break is the `:nth-child` selector. The `:nth-child` selector allows any particular element to be selected out of a list of elements. For example, I want to customize the third navigation element to look like a button. I could use `li:nth-child(3)` to select the third item. In Figure 9-6 the third menu item, Register, has the button style. If the my client changes the menu order, making Register the second menu item, the button style stays applied to the third element. Therefore the About menu item now has the button style. The CSS selector would have to be updated to `li:nth-child(2)` in order to apply the button style to the Register menu item again.

Home   About   Register   Contact   Home   Register   About   Contact

Figure 9-6. Menu item styled using nth-child selector

In addition to user risk, there is also risk to custom code from Squarespace. Squarespace will update the template and core system components without any warning. Squarespace tries to minimize this impact, but in order to add new features sometimes they have to make major updates to the templates. An example of this is when the Brine template was updated spring 2016. Squarespace added a number of new Tweaks to the template including a Tweak to adjust the spacing between menu items. Squarespace had to change the HTML structure of the header area to accommodate these new Tweaks. Websites that had custom CSS controlling the spacing of the navigation menu items all had to be updated. For me personally this was a handful of sites that I updated. I know some web shops had to update many more sites than that.

Another instance of Squarespace updates breaking custom code occurred with my translation scripts. I have a package I put together that translates Event, Blog post, and Summary Block dates into other languages. The code works by grabbing the date out of a data attribute and manipulating it to get translated dates. The data attribute was originally formatted as `yyyy-mm-dd`. My code took that date attribute and parsed it into the format the JavaScript date function could understand. Then Squarespace updated the template and system files. The new data attribute has the format `mm/dd/yyyy`. I noticed the problem when my translation scripts were producing invalid dates. I had to go back into my code and update the parsing to reflect the new date attribute format. When I created my translation script package, I knew that there would be this risk. However, the benefit to the international Squarespace community outweighed the risk of occasionally having to update the code.

When working through the risk of particular custom code, think through the impact on your client when the code fails. In the above examples the problems were not a big deal. Some of my clients hadn't even noticed the menu item spacing had changed. The invalid dates were a little more problematic. However, the fixes also were easy to implement because it only required updating a few CSS selectors or a couple lines of parsing code. If a fix for the code would be major work, equivalent to rewriting the whole thing, then I would look at other options. In the world of web development, there is rarely only one way to do something. There are typically many choices and you can weigh the risk verses reward for each one.

Scoping the Project

Another important aspect of respecting the limits is scoping the project. The scope of the project consists of all the functionality the website will have, page layouts, and design elements. Determine the scope of the project at the beginning, before starting the project. This allows you to make solid recommendations for the platform to build the site on and the third-party tools to use. There will always be the occasional client who decides that they want something out of scope at the last moment. However, life is easier when we minimize such scope surprises.

E-commerce Scope

When considering the scope of an e-commerce website there are a number of factors I take into account. The first factor is the number of products. Squarespace works well for smaller online stores. However, a site that had hundreds of products would be very difficult to manage. There is also the question of inventory management. Will all orders be processed through the Squarespace store or will there be in-person sales as well? If there are in-person sales, what software will be used to manage the inventory?

The company may want to manage inventory in their existing Point of Sale software system. In this case they would need to update the inventory levels in Squarespace on a regular basis. For a handful of products, or products with slow turnover, that is not a problem. However if the store had 1000 products, manual inventory management becomes impossible. Squarespace does have a product importer but it only adds new products to the site. It will not update existing products.

Another important factor with e-commerce is the payment processor options. Currently Squarespace is integrated with Stripe and PayPal. If your client requires the system to integrate with a different payment provider, then you need to look at other e-commerce options.

Shipping rates are another major factor that tends to come up toward the end of the project. Some stores need simple flat rate shipping, or rates calculated by package size. Sometimes stores require more finite control over the shipping rates or offer different shipping rates based on the product. In these cases Squarespace wouldn't be a good fit for the client. I would research other e-commerce platforms that meet the specific shipping needs.

Sales tax rates are another major factor that is often forgotten until the end of the project. Sales tax requirements vary greatly depending on the company's location. Squarespace does not offer product-specific sales tax rates. All products in a given product type, physical, digital, or service, are subject to the same sales tax in Squarespace. Make sure you understand your client's requirements for collecting sales tax. Medical supplies and food are often exempt from sales tax. If an online store consists of taxable and non-taxable products then you may have get creative, or switch to a different e-commerce provider. It is up to your client to determine their tax obligations.

Some online retailers are required to only sell their products to adults 18 years and older. For those stores there are script services that pop up asking the user to verify their age. These scripts usually meet the legal requirement for blocking access to minors. Like all JavaScript blocking services, they are not perfect. If JavaScript is disabled or the user knows how to edit the code then they can still access the site. Figure 9-7 shows an example of the age verification script. If the user selects "I am 18 or Older" they can see the product page. If the user clicks "I am Under 18" then they are redirected to another page.

Figure 9-7. *Age verification script*

Customer communication is another area that Squarespace has limited functionality. There is limited ability to customize the emails that the customer gets. For example, in Figure 9-8 the blue box surrounds the content that can be customized. The rest of the body content of the order confirmation email cannot be updated. The header and footer area can be customized with HTML. The customization will appear on all notification emails. The header and footer cannot be customized on a per notification basis.

River Stone Digital: New Order Confirmed #00000

Order Confirmed: #00000

Thank you for your order at River Stone Digital. Once your package ships we will send you a notification email. Your order confirmation is below.

Order Number: **#00000** (placed on August 9, 2017 05:07PM CDT)

BILLED TO:	SHIPPING TO:
John Doe	John Doe
123 Main Street	123 Main Street
Apt 1	Apt 1
State, City, 12121	State, City, 12121
United States	United States
CC: XXXX-1234	Standard Shipping
john.doe@example.com	

Order Summary

ITEM	QTY	UNIT PRICE	SUBTOTAL
Sample Product SK12345	1	$1.00	$1.00
Sample Product 2 SK456789 Black / 45	5	$1.00	$5.00

Item Subtotal		$6.00
Shipping & Handling		$0.00
Sales Tax		$0.60
TOTAL		**$6.60**

http://www.riverstonedigital.com

Figure 9-8. *Order Confirmation email customization area*

Third-party tools can be used to get around some of these limits. I have used Zapier to send product-specific emails to customers. However, the Zapier approach required a lot of custom code that would need to be updated for every product change. The checkout page and payment screens are another area of often-requested wording changes. The only changes that can be made to the checkout pages are within the Checkout Page Style Editor. These pages cannot be accessed by custom code in order to protect the security of the payment transaction. If detailed customization of all payment screens is needed, a platform like Shopify would be the better choice.

Dynamic Content

The need for dynamic content is another scoping factor to consider. Dynamic content is the website's ability to pull content from one location into another. For example, our client is a performing arts venue. Each performance has its own page for selling tickets. The performance is also listed on a season calendar page and in a slideshow on the homepage. Ideally the client wants to update the information on the Event page and have it updated in the slideshow and on the season calendar. This would mean that the performance name, date, image, and description would populate form the performance pages to other pages. Figure 9-9 shows the client's ideal dynamic content capabilities.

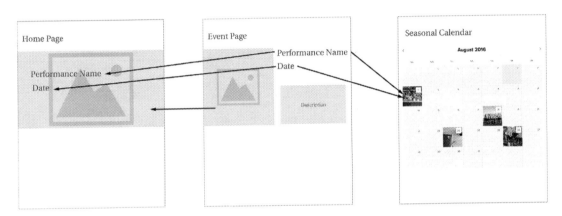

Figure 9-9. Client's ideal dynamic content for performance information

In this scenario the performance pages could be built as Events. When the individual Event is updated the corresponding season calendar is also updated. The Season Calendar page could be the Event List page or it could be a Calendar Block added to a page. However, making the homepage slideshow work is more difficult. Squarespace doesn't currently have a block that can pull all the event information from the Event page and display it as a slideshow. Figure 9-10 shows the closest we can get using built-in Squarespace functionality.

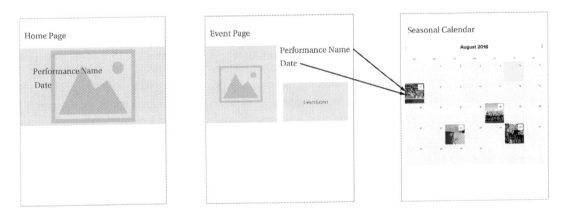

Figure 9-10. Dynamic content with built-in Squarespace tools

At this point our client will have to choose from a few options. The first option is for the client to live with the Squarespace built-in limitations. The second option would be for us to build a custom homepage slideshow that loaded the event information via AJAX. The third option would be to switch to a platform that is better able to handle that type of content.

Squarespace tools are great for supporting visual dynamic content. Artists, photographers, and other visual mediums will find it pretty easy to manage the images in a single location and have them populate across the site. Art galleries and creative professional agencies often have the need to group images by artist, and then group the artists together. There is often the desire to then be able to sort the artists by genre, style, services, or other categories. I have worked on several sites where I have used the following dynamic content setup. The images are all stored in Gallery Pages named by artist. Then the Artist pages are each an individual Blog Post. This allows the Artists to be filtered by categories and tags. Then within the Blog Post for a given artist, I add a Gallery Block of their work. Then all the Artists are listed together on the Blog List page. Subsets of the artists can be displayed in Summary Blocks on other pages of the site as well. Figure 9-11 illustrates this setup.

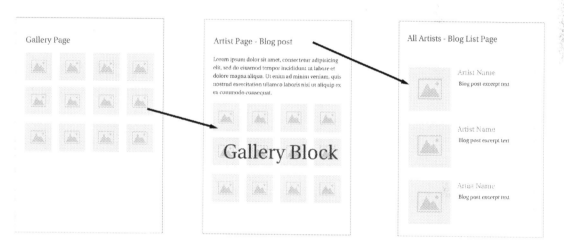

Figure 9-11. *Artist and artwork dynamic content setup*

Highlighting audio and text-based content is a little more difficult. There are not as many options for displaying the content. Audio and text content is also much less engaging visually. A recent for a writer had me contemplating how to highlight the writing in an engaging way. I opted to use a template with a Portfolio function. The portfolio was populated with projects. Each project focused on writing that she did for a particular client. To showcase the writing, while allowing the writing to be readable, I created a preview image and a high-resolution PDF of each piece. The preview images I added to a gallery block on each project page. I uploaded the high-resolution PDFs to the file management system of Squarespace. Then I linked the preview images in the Gallery Block to the corresponding PDFs and set the links to open in a new window. This created a visually compelling display of the writing while allowing prospective clients to easily read it. Figure 9-12 shows an example of this structure.

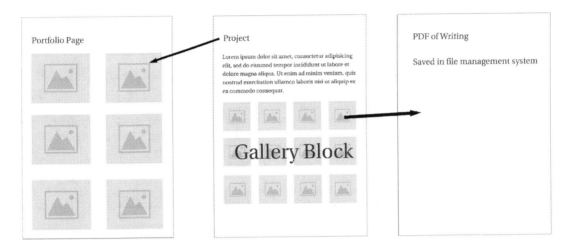

Figure 9-12. Writing portfolio content design

Contributor Permissions

Another important part of respecting the limits is determining the needs for contributor permissions. Currently Squarespace has seven different permission levels: Administrator, Content Editor, Store Manager, Billing, Reporting, Comment Moderator, and Trusted Commenter. The most common of these roles are Administrator and Content Editor.

The Site Owner is a special type of Administrator. Administrators have access to all areas of the site, all settings, and all functionality. The Site Owner has the additional ability to assign the ownership of a site to someone else. The Site Owner also receives the domain verification emails. Typically when starting a new project I will create the new site in Squarespace from my account. Since I start the trial for the site, I start out as the Site Owner. When the project is ready to launch, I will transfer ownership of the site to my client. Then my client can enter their billing information and manage the subscription going forward. I continue to remain an Administrator on the account to help with content update and any future needs they have.

The Content Editor is the next step of access down from Administrator. The Content Editor role is fairly limited. The Content Editor, as the name suggests, can edit content on the site. The Content Editor can add pages and content blocks. The Content Editor cannot delete pages. The Content Editor can add, delete, or reorder most collection items like blog posts, products, and events. Content Editors cannot access the announcement bar or the promotional popup feature since both of those features exist in menu items that are hidden for Content Editors. Typically a small business will have their main website manager be an Administrator. Content Editor role would be assigned to an intern or other employee who helps update content but doesn't manage the site.

The Store Manager role is similar to the Content Editor's permissions. The Store Manager has additional access to store functionality beyond the Content Editor's permissions. The Store Manager can fulfill orders and view orders. The Store Manager role is the only other role to receive order notification emails besides Administrators. I have set up the Store Manager role for the business's accountant so that they can receive the order notification emails and correctly account for the payments processed by PayPal or Stripe.

The Billing and Reporting user permissions grant access to just those portions of the site. The Billing user can update payment information and change the subscription plan. The Reporting user can view the Analytics of the site and comment without moderation. The Trusted Commenter can comment without moderation and reply to comments. The Comment Moderator reviews new comments before making the comments live.

What is notably missing from the user permissions is a Blogging user. The users either have access to all content as a Content Editor or no access to the content. Ideally a Blogging user would only have access to the blog, and not other parts of the site. A Blogging user is a fairly standard user-permission level that your client might be surprised doesn't exist in Squarespace.

If a company needs more granular control over the contributor permissions, then they need a different platform. Examples of this type of granular control include the previous example of a Blogging user. Another example is giving editing access to only a few pages in the site. For example, allowing the education department to update their pages, but not other pages on the site. Another example is giving a guest blogger access to only their blog post.

Squarespace's current user permissions fit the needs of most small businesses and individuals. They are simple, easy to understand, and easy to update. The need for more complicated user permissions comes with medium- to large-size companies. These companies will often have other needs that are beyond the scope of Squarespace. If user permissions are an issue then it is a good indication that the company is looking for a more enterprise-level solution.

Scope Creep

Scope creep is where the client changes the project scope as the project progresses. Scope creep delays projects and often results in less-than-optimal sites. I have had projects that crept their way right out of the Squarespace platform. Nothing is more painful than getting to the end of a project cycle only to realize you can't deliver what you client needs with Squarespace. The website either needs to be rebuilt on a different platform, or your client lives with the current limitations and is unhappy.

Oftentimes the scope creep occurs because the client has unreasonable expectations about what they can have for the price they want to pay. A frequent scenario I encounter is a DIY user starts the website on Squarespace. The DIY user realizes that they can't get the professional results that they want on their own and seek my help. The requests often start with Custom CSS edits and minor amounts of JavaScript. However, as the project gets closer to completion, the DIY user realizes that Squarespace has limitations. The e-commerce isn't as robust as they anticipated or they can't easily add a unique feature they saw on another website. My favorite is when the DIY user expects me to be able to add a WordPress plugin to Squarespace.

I have had projects go the other way as well. I have been brought into projects that were started on WordPress. In some cases it has been easier and faster for me to rebuild the site in Squarespace than to finish the project in WordPress. Sometimes I have rebuilt the site in Squarespace. Sometimes the client wanted to stick with WordPress. All I can do is educate my client about their options and let them make the decision.

Wrap-Up

You should now have a good idea of what to look for when scoping a project. You should know when Squarespace is the right platform to use, or when you may have to look for a different option. Third-party tools were mentioned a number of times in this chapter. The next chapter will go into specifics about these tools. We will look at the different types of third-party tools and I will share some of my favorites.

■ ■ ■

CHAPTER 10

Third-Party Tools

In this chapter we will go over the different types of third-party tools. When I talk about third-party tools, I am referring to any code from an outside source that you will add to a Squarespace website. There are many different words that get used for this type of code: plugin, widget, add-on, and code snippet. A lot of these terms have platform-specific meanings, which is why I will avoid using them. For example, plugins became a very popular term due to the WordPress platform. In WordPress, plugins have a specific interface inside the WordPress dashboard where they are added. Plugins are also referenced in the WordPress documentation. There is no corresponding interface in Squarespace.

Types of Third-Party Tools

There are many different ways to classify third-party tools. The first classification we will use is Squarespace specific tools versus general tools. Squarespace specific tools can only be used with a Squarespace website. General tools can be applied to any website and are not platform specific. The second way to classify third-party tools is by what they do. Some third-party tools are stand-alone codes that add functionality or a user experience effect to the Squarespace website. Other third-party tools integrate the Squarespace website with another system.

Squarespace Specific

The first group of third-party tools we will discuss is the Squarespace specific tools. There are three main providers of Squarespace specific tools that I would recommend. I have personally tested out the products and interacted with the developers as part of the Squarespace Circle Forum. There are many other smaller providers as well but I don't have personal experience with them.

The first provider I will talk about is MemberSpace, `www.memberspace.com`. Figure 10-1 shows the MemberSpace homepage. Squarespace does not include any kind of public-facing user functionality. There is no way for your website visitors to create a user account and gain access to restricted content or manage their account subscription. MemberSpace was created to fill this need. MemberSpace acts as the gateway that requires users to log in before accessing protected content. MemberSpace includes all the major functionality you would expect from a membership platform. This includes recurring and one-time payments via Stripe, multiple membership plan levels, custom sign-up forms, drip content for new members, custom styling, custom wording, and much more.

© Sarah Martin 2017
S. Martin, *The Definitive Guide to Squarespace*, https://doi.org/10.1007/978-1-4842-2937-8_10

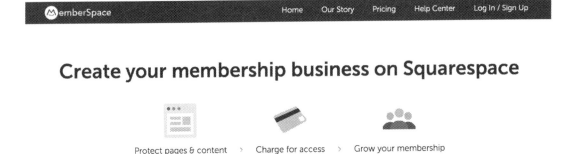

Figure 10-1. MemberSpace at www.memberspace.com

MemberSpace pricing is based on the number of active members. There are multiple price tiers. The tiers that have fewer active members are less expensive than the tiers with more active members. This model works great for recurring billing where a member pays a monthly or annual fee for access to content. It also allows small membership businesses to gain members before the subscription cost becomes significant. There are a few membership-model businesses that this doesn't work well for. An example is a business with a pay once – access forever model. In this case the number of active members would always be increasing without increased revenue. For that scenario it may be better to use a password-protected page inside the Squarespace site instead of a membership platform.

Squarespace Websites, `www.squarewebsites.org`, is another resource of Squarespace specific tools. Figure 10-2 shows the Squarespace Websites homepage. Squarespace Websites picked an SEO driven business name, and is not affiliated or endorsed by Squarespace. Squarespace Websites is incredibly generous and offers many tools for free. The most popular tool they offer is a Chrome browser extension that allows content to be exported and imported between Squarespace websites. Squarespace Websites also provides a script that allows files to be uploaded via a Squarespace form. The files are then stored in Google Drive.

Figure 10-2. *Squarespace Websites* `www.squarespacewebsites.org`

There are a few other products offered by Squarespace Websites. There is a custom table block, product filtering, and a few other tools that are added to the Squarespace interface. There is also a code connector tool that many web developers find useful. The code connector streamlines the interface between coding in a code editor and uploading it to Squarespace. I am sure that their list of offerings will continue to grow as well.

The third Squarespace specific resource provider is Square Studio. Figure 10-3 shows the Square Studio homepage. Square Studio offers a wide variety of user experience tools that they call plugins. These plugins range from specific block styles to animation effects. If one of my clients requests a fairly common visual effect, like skill bars, I will usually check to see if Square Studio has already created it. Square Studio's Tabs plugin is also very popular. It allows you to create a section with its own navigation and multiple content panels.

Figure 10-3. *Square Studio squarestud.io*

All of Square Studio's plugins work with AJAX page loading. They are one of the few sources of user-experience effects that consistently work with the AJAX based templates. When I am working on a site that already includes Square Studio's mutation observer I will incorporate their mutation observer into my code. As I mentioned before, it isn't good to run multiple mutation observers at the same time. Square Studio offers membership a membership plan as well as offering their plugins à la carte through their store.

General

The general category of third-party tools includes stand-alone code. This code is not platform dependent and doesn't connect Squarespace to any other platform. While this code can be used on any website, it may require some modifications to work well on Squarespace. The general third-party tool may add functionality or just create a user experience effect.

One of my favorite third-party tools is the Isotope JavaScript library found at `https://isotope.metafizzy.co/`. Figure 10-4 shows the Isotope homepage. Isotope allows me to add filtering and sorting functionality to a website. Within Squarespace I have used it to add dynamic filters to blogs and online stores. It is great for filtering gallery images by multiple tags as well. Since Isotope is not platform specific I have used Isotope on WordPress sites. Isotope is also built into the Shopify platform.

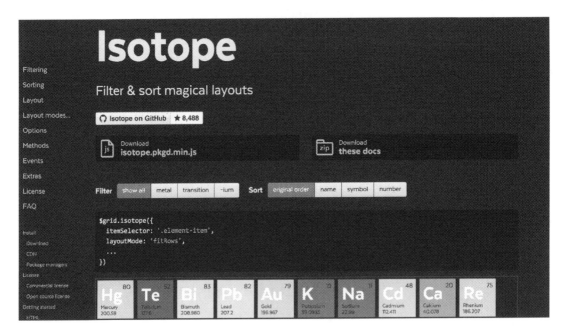

Figure 10-4. *Isotope JavaScript library,* `https://isotope.metafizzy.co/`

When using Isotope with Squarespace I will usually use the jQuery implementation. That means before I can write the Isotope code, I need to include both the jQuery library and the Isotope library. The Isotope JavaScript file will get uploaded to the file management section. You will be able to use it from there. If you are using Isotope on multiple pages, or with an AJAX based template you will include these library in the site-wide header code injection.

Listing 10-1. Isotope and jQuery script to add libraries

```
<script src="https://ajax.googleapis.com/ajax/libs/jquery/3.2.1/jquery.min.js"></script>
<script src="/s/isotopepkgdmin.js"></script>
```

The next part of using the Isotope library is to add the controls for the filtering. This can be done in a few different ways. The first way, where possible, is to add a code block to the page with the filter controls. These controls can also be added via code injection. Listing 10-2 shows an example of how the controls can be added to a code block. The Isotope website has additional samples of the filter controls. In my experience drop-down menus and buttons are the most popular controls.

Listing 10-2. Isotope filter buttons example

```
<div class="button-group filter-button-group">
  <button data-filter="*">Show All</button>
  <button data-filter=".Services">Services</button>
  <button data-filter=".Food_Drink">Food &amp; Drink</button>
  <button data-filter=".Groceries">Groceries</button>
  <button data-filter=".Health">Health</button>
  <button data-filter=".Beauty">Beauty</button>
</div>
```

The Isotope library works by hiding or displaying the items inside the grid. In order to do so the filter property has to be included as a class on those items. In this example, we are filtering based on category. Therefore the next part of implementation is adding the category tags to the outer item. If you are using summary blocks to display your items then the categories need to be added to the `.summary-item` elements. First we get the categories from the metadata. Then we add them to the `.summary-item`. Then we can add the standard Isotope code to initialize the Isotope script and add the filtering functionality. Listing 10-3 shows this code.

Listing 10-3. Adding categories to summary-item and initializing the Isotope script

```
<script>
$(function(){
  $('.summary-item').each(function(){
    var cat = $(this).find('.summary-metadata-item--cats a').html();
    $(this).addClass(cat);
  });

  var $grid =   $('.summary-item-list').isotope({
    // options
    itemSelector: '.summary-item'
  });

  $('.filter-button-group').on( 'click', 'button', function() {
    var filterValue = $(this).attr('data-filter');
    $grid.isotope({ filter: filterValue });
  });

});
</script>
```

Another example of a general third-party tool is the Font Awesome icon library, fontawesome.io. Figure 10-5 shows the Font Awesome homepage. Font Awesome is an icon library that allows you to add hundreds of scalable vector icons to a website. Implementation includes adding the files to your site directly or getting a CDN script code from Font Awesome. I have used Font Awesome on a number of sites to create custom sharing functionality or other custom user experience effects.

Figure 10-5. *Font Awesome homepage*

There are a few different ways to use the Font Awesome library in your site. The icons can be added directly inside a code block or markdown block using HTML. The approach uses the following HTML structure where the class name corresponds to the icon `<i class="fa fa-leaf" aria-hidden="true"></i>`. The second approach uses exclusively custom CSS. The icon is typically added as a `:before` or `:after` pseudo element. Listing 10-4 shows the CSS to add the leaf next to a menu item to indicate it is vegetarian. The icon can then be styled just like any other text element on the page.

Listing 10-4. Font Awesome CSS example

```
.menu-item-title:before{
  content: "\f06c";
  font-family: 'FontAwesome';
}
```

Squarespace does include its own icon font library; however, there are far fewer icons in the Squarespace icon font. To ensure consistency I will use the Squarespace font icon when available. An example of this is when I code custom lightboxes. I will use the Squarespace close-x icon in my lightbox code. Erica Heinz has a great write-up about the Squarespace UI font on her site http://ericaheinz.com/notes/symbol-fonts-on-squarespace.

Platform Integration

The final category of third-party tools is platform integration tools. Platform integration tools connect Squarespace to another platform or service. There are a number of ways that integrations can be done. The platform may offer a JavaScript integration where the JavaScript loads the integration into the Squarespace website. Other platforms use HTML elements to add the third-party functionality to Squarespace. Platforms can also connect directly by linking between them with navigation links. While the link approach isn't technically integrating the sites, it can provide a seamless user experience that serves the same purpose.

Shopify is commonly integrated with Squarespace for additional e-commerce functionality. The Shopify Lite plan with Buy Buttons is a perfect example of platform integration. I recently worked on a website that used Buy Buttons to sell ready-to-cook meal plans. Shopify Lite allowed my client to also sell on their social media platforms while managing inventory in a single location.

The Shopify Buy Button can be added to any webpage. I have seen Buy Buttons used on regular pages as well as with Squarespace Product pages. When the Buy Button is used with a Squarespace Product page, the Squarespace add-to-cart button needs to be hidden with custom CSS. Shopify provides the following example code, in Listing 10-5 for embedding a Buy Button onto a website. Figure 10-6 shows the Shopify page that the example script is from: https://www.shopify.com/buy-button. Looking at the below code we see there are three parts. The first function initializes, or sets up, the Shopify script. It also includes some styling for the Buy Button. The second function loads the Shopify JavaScript library and then calls the first function to run. The third part of this integration is the `<div id='product-component-05cfb487fb6'></div>` that indicates where the Buy Button will be added.

Listing 10-5. Shopify Example Buy Button code

```
<script type="text/javascript">
  function ShopifyBuyInit() {
    var client = ShopifyBuy.buildClient({
      domain: 'embeds.myshopify.com',
      apiKey: '952162710f94aa7b7644b14b2a94f4a3',
      appId: '6',
    });

    ShopifyBuy.UI.onReady(client).then(function (ui) {
      ui.createComponent('product', {
        id: [3030475907],
        node: document.getElementById('product-component-05cfb487fb6'),
        moneyFormat: '%24%7B%7Bamount%7D%7D',
        options: {
          "product": {
            "styles": {
              "button": {
                "background-color": "#292929",
                ":hover": {"background-color": "#464646"},
                ":focus": {"background-color": "#464646"}
              },
            }
          }
        }
      });
    });
  }
```

```
(function () {
  var scriptURL = 'https://sdks.shopifycdn.com/buy-button/latest/buy-button-storefront.min.js';
  window.ShopifyBuy && window.ShopifyBuy.UI ? ShopifyBuyInit() : loadScript();

  function loadScript() {
    var script = document.createElement('script');
    script.async = true;
    script.src = scriptURL;
    (document.getElementsByTagName('head')[0] || document.getElementsByTagName('body')[0]).
    appendChild(script);
    script.onload = ShopifyBuyInit;
  }
})();
</script>
<div id='product-component-05cfb487fb6'></div>
```

Figure 10-6. *Shopify example code and buy button:* $https://www.shopify.com/buy-button$

For Squarespace websites that do not use AJAX page loading, the entire integration script in Listing 10-6 can be added to a code block anywhere on the site. For Squarespace websites that do use AJAX page loading some changes need to be made to make it work. When we talked about AJAX page loading in Chapter 7 we discussed how all the JavaScript needs to be in the Site-wide Code Injection locations. The Shopify script will need to be modified to run after the AJAX page load changes as well. Therefore the only part that should remain in a code block is the `<div id='product-component-05cfb487fb6'></div>` since the `<div>` indicates where the Buy Button is to be added.

In order to make the Shopify script work with AJAX, we first need to figure out what needs to load once, and what needs to load after the page change. The first function `ShopifyBuyInit()` contains information specific to the Buy Button. Therefore this will need to be loaded every time the AJAX page changes. The second function loads the Shopify script and then calls the first function. So the second function only needs to run on the initial page load since the Shopify script will stay loaded on the AJAX page change. Listing 10-6 shows how we are breaking down the Shopify script and includes comment indicating the additional script modification needed for AJAX page change.

Listing 10-6. Modified Shopify Script with comments indicating code needed

```
<script type="text/javascript">
/*Shopify Buy Button function that needs to run for regular and AJAX page changes */
  function ShopifyBuyInit() {
    var client = ShopifyBuy.buildClient({
      domain: 'embeds.myshopify.com',
      apiKey: '952162710f94aa7b7644b14b2a94f4a3',
      appId: '6',
    });

    ShopifyBuy.UI.onReady(client).then(function (ui) {
      ui.createComponent('product', {
        id: [3030475907],
        node: document.getElementById('product-component-05cfb487fb6'),
        moneyFormat: '%24%7B%7Bamount%7D%7D',
        options: {
          "product": {
            "styles": {
              "button": {
                "background-color": "#292929",
                ":hover": {"background-color": "#464646"},
                ":focus": {"background-color": "#464646"}
              },
            }
          }
        }
      });
    });
  }

  /* Function that loads the Shopify script and calls the ShopifyBuyInit() function on
regular page load */

(function () {
  var scriptURL = 'https://sdks.shopifycdn.com/buy-button/latest/buy-button-storefront.min.js';
```

```
  window.ShopifyBuy && window.ShopifyBuy.UI ? ShopifyBuyInit() : loadScript();

  function loadScript() {
    var script = document.createElement('script');
    script.async = true;
    script.src = scriptURL;
    \(document.getElementsByTagName('head')[0] || document.getElementsByTagName('body')[0]).
appendChild(script);
    script.onload = ShopifyBuyInit;
  }
})();

/* Call ShopifyBuyInit() after AJAX page change */
 window.addEventListener("mercury:load", ShopifyBuyInit);
</script>
```

Most sites that use Shopify will have more than one product. The next question becomes how do we modify this script so that it works for multiple Shopify Buy Buttons and the script only runs on the correct pages? Making this script work with AJAX page loading and multiple buttons takes some more planning but is doable. The big changes we need to make include checking that a page contains the <div> container before running the script and running the correct script version for that button. The first change we is renaming the ShopifyBuyInit() function to ShopifyBuyInit1() and ShopifyBuyInit2(). This allows us to keep track of which button we are loading. We also remove the script.onload = ShopifyBuyInit function call from the Shopify script loading page. We no longer want that to run automatically. We need to be able to check if we should load it and then call the correct function.

Next we will add a new function called loadShopifyBuyButtons(). This script will check to see if a page has a Buy Button and if it does load the corresponding ShopifyBuyInit() script. Then we will call loadShopifyBuyButtons() on page load and on AJAX page changes. Listing 10-7 shows this updated version of the script. As many Buy Buttons as you need can be added this way.

Listing 10-7. Multiple Shopify Buy Buttons

```
<script type="text/javascript">
/*First Buy Button */
  function ShopifyBuyInit1() {
    var client = ShopifyBuy.buildClient({
      domain: 'embeds.myshopify.com',
      apiKey: '952162710f94aa7b7644b14b2a94f4a3',
      appId: '6',
    });

    ShopifyBuy.UI.onReady(client).then(function (ui) {
      ui.createComponent('product', {
        id: [3030475907],
        node: document.getElementById('product-component-05cfb487fb6'),
        moneyFormat: '%24%7B%7Bamount%7D%7D',
        options: {
          "product": {
            "styles": {
              "button": {
                "background-color": "#292929",
                ":hover": {"background-color": "#464646"},
```

```
                ":focus": {"background-color": "#464646"}
              },
            }
          }
        }
      });
    });
  }

  /* Second Buy Button */

  function ShopifyBuyInit2() {
    var client = ShopifyBuy.buildClient({
      domain: 'embeds.myshopify.com',
      apiKey: '952162710f94aa7b7644b14b2a94f4a3',
      appId: '6',
    });

    ShopifyBuy.UI.onReady(client).then(function (ui) {
      ui.createComponent('product', {
        id: [3030475907],
        node: document.getElementById('product-component-05555555'),
        moneyFormat: '%24%7B%7Bamount%7D%7D',
        options: {
          "product": {
            "styles": {
              "button": {
                "background-color": "#292929",
                ":hover": {"background-color": "#464646"},
                ":focus": {"background-color": "#464646"}
              },
            }
          }
        }
      });
    });
  }

  /* Function that loads the Shopify script */

(function () {
  var scriptURL = 'https://sdks.shopifycdn.com/buy-button/latest/buy-button-storefront.min.js';
  window.ShopifyBuy && window.ShopifyBuy.UI ? ShopifyBuyInit() : loadScript();

  function loadScript() {
    var script = document.createElement('script');
    script.async = true;
    script.src = scriptURL;
    (document.getElementsByTagName('head')[0] || document.getElementsByTagName('body')[0]).
    appendChild(script);
```

```
  }
})();

/* load correct buy button based on page content */
function loadShopifyBuyButtons(){
//Check if page has first Buy Button and load script if it does
  if(Y.one('#product-component-05cfb487fb6')){
    ShopifyBuyInit1() ;
  }
 // Check if the page has second Buy Button and load script if it does
  if(Y.one('#product-component-05555555')){
    ShopifyBuyInit2()
  }
}

//Call loadShopifyBuyButtons script on initial page load.
window.addEventListener("load", loadShopifyBuyButtons);

//Call loadShopifyBuyButtons script after AJAX page changes
 window.addEventListener("mercury:load", loadShopifyBuyButtons);

</script>
```

Most platform integrations that involve a script embed will follow the same process as the Shopify Buy Buttons. The other option for integration is using an `<iframe>` element. The `<iframe>` adds functionality to a page without requiring JavaScript. The Google Maps Embed API is a good example of an `<iframe>` embed. Google Maps is integrated using the JavaScript approach when you use the Squarespace map block, so this example is purely for demonstration purposes.

Google includes the following example, seen in Figure 10-7, on their website at `https://developers.google.com/maps/documentation/embed/guide`. The HTML consists of an `<iframe>` with its corresponding attributes. The `<iframe>` is a simple, easy integration because it is just added into a code block. There is no need to worry about AJAX page loading.

```
<iframe
  width="600"
  height="450"
  frameborder="0" style="border:0"
  src="https://www.google.com/maps/embed/v1/place?key=YOUR_API_KEY
    &q=Space+Needle,Seattle+WA" allowfullscreen>
</iframe>
```

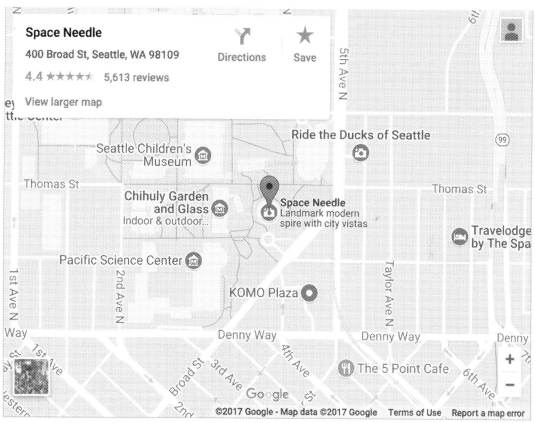

Figure 10-7. *Google Map <iframe> example*

The <iframe> approach, while simpler, does come with limitations. The content inside of an <iframe> cannot be styled with Custom CSS. The style of the <iframe> content would need to be updated within the originating platform, if that is even possible. Therefore web professionals will usually opt for the JavaScript embed to allow the integration to be styled to match the website.

Evaluating Third-Party Tools

Another important factor of using third-party tools is using quality tools. There is a lot of bad code floating around out on the Internet. Poorly coded third-party tools can have unintended side effects and cause bizarre problems with a website. One tool I worked with recently would work fine when initially added to a page. However, when I went back into the Squarespace page editor to update the page I could no longer make changes. The third-party script prevented Squarespace from fully loading the page editor.

When evaluating third-party tools I look at three main factors: source, customer reviews, and the Squarespace Circle Forum. First and foremost, I evaluate the source of the code. Is it coming from a reliable company? What other products do they offer? Is this code within their wheelhouse or a one-off project? Reliable code comes from reliable companies. The second factor is customer reviews. Do people actually use this tool? If people express concerns about a limitation of the tool, is it a limitation you also face? You can learn a lot about how easy or difficult it is to implement a tool from the customer reviews. The final factor is information inside the Squarespace Circle Forum. There is a wealth of knowledge for integrating third-party tools indie the Circle Forum. I will often start my search with tools that other Circle Forum members have successfully used in their projects.

Wrap-Up

Now that we have finished our discussion about third-party tools, you should feel comfortable adding third-party tools to the site. You may not be ready to create your own code, but you should be able to understand how to use existing code. The final chapter of this book will introduce Developer Mode. Some Squarespace professionals choose not to use Developer Mode, while others use it exclusively. No matter what your preference is, it is beneficial to understand the Developer Mode capabilities.

■ ■ ■

CHAPTER 11

Developer Mode

In this final chapter we will cover Developer Mode. Developer Mode tends to seem very mysterious to new Squarespace users. There isn't much documentation on Developer Mode, and web developers often learn how to use the system as they go. It does take a serious understanding of HTML, CSS, and JavaScript to safely use Developer Mode. Even if you don't plan on using Developer Mode, it is good to understand the capabilities of the system! By the end of this chapter you should have a solid understanding of what Developer Mode is, how to use it, and when to use it.

What Is Developer Mode?

Developer Mode gives web developers access to the template files for a particular website. It provides developers a way to modify the website outside of the Style Editor and Code Injections. Using Developer Mode provides increased control over the website and allows the coding of completely bespoke templates.

One major benefit of using Developer Mode is that trial sites in Developer Mode never expire. This allows web professionals to keep two versions of the website – a production site and a development site – without paying for a second website subscription. For bespoke templates it is best practices to have a development site and a production site. When using a development site, all changes are made to the development site first. This allows the client to see the changes, interact with the development site, and approve the changes. Once the changes are approved, the files are then moved to the production site and any content updates are made.

While Developer Mode gives increased control of the template, it also takes away some nice features. When Developer Mode is enabled, the template will not receive any automatic updates to the template files. The reasoning behind this is that Squarespace does not want to overwrite any of the custom code. The core files for the website, the Squarespace platform, Blocks, and menu features will still receive updates. This works really well for truly bespoke templates. For templates that are based off of a Squarespace template, like the Brine family templates, it is important to understand they won't automatically be updated. The Squarespace template updates can be incorporated into the Developer Mode template, but it takes careful consideration and planning to integrate the new template code into the custom template. A good example of this is when the Brine template family was updated to include videos as banner backgrounds. The update included a restructuring of the JavaScript code for the entire template. Therefore it wasn't an easy task to integrate the video background feature into the existing Developer Mode template. Clients need to know that future updates like this will take time and cost money.

© Sarah Martin 2017
S. Martin, *The Definitive Guide to Squarespace*, https://doi.org/10.1007/978-1-4842-2937-8_11

When to Use Developer Mode

Like most powerful tools, it is important to know when to use Developer Mode and when to not use it. The best time to use Developer Mode is when you are building a truly bespoke template. Bespoke templates could include unique navigation, animations, layouts, or other interactive features. , Before starting a Developer Mode project I make sure that I cannot create the bespoke element using an existing Squarespace template. I used Developer Mode more frequently a few years ago when the Squarespace templates were less flexible. Since the release of the new style template families, Brine, Skye, Farro, Tremont, and York, are so flexible, I use Developer Mode less often.

Enabling Developer Mode also is helpful for projects with a large amount of custom CSS or other code injections. This is especially true if the custom CSS depends on template-specific classes or ids. When using a Squarespace template without Developer Mode, there is always the risk that an automatic template update will break the custom code. For sites that extensively customize a Squarespace template, this risk can be minimized by enabling Developer Mode. Some Squarespace developers will always enable Developer Mode for this very reason. However, when browsers change, the web developer has to make those updates to the bespoke template. If the template is not updated as browsers change the user experience can slowly degrade over time.

Developer Mode really requires having an ongoing relationship with the client. Squarespace is always working on improving the platform and templates. Therefore it is safe to assume new features will be added that your clients will eventually want to use. I have several clients whom have been with me for years running Developer Mode templates. There are other clients that I have steered away from Developer Mode since they were going to do all ongoing site management themselves.

For web developers switching to the Squarespace platform from other web platforms, Developer Mode can feel more natural. The ability to see all the template files, modify them, and upload them to the site is a common way to edit websites on many platforms. It also allows the developer to see all the code in one location. When I first used Squarespace I found it easier to use Developer Mode and over time grew my understanding of the Style Editor and Code Injections.

Sometimes clients really want all the automatic updates that Squarespace provides. These clients often update their site and will use new features as soon as they are released. For these clients I will make the customizations work with the Code Injections, even if it would have been easier to use Developer Mode.

Turning On Developer Mode

The first step in using Developer Mode is to choose a starting point. You can start with any of the Squarespace templates or with the Squarespace Base Template, `https://base-template.squarespace.com/`. The Base Template is a skeleton of a template. It has all the necessary files and almost no styling or frills. The other Squarespace templates are all very complicated, and often a lot of code needs to be removed for customizations to work correctly. It is often easier to start with a blank slate than to work around existing code. Developer Modes sites are started just like regular Squarespace websites by selecting "create a site like this" and walking through all the initial steps we covered in earlier chapters.

Once the website has been created in the Squarespace platform, Developer Mode can be enabled. Developer Mode can be enabled by going to the Settings Menu, selecting the Advanced option under Website, and finally selecting Developer Mode. The Developer Mode area will initially be set to "off." Figure 11-1 shows how the Developer Mode menu will initially appear. Toggling the switch to "on" enabled Developer Mode. A popup will appear making sure that you understand the basics of Developer Mode before continuing. This popup is also shown in Figure 11-1.

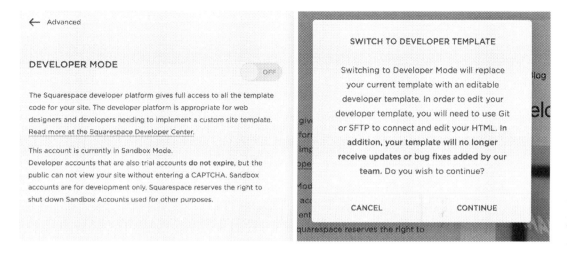

Figure 11-1. *Developer Mode toggle switch and popup message*

Once you select continue, Squarespace will switch the template to developer mode and provide the connectivity details. Figure 11-2 shows how the Developer Mode area now appears. The Developer Mode area now displays all the information needed to access the template files for the site.

Figure 11-2. *Developer Mode area enabled*

Getting Started with SFTP

The next step in the process is accessing the template files. There are two ways to access the template files, SFTP and GIT. In this chapter we will use SFTP to access the template files. SFTP uses a visual user interface and is usually easier to learn. However, SFTP is not as powerful as GIT and most seasoned web developers will use GIT. When I use SFTP to access a Developer Mode website I still use GitHub https://github.com/ to keep track of my code.

The template files are accessed via SFTP using an FTP client. An FTP client is a program that can connect to the remove server and allows you to browse, upload, and download files. There are many different FTP clients. I will be using the Cyberduck FTP client in my examples. Cyberduck is a free FTP client that is available for both Mac and Windows https://cyberduck.io/. If you do not have an FTP client then you will need to download and install one before accessing the template files.

Once you have a FTP client installed it is time to set up the connection to the Squarespace server. The first step is to select the Open Connection button. In Cyberduck the screen in Figure 11-3 is then displayed. The default value in Cyberduck is to use FTP as the protocol. However Squarespace uses SFTP so the first change I make is selecting SFTP (SSH File Transfer Protocol) from the drop-down menu. Next I will put in the configuration information found in the Developer Mode area. Figure 11-2 shows that the host name is dev.squarespace.com. In Cyberduck the host name goes in the Server field. Figure 11-2 also shows that the SFTP port is 2030. Therefore 2030 should be entered into the Port field in Cyberduck. The username and password are the same as your Squarespace account login. Figure 11-3 shows the completed Cyberduck form. Make sure you double check the port value. There are multiple port values that Squarespace uses.

Figure 11-3. *Default Cyberduck form and completed Cyberduck form*

Once you have successfully connected to the Squarespace server, Cyberduck will display a list of folders. If this is your first Developer Mode website then only one folder will be present. Figure 11-4 shows my list of websites in Cyberduck. I currently have 11 websites in Developer Mode. The folder sarah-martin-t54n is the example I am using in this chapter. You can also see how I have development and production versions of multiple websites.

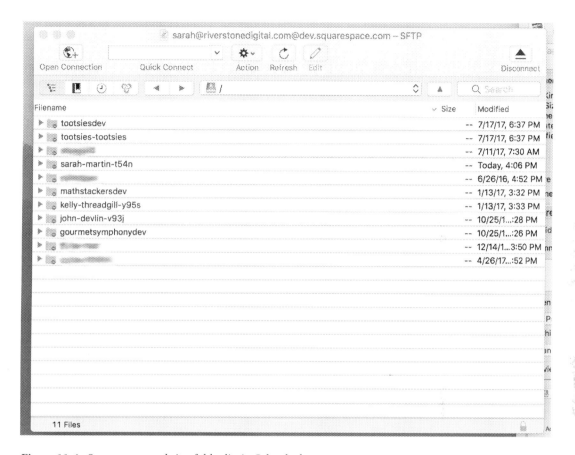

Figure 11-4. *Squarespace websites folder list in Cyberduck*

Inside the Folder Structure

All Squarespace templates share the same basic structure. When I expand the folder in Cyberduck you can see all the parts of the template. Figure 11-5 shows the expanded Base Template and an expanded Brine family template. As you can see the only difference between the two templates is that the Brine template has an additional folder called assets and the Base Template has a file called readme.md. Once you have access to the folder, you can then download it to your computer to work with.

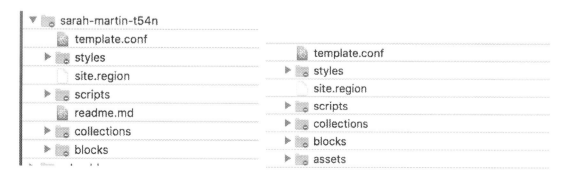

Figure 11-5. *Template folder contents of Base Template and Brine Template*

It is always good to start by reading the readme file. Many developers will skip over the readme file and only go back to it when they get stuck. I find that I save time if I at least skim the readme file before working with new code or software for the first time. The readme file contains a basic overview of the Squarespace template structure as well as links to additional resources. Figure 11-6 shows the readme file as it appears in my code editor. We will cover all the same material in this chapter so the readme file serves as a nice point of reference later when you are working on your own projects.

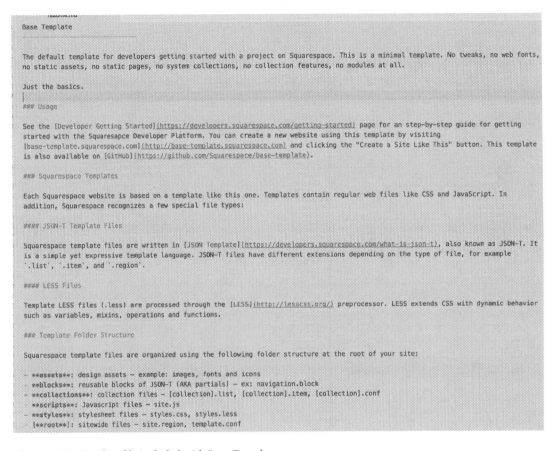

Figure 11-6. Readme file included with Base Template

The first file we will take a look at is the site.region file. Listing 11-1 shows the contents of the site. region file. Taking a look at the file content we see that it is mostly written in HTML. However, there are definitely portions that are clearly not HTML. For example, this code found in the header {squarespace-headers} is definitely not HTML. The curly brackets denote areas of JSON Template, also known as JSON-T, programming language. JSON-T is potentially the most mysterious aspect of Developer Mode. JSON-T is a minimalist template language Squarespace uses to render the website. If you are familiar with other web programming languages JSON-T is the equivalent of PHP. It is the server-side programming language that the platform uses to take data stored in a database and turn it into a webpage.

Listing 11-1. site.region file

```html
<!doctype html>
<html>
  <head>
    <meta http-equiv="X-UA-Compatible" content="IE=edge,chrome=1">
    <meta name="viewport" content="width=device-width, initial-scale=1.0, shrink-to-fit=no">

    <!-- include system scripts, page meta, and header code injection -->
    {squarespace-headers}
  </head>
  <body id="{squarespace.page-id}" class="{squarespace.page-classes}">

    <div class="site-container">

      <header class="site-header">
        <!-- site navigation -->
        <squarespace:navigation navigationId="siteNav" template="site-navigation" />

        <!-- site title or logo -->
        {.section website}
          <h1 class="site-title-heading" data-content-field="site-title">
            <a href="/" class="site-title-link">{siteTitle}</a>
          </h1>
        {.end}
      </header>

      <!-- cms content injection point -->
      <main class="content-container" role="main" data-content-field="main-content">
       {squarespace.main-content}
      </main>

      <!--Footer with open block field -->
      <footer class="site-footer">
        <squarespace:block-field id="footerBlocks" columns="12" />
      </footer>

    </div>

    <!-- combo and minify scripts when not logged in -->
    <squarespace:script src="site.js" combo="{.if authenticatedAccount}false{.or}true{.end}" />

    <!-- other scripts, and footer code injection -->
    {squarespace-footers}

  </body>
</html>
```

Looking at site.region in Listing 11-1 we see that it contains the basic structure of the website. The site.region file defines the areas for the header, body content, and footer. The Base Template and Brine template each have a single site.region file. However it is possible to have multiple page layouts by having multiple .region files. The files could be broken out into a header.region, footer.region, full-width-content.region, and left-column.region. All of the .region files would need to be included in the top-level folder. Figure 11-7 shows the multiple regions that one of my Developer Mode sites has. The site has three page layouts: one with a sidebar (sidebar.region), one without a sidebar (regular.region), and a special one for the homepage (home.region).

Figure 11-7. *Developer Mode website with multiple regions*

The next file we will look at is the template.conf file. The template.conf file defines the configuration of the page layouts, the navigation menus, style sheets, and system collections to be used by the site. Listing 11-2 shows the Base Template template.conf file and Listing 11-3 shows the template.conf file from the Math Stackers website. In Listing 11-3 you can see where I defined the additional page layouts by providing a name for the layout and a list of the regions that make up the layout. Listing 11-4 is the template.conf file from the Brine template. You can see where the Brine template defines the three navigation areas, includes all the system files, and a lot of style sheets. You can also see that the Brine family of templates is actually called the Wright famework by Squarespace.

Listing 11-2. Base Template template.conf file

```
{
  "name" : "Basic Template",
  "author" : "Squarespace",

  "layouts" : {
    "default" : {
      "name" : "Default",
      "regions" : [ "site" ]
    }
  },

  "navigations" : [ {
      "title" : "Site Navigation",
```

```
      "name" : "siteNav"
  } ],

  "stylesheets" : [ "base.less" ]
}
```

Listing 11-3. *Math Stackers template.conf file*

```
{
  "name" : "Math Stackers",
  "author" : "Sarah Martin",

  "layouts" : {
    "default" : {
      "name" : "Default",
      "regions" : [ "header", "regular", "footer" ]
    },
    "homepage" : {
      "name" : "Home Page",
      "regions" : ["header", "home", "footer"]
    },

    "sidebar" : {
      "name" : "Sidebar",
      "regions" : ["header", "sidebar", "footer"]
    }
  },

  "navigations" : [ {
      "title" : "Main Navigation",
      "name" : "mainNav"
  } ],

  "stylesheets" : [ "base.less", "animation.less" ],

  "systemCollections" : [ "products" ]
}
```

Listing 11-4. *Brine template.conf file*

```
{
  "name": "Wright",
  "author": "Squarespace, Inc.",
  "layouts": {
    "default": {
      "name": "Default",
      "regions": [
        "site"
      ]
    }
  },
```

```
  "navigations": [
    {
      "title": "Main Navigation",
      "name": "mainNavigation"
    },
    {
      "title": "Secondary Navigation",
      "name": "secondaryNavigation"
    },
    {
      "title": "Footer Main Navigation",
      "name": "footerMainNavigation"
    }
  ],
  "stylesheets": [
    "site.less",
    "ancillary.less",
    "cart.less",
    "footer.less",
    "header.less",
    "index.less",
    "mobile-styles.less",
    "tweak.less",
    "ui-icons.less",
    "util.less",
    "social-links.less",
    "sqs-video-background.less"
  ],
  "systemCollections": [
    "blog",
    "products",
    "gallery",
    "events",
    "album"
  ],
  "systemPartials": [
    "sqs-share-buttons"
  ]
}
```

The template folder also contains a number of subfolders. The assets folder contains static images for the website. These images are ones that are part of the template itself. You could also use the assets folder for font files or content images. However, the items in the assets folder cannot be updated or changed from the Squarespace interface. Therefore don't add anything to the assets folder that your client would need to access or update.

The styles folder contains all the style sheets for the website and for the Base Template that includes the files base.less and reset.css. The Brine template has many more style sheets that are included. The scripts folder should contain any JavaScript that the site uses. On the Math Stackers website, which has an animation on the homepage, I included the animation.js file. The animation.js file has all the custom JavaScript for the homepage. The pages folder would contain any static HTML pages that you want to include on your site. This would be the way to add a stand-alone splash page that was completely different from the rest of the website.

The blocks folder contains template partials to reuse throughout the website. This is not to be confused with the Squarespace content Blocks in the page layout. In the Base Template the blocks folder contains the code that defines the site navigation structure. Listing 11-5 shows the contents of the Base Templates site-navigation.block. You will see that the site-navigation.block file contains the same mix of HTML and JSON-T that we saw in the site.region file. If you look back at Listing 11-1 you will see `<squarespace:navigation navigationId="siteNav" template="site-navigation" />` in the site.region file for the Base Template. This bit of code is what tells the site.region file to include the contents of the site-navigation.block file.

Listing 11-5. site-navigation.block

```
<nav class="site-navigation">
  <ul class="site-navigation-list">
    {.repeated section items}

      <li class="site-navigation-item {.section active} active-link{.end}">

        <!-- collection link -->
        {.section collection}
          <a href="{fullUrl}">{navigationTitle}</a>
        {.end}

        <!-- external link -->
        {.section externalLink}
          <a href="{url}"{.section newWindow} target="_blank"{.end}>
            {title}
          </a>
        {.end}

      </li>

    {.end}
  </ul>
</nav>
```

The final folder is the collections folder. There are two types of collection files. There are system collections that are used across multiple Squarespace template and are included in the template.conf file under the `systemCollections` definition. The second type of collections is template-specific collections. If files are included in the collections folder then they will be used instead of the systems collection files. There are three parts to a collection. There is the .conf file, which defines the collection. The .list file defines how the list of items displays. The final file is the .item file. The .item file defines how the single item displays. Listing 11-6 shows the blog.conf file for the Base Template. The blog.conf file defines the name of the collection as Blog. It also sets the ordering to chronological and defines the text on the add new item button and the type of content it takes. We will go into editing the collection files in more detail later in this chapter.

Listing 11-6. blog.conf file for Base Template

```
{
  "title" : "Blog",
  "ordering" : "chronological",
  "addText" : "Add Post",
  "acceptTypes": ["text"]
}
```

Editing CSS

The styles folder in the theme can contain both LESS and CSS style sheets. As mentioned earlier LESS is a CSS pre-compiler language. That means you write the style rules using the LESS language and it gets compiled into CSS. LESS allows style rules to be nested as well as variable names used. This allows you to write less styling code, hence the name. When used with other websites the LESS language has to be compiled into CSS before being added to the website. With Squarespace all LESS files that are in the styles folder are combined and then run through the LESS compiler by Squarespace. This saves you the step of pre-compiling the code. The final compiled style sheet generated by Squarespace is the site.css file. Since all the style sheets are combined it can be difficult to debug the style code.

Listing 11-7 shows the base.less file included in the Base Template. As you can see the base.less file is a very basic skeleton for the site styling. The use of variables in LESS is one of my favorite parts of the language. It allows me to define all my major style colors in one place and update them throughout the code if needed. In Listing 11-8 you will see where I have added some color variables to the top of the base.less file. Then I have used the color variables in the base.less file to define the color of links and headers. You can learn more about the LESS language at http://lesscss.org/.

Listing 11-7. Base Template base.less file

```
/* CSS pre-processing by {less}. http://lesscss.org/
**********************************************/

/* General styles
**********************************************/

body {
  font-family: -apple-system, BlinkMacSystemFont,
    "Segoe UI", "Roboto", "Oxygen", "Ubuntu", "Cantarell",
    "Fira Sans", "Droid Sans", "Helvetica Neue",
    sans-serif;
  font-size: 100%;
  font-weight: normal;
}

.site-container {
  line-height: 1.6em;
  color: #777;
  max-width: 1020px;
  padding: 6vw;

  h1, h2, h3 {
    font-weight: normal;
    line-height: 1.2em;
  }

  a {
    color: cornflowerblue;

    &.disabled {
      color: #ccc;
    }
```

```
  }
}

.site-header {
  margin-bottom: 4vw;
}

.site-navigation { }

.site-navigation-list {
  padding: 0;
}

.site-navigation-item {
  display: inline-block;
  font-size: 87.5%;

  & + .site-navigation-item {
    margin-left: 1em;
  }

  a {
    color: #111;
    text-decoration: none;

    &:hover {
      color: #999;
    }
  }

  &.active-link > a {
    color: #999;
  }

}

.site-title-heading {

  .site-title-link {
    color: #111;
    font-weight: 400;
    text-decoration: none;
  }
}

.content-container { }

.site-footer {
  font-size: 75%;
  margin-top: 4vw;
  margin-bottom: 4vw;
}
```

```
/* Homepage
**************************************************/

body.homepage { }

/* Blog list
**************************************************/

body.collection-type-blog.view-list {

  .blog-list-item + .blog-list-item {
    margin-top: 3vw;
  }
}

/* Break grid and stack blocks on small screens
**************************************************/

@media screen and (max-width: 640px) {
  @import 'sqs-grid-breaker';
}
```

Listing 11-8. Base Template base.less with color variables

```
/* CSS pre-processing by {less}. http://lesscss.org/
**************************************************/
@tealBlue: #00cace;
@darkBlue: #0b1699;

/* General syles
**************************************************/

body {
  font-family: -apple-system, BlinkMacSystemFont,
    "Segoe UI", "Roboto", "Oxygen", "Ubuntu", "Cantarell",
    "Fira Sans", "Droid Sans", "Helvetica Neue",
    sans-serif;
  font-size: 100%;
  font-weight: normal;
}

.site-container {
  line-height: 1.6em;
  color: #777;
  max-width: 1020px;
  padding: 6vw;

  h1, h2, h3 {
    font-weight: normal;
    line-height: 1.2em;
    color: @darkBlue;
  }
```

```
  a {
    color: @tealBlue;

    &.disabled {
      color: #ccc;
    }
  }
}

.site-header {
  margin-bottom: 4vw;
}

.site-navigation { }

.site-navigation-list {
  padding: 0;
}

.site-navigation-item {
  display: inline-block;
  font-size: 87.5%;

  & + .site-navigation-item {
    margin-left: 1em;
  }

  a {
    color: #111;
    text-decoration: none;

    &:hover {
      color: #999;
    }
  }

  &.active-link > a {
    color: @tealBlue;
  }

}

.site-title-heading {

  .site-title-link {
    color: #111;
    font-weight: 400;
    text-decoration: none;
  }
}
```

```css
.content-container { }

.site-footer {
  font-size: 75%;
  margin-top: 4vw;
  margin-bottom: 4vw;
}

/* Homepage
***********************************************/

body.homepage { }

/* Blog list
***********************************************/

body.collection-type-blog.view-list {

  .blog-list-item + .blog-list-item {
    margin-top: 3vw;
  }
}

/* Break grid and stack blocks on small screens
***********************************************/

@media screen and (max-width: 640px) {
  @import 'sqs-grid-breaker';
}
```

Editing JavaScript

All JavaScript included in the template should be added in the scripts folder. In the Base Template there is only a very basic site.js JavaScript file. Listing 11-9 shows the site.js file. The only thing included in this file is a function that loads all of the images for the website. The function `loadAllImages()` tells the Squarespace ImageLoader function to load the images. Then there are two event handlers. The first event hander `document.addEventListener('DOMContentLoaded', loadAllImages);` tells Squarespace to load the images when the page changes. The second event handler, `window.addEventListener('resize', loadAllImages);` tells Squarespace to load the images when the browser window resizes.

Listing 11-9. Base Template site.js file

```javascript
/**
 * This script wrapped in a Immediately-Invoked Function Expression (IIFE) to
 * prevent variables from leaking onto the global scope. For more information
 * on IIFE visit the link below.
 * @see http://en.wikipedia.org/wiki/Immediately-invoked_function_expression
 */

(function() {
  'use strict';
```

```
// Load all images via Squarespace's Responsive ImageLoader
function loadAllImages() {
  var images = document.querySelectorAll('img[data-src]' );
  for (var i = 0; i < images.length; i++) {
    ImageLoader.load(images[i], {load: true});
  }
}

// The event subscription that loads images when the page is ready
document.addEventListener('DOMContentLoaded', loadAllImages);

// The event subscription that reloads images on resize
window.addEventListener('resize', loadAllImages);
```

```
}());
```

Most of the Squarespace templates have extensive amounts of JavaScript in the site.js file. The Brine template has all the JavaScript for parallax images, navigation, background videos, and many other features in the site-bundle.js file. The unbundled version of the scripts can be found on GitHub as part of the template frameworks provided by Squarespace.

Editing the Layout with JSON-T

Earlier in this chapter we looked at the site.region files. The region files allow you to change the HTML structure for the entire template. You could change the header layout, add body content areas, and customize the footer layout. In addition to the site.region files I also introduced the three type of collection files. The three types of files are the .conf, .list, and .item files. In the Base Template the blog.conf, blog.list, and blog.item files are included in the website folder.

The collection files can be used to customize the corresponding part of the collection. For example, Listing 11-10 shows the blog.list file included in the Base Template. The top of the file contains three tags that populate the content at the top of the Blog List page. These tags display the text Filtered by Category: xxxx. There are filters for category, tag, and author. If my desired layout doesn't include the filtered text then I could remove it by deleting the first 12 lines from the blog.list file.

Listing 11-10. Base Template blog.list

```
{.section categoryFilter}
  <p class="filtered-by">Filtered by Category: {@|safe}</p>
{.end}

{.section tagFilter}
  <p class="filtered-by">Filtered by Tag: {@|safe}</p>
{.end}

{.if authorFilter}
  <p class="filtered-by">Filtered by Author: {author.displayName}</p>
{.end}

<!-- item loop -->
{.repeated section items}
```

```
<article id="post-{id}" class="blog-list-item {@|item-classes}" data-item-id="{id}">
  <!-- main image (thumbnail) -->
  {.main-image?}
    <a href="{fullUrl}" class="main-image content-fill">
      <img {@|image-meta} />
    </a>
  {.end}
  <!-- post title -->
  <h1 class="title" data-content-field="title">
    {.passthrough?}
      <a href="{sourceUrl}" target="_blank">{title}</a>
    {.or}
      <a href="{fullUrl}">{title}</a>
    {.end}
  </h1>
  <!-- excerpt or body -->
  {.if excerpt}
    {excerpt}
    <a class="link" href="{fullUrl}">Read More</a>
  {.or}
    {body}
  {.end}
</article>

{.or}

  <!-- no items means no blog posts -->
  <p><em>No blog posts yet.</em></p>

{.end}

<!-- pagination -->
{.if pagination}
  <nav class="blog-list-pagination">

    <!-- newer page -->
    {.if pagination.prevPage}
      <a href="{pagination.prevPageUrl}">Newer</a>
    {.or}
      <a class="disabled">Newer</a>
    {.end}

    <!-- older page -->
    {.if pagination.nextPage}
      <a href="{pagination.nextPageUrl}">Older</a>
    {.or}
      <a class="disabled">Older</a>
    {.end}

  </nav>
{.end}
```

Individual blog posts can also be customized within the blog.item file. Listing 11-11 shows the Base Template blog.item file. Looking through the file we can see where the post title, body content, categories, tags, sharing, and commenting are added to the blog post. At the bottom of the file is the pagination to navigate between blog posts. The navigation is a great example of how to easily customize the text for a blog post. In this file the navigation uses the words Newer and Older to define the pagination. However if you wanted to have the pagination say Next Event and Previous Event you could easily change it here. The original newer post link is `<a href="{fullUrl}">Newer</a>` . To update the text all that needs to change is the text. The JSON-T surrounding it will take care of populating all the other data. Therefore the updated newer post link would look like `<a href="{fullUrl}">Next Event</a>` . Changing text is a great place to get started with custom updates in Developer Mode. Changing text creates meaningful changes to the template without too much risk of breaking the site.

Listing 11-11. Base Template blog.item file

```
{.section item}

  <!--WRAPPER-->
  <article id="post-{id}" class="{@|item-classes}" data-item-id="{id}">

    <!--POST TILE-->
    <h1 class="title" data-content-field="title">
      {.passthrough?}
        <a href="{sourceUrl}" target="_blank">{title}</a>
      {.or}
        {title}
      {.end}
    </h1>

    <!--AUTHOR AND DATE-->
    <p class="meta">
      <a href="{fullUrl}" class="permalink"><time datetime="{addedOn|date %F}">{addedOn|date
      %B %d, %Y}</time></a> by <a href="{collection.fullUrl}?author={author.id}">{author.
      displayName}</a>
    </p>

    <!--MAIN CONTENT-->
    {body}

    <!--BLOG INJECTION-->
    {postItemInjectCode}

    <!--CATEGORIES-->
    {.repeated section categories}
      <a class="category" href="{collection.fullUrl}?category={@|url-encode}">{@}</a>{.
      alternates with},
    {.end}

    <!--TAGS-->
    {.repeated section tags}
      <a class="tag" href="{collection.fullUrl}?tag={@|url-encode}">{@}</a>{.alternates with},
    {.end}
```

```
    <!--SHARE AND LIKE-->
    {@|like-button}
    {@|social-button}

    <!--LOCATION-->
    {.section location}
      {.section addressTitle}
        {addressTitle}
        {addressLine1}
        {addressLine2}
        {addressCountry}
      {.end}
    {.end}

    <!--COMMENTS-->
    {@|comments}

  </article>

{.end}

<!--PAGINATION-->
{.section· pagination}
  <nav class="blog-item-pagination">

    <!--NEWER PAGE-->
    {.section prevItem}
      <a href="{fullUrl}">Newer</a>
    {.or}
      <a class="disabled">Newer</a>
    {.end}

    <!--OLDER PAGE-->
    {.section nextItem}
      <a href="{fullUrl}">Older</a>
    {.or}
      <a class="disabled">Older</a>
    {.end}

  </nav>
{.end}
```

Custom Post Types

In addition to changing existing collection types, Developer Mode allows you to create custom post types. The custom post type first is defined in the template.conf file. In this example we will create a custom post type called Sponsored Post. This type of custom post will have an additional field that links to the sponsor's website. Listing 11-12 shows the code that is added to the template.conf to add the Sponsored Post type to the template. The key of "customTypes" is added so that Squarespace knows you are creating a custom type. Then the custom post type has to have a title, name, and base type. In this example the base type is text since it is a type of blog post. The base type can also be image or video. Finally the additional custom fields are defined. The fields can be text, wysiwyg, image, checkbox, or gallery. In the Listing 11-12 example the custom field is a text field since it contains the text URL of the link.

Listing 11-12. Code for Sponsored Post to add to template.conf file

```
"customTypes" : [
  {
    "title" : "Sponsored Post",
    "name" : "sponsoredPost",
    "base" : "text",
    "fields" : [
      {
        "name" : "sponsorLink",
        "title" : "Sponsor Link",
        "type" : "text"
      }
    ]
  }
]
```

The next step is to add the custom post type to a collection. The custom post type can also be added to multiple collections. Some developers have created custom post types that are a hybrid of an event and a blog post.

Squarespace also offers custom collections. Custom collections have to have a .conf, .item, and .list file just like the regular template collections. The custom collection functionality is fairly limited. The custom collections can be ordered chronologically or user ordered. It is not possible to have alphabetical, reverse-chronological, or any other type of sorting. This severely limits the usefulness of custom collections compared to other platforms. The post types are also limited to text, image or video.

Style Editor Tweaks

A special type of LESS file found in Squarespace templates is the tweaks.less file. The tweaks.less file defines everything found in the Style Editor. The tweaks.less file also defines the default values for the Style Editor Tweaks. The tweak.less file can be used in a couple of different ways. The first option would be to add more Tweaks to the Style Editor. I could see this being useful for changing the template colors seasonally or providing very specific options to the client. The more common use for the tweak.less file is to remove options from the Style Editor. When starting a bespoke website from a Squarespace template it is often a good idea to remove the Style Editor tweaks. This prevents the client from significantly changing the style of their custom template.

There are a few parts to each tweak. Listing 11-13 shows the beginning part of the tweak.less file for the Brine family template. The first part of the tweak is the tweak definition that is used in the Style Editor. The tweak definition opens with //tweak: telling Squarespace that a tweak will be defined. Next the category, label, variable name, type of tweak, and options are defined in name-value pairs. The second part of the tweak is the default value of the tweak. The default value is defined by a LESS variable and value. In Listing 11-13 the first tweak is the body background color tweak. The name of the variable is @tweak-site-body-background-color and the value is #f5f5f5. I can change the default background color by changing the color code. I can also remove the background style editor tweak by removing the tweak definition. The variable will need to be kept or replaced throughout all the style sheets. I will typically move the variable definitions to the main less file that I am working with, for easy reference. In this example I would move @tweak-site-body-background-color: #f5f5f5; to the base.less file.

Listing 11-13. First 30 lines from the Brine template tweak.less file

```less
// ==========================================================

//    Site

// ==========================================================

// tweak: { "category" : "Site", "label" : "Background", "title" : "tweak-site-body-
background-color", "type" : "color", "disableTransparency" : "true", "showOnlyWhenPresent" :
".tweak-site-width-option-constrained-width" }
@tweak-site-body-background-color: #f5f5f5;

// tweak: { "category" : "Site", "label" : "Design", "title" : "tweak-site-width-option",
"type" : "dropdown", "options" : [ "Full Width", "Full Background", "Constrained Width" ],
"default" : "Full Background" }

// tweak: { "category" : "Site", "label" : "Width", "title" : "tweak-site-width", "type" :
"value", "step" : 10, "min" : 640, "max" : 1920, "showOnlyWhenPresent" : "body:not(.tweak-
site-width-option-full-width)" }
@tweak-site-width: 1440px;

// tweak: { "category" : "Site", "label" : "Side Padding", "title" : "tweak-site-side-
padding", "type" : "value", "step" : 1, "min" : 17, "max" : 240 }
@tweak-site-side-padding: 40px;

// tweak: { "category" : "Site", "label" : "Icons", "title" : "tweak-icon-weight", "type" :
"dropdown", "options" : [ "Hairline", "Light", "Medium", "Heavy" ], "default" : "Hairline",
"target" : ".Icon", "showOnlyWhenPresent" : ".Icon" }

// ----------------------------------------

//    Border

// tweak: { "category" : "Site: Border", "label" : "Show Border", "title" : "tweak-site-
border-show", "type" : "checkbox", "active" : false }

// tweak: { "category" : "Site: Border", "label" : "Width", "title" : "tweak-site-
border-width", "type" : "value", "step" : 1, "min" : 1, "max" : 120, "target" : ".Site",
"showOnlyWhenPresent" : ".tweak-site-border-show" }
@tweak-site-border-width: 5px;

// tweak: { "category" : "Site: Border", "label" : "Color", "title" : "tweak-site-border-
color", "type" : "color", "disableTransparency" : "true", "showOnlyWhenPresent" : ".tweak-
site-border-show" }
@tweak-site-border-color: #dddddd;
```

Error Reporting

Squarespace does provide some built-in error reporting when working in developer mode. Any LESS compilation errors will be written at the bottom of the site.css file. Therefore you can use the inspector tool to read the error and fix it in the LESS file. The error message can also be seen by going to the /site.css URL. You can also see that Figure 11-8 shows how the LESS errors appear in the site.css file. It is typically pretty obvious that you have a LESS error; the site will look completely wrong. LESS errors also typically appear in the Developer Mode area.

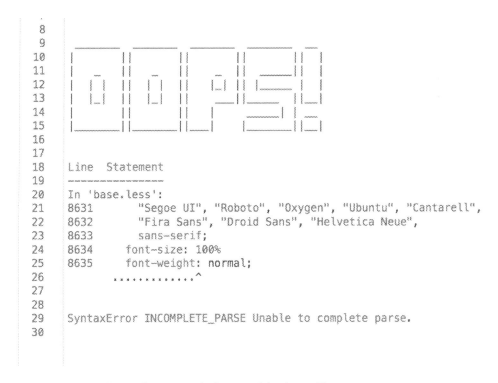

Figure 11-8. *LESS compiler error at the bottom of the site.css file*

The second type of error reporting is template structure errors. These types are errors are usually due to typos in the region, collection, or block files. The template structure errors are displayed in the Developer Mode section of the menu, under the server connection settings. The error will also be large and red; it is very hard to miss! The error message will also explain exactly where the error was found. Figure 11-9 shows an example of a template structure error message.

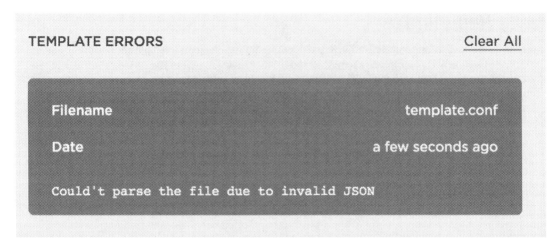

Figure 11-9. Template Structure Error message

The final type of error message is an error with the JSON-T. Serious JSON-T errors appear as a black screen of death, with the error message rendered directly into the front end of the website. Figure 11-10 shows how the JSON-T error message looks. Squarespace calls it the black screen of death since you cannot view the website until you have fixed the error. For minor JSON-T errors, the error may be written inside the website HTML inside of a comment block.

Figure 11-10. JSON-T error message

Development Tools

Squarespace also provides a number of development tools to the Squarespace developer community. I won't walk through all of the tools in detail, just provide you with an overview. The first tool is the Local Development Server. Squarespace's Local Development Server is a little different than regular local servers. The Squarsepace's Local Development Server still requires an Internet connection to pull content down from the website. The Local Development Server also does not allow you to log in or make edits to the site. It is purely a way to view changes to the template files locally. Nothing else can be changed locally. I have found the Local Development Server to be useful when doing extensive CSS work since it saves the time spent on multiple SFTP file uploads. However, I have found that I tend to update content as I work on the template and therefore the Local Development Server didn't fit my workflow well. You can find out more about the Local Development Server, as well as set up instructions at `https://developers.squarespace.com/local-development/`.

Squarespace has also provided a number of development code helpers they call the Squarespace Toolbelt. You can find the full definition of the Squarespace toolbelt tools on GitHub or npm. There are also a number of front-end modules available on GitHub and npm as well. The front-end modules include the AJAX page loading code, video background code, layout helpers, and the core code files. All of these tools have extensive documentation provided within the GitHub or npm platform. Using these tools also takes a considerable amount of programming language. I would suggest mastering the basics of updating a template before diving into the more complex tools.

The final resource that Squarespace provides is the template frameworks. The template frameworks are the uncompressed versions of the five new template families. The frameworks are listed by their framework name but have the common template family name included in the description. If you look at the Wright Framework, also known as Brine family template, in GitHub you will see that there are three folders and two additional files that all get combined into the site-bundle.js file that we saw in Cyberduck. Figure 11-11 shows the side-by-side comparison of the scripts folder of the framework on GitHub and the scripts folder in Cyberduck.

Figure 11-11. *Brine template scripts folder in GitHub and in Cyberduck*

Join the Squarespace Community

Congratulations on reaching the end of the book! To continue exploring Developer Mode and other advanced customizations, get involved with the Squarespace Community. The Squarespace Circle Forum is for active web professionals and provides a wealth of resources. Inside the Squarespace Circle Forum you can find hundreds of my code solutions. You can also continue learning by following my blog at `www.riverstonedigital.com/blog`. My blog contains additional Squarespace customizations. The format of learning will be the same as this book. Each blog post explores a customization and breaks it down into the code needed with step-by-step explanations.

Index

Get the eBook for only $5!

Why limit yourself?

With most of our titles available in both PDF and ePUB format, you can access your content wherever and however you wish—on your PC, phone, tablet, or reader.

Since you've purchased this print book, we are happy to offer you the eBook for just $5.

To learn more, go to http://www.apress.com/companion or contact support@apress.com.

Apress®

Printed in the United States
By Bookmasters